D0805725

Releasing Prisoners,
Redeeming Communities

Releasing Prisoners, Redeeming Communities

Reentry, Race, and Politics

Anthony C. Thompson

NEW YORK UNIVERSITY PRESS
New York and London

NEW YORK UNIVERSITY PRESS
New York and London
www.nyupress.org

© 2008 by New York University

Library of Congress Cataloging-in-Publication Data
Thompson, Anthony C.
Releasing prisoners, redeeming communities : reentry, race, and
politics / Anthony C. Thompson.
p. cm.
Includes bibliographical references and index.
ISBN-13: 978-0-8147-8303-0 (cloth : alk. paper)
ISBN-10: 0-8147-8303-1 (cloth : alk. paper)
1. Ex-convicts—United States. 2. Criminals—Rehabilitation—
United States. 3. Minorites—United States—Social conditions.
I. Title.
HV9275.T56 2008
365'.6470973—dc22   2007043248

New York University Press books are printed on acid-free paper,
and their binding materials are chosen for strength and durability.

Manufactured in the United States of America

10 9 8 7 6 5 4 3 2

For My Parents,
Elena and Leo Hopkins and Teddi and Billy Taylor.
You have taught me a great deal about love, faith,
and redemption.

Contents

Acknowledgments

I gratefully acknowledge financial support from the Filomen D'Agostino and Max E. Greenberg Research Fund at the New York University School of Law as well as the continued support from a number of colleagues, especially Professor Deborah Schenck, who has been a great support in this project. I would like to thank Susan Hodges and Damaris Marrero for their impeccable administrative support. I would like to thank Michael Chen, Tom Leith, Tara Mikkilineni, Cynthia Pong, and Andrew Stanner for their research assistance. I would also like to thank Jenna Johnson for her edits of an early draft. I would like to thank Oscar Bobrow and Jennifer Gonnerman for their comments on an earlier draft. I want to thank my editor, Debbie Gershenowitz, for identifying the importance of the issue and for her insightful editorial assistance. Finally, I want to especially thank Kim Taylor-Thompson for her support and substantive assistance in this effort.

Introduction

Reentry is a term few people outside the criminal justice system know. Some individuals and communities have experienced firsthand the consequences of our national failure to facilitate meaningful reintegration of recently released prisoners. Far too few individuals can either articulate or imagine the benefits of a comprehensive approach to reentry. This is due largely to the fact that this country has never devoted the time, care, or attention necessary to create such an approach. Instead, our efforts to address reentry have, at best, remained an afterthought and, at worst, have been dismissed as someone else's concern. What has led our choice as a nation to ignore this crisis is the pervasive interplay of race, power, and politics that infuse and confuse our attitudes about crime.

So permit me to begin with a definition to ground our discussions. Reentry is the process by which individuals return to communities from prison or jail custody. The focus of this book is the way that race, power, and politics all conspire to make reintegration more difficult, if not impossible. In conversations, studies, and reports, we often discuss crime statistics, drug use, and incarceration rates. In addition, significant attention has been paid to prison conditions and to the philosophy and approach to incarceration. Whether we are talking about rehabilitation, retribution, or incapacitation, we have spent precious little time considering what happens when individuals leave custody. We rarely consider, for example, the obstacles for men and women who have been separated from family and community for significant periods of time. Alternatively, we have also failed to examine in depth the communities themselves. The cycle of poverty, incarceration, and frequent removal of large numbers of people to jail and prison generate instability in the fabric of the community. Racial and ethnic bias, the War on Drugs, and the portrayal of young men of color as predators all conspire to blur our focus on the issue.

The United States is in the midst of the largest multiyear discharge of prisoners from state and federal custody in the history of its prison system. This release is a direct consequence of the explosion in incarceration that this country experienced and endorsed over the last two decades. The repercussions of this massive release effort are only now beginning to be felt. Staggering numbers of ex-offenders, having completed their sentences, are returning to the communities from which they originally came.[1] In 2001 alone, corrections officials discharged over six hundred thousand individuals, with most returning to the core communities of their incarceration.[2] As a result of the War on Drugs and the almost single-minded focus in the 1980s and 1990s on targeting, denouncing, and dehumanizing those convicted of drug offenses, we banished hundreds of thousands of individuals to prisons and jails. Now we have created an explosive situation of individuals being returned to communities that, for the most part, are barely surviving. These communities, already in dire need of health care, affordable housing, drug treatment, social services, and, most of all, jobs draw even closer to the precipice when they are inundated by recent parolees who have not been prepared for reentry into society.

The importance of reentry and reintegrating formerly incarcerated individuals back into society has belatedly emerged as a major issue among criminal justice policy makers. Although prisoner reentry is not a new criminal justice matter, its importance is exacerbated by correctional policies that have resulted in the incarceration of large numbers of persons for significant periods of time, the release of prisoners who have not received treatment, and the failure to provide adequate services and surveillance in the communities after release.[3] Recently, prisoner reentry has garnered bipartisan attention. Both Republican[4] and Democratic[5] elected officials have recognized the importance and impact of prisoner reentry. Congress is in the process of considering "The Second Chance Act,"[6] which boasts both liberal and conservative support and offers a wide range of reentry activities. But this belated political attention may prove too little, too late.

The public debates over reentry that have emerged have begun to offer an important glimpse into the challenges of life after prison. Still, as important as these discussions are, they have too often missed the mark. These debates have frequently taken place in a race-neutral context, thereby ignoring the elephant in the room—the fact that we are talking about a problem that predominantly affects only certain populations in this country. This book aims both to rectify this oversight and to advance the public debate by situating the issue of reentry squarely in its peculiarly U.S. context: one influenced by race, power, and the media. This book examines the ways in which political leaders have successfully wielded the twin weapons of racial bias and raced-based fear to launch their political agendas and propel their careers. Elected officials have built electoral platforms on the backs of communities of color, waging wars on crime and drugs with little consideration of, or concern for, the communities that would suffer the greatest casualties. And, despite full-throated claims of objectivity and neutrality in reporting, the media has been complicit in our prison boom and the subsequent reentry crisis. By demonizing men of color and spreading misconceptions about crime and men of color, the media has played a vital role in dooming efforts at reentry. Finally, this book aims to move to the foreground considerations of the disproportionate impact of race-based policies on communities of color. The individual and collective stories of reentry and its relentless challenges can no longer be relegated to the background.

I have chosen to write this book because the subject is personal to me. The intersection of race, reentry, and politics has always shaped my perceptions of, and approach to, the criminal justice system. Pretty early in my personal life and then again later in my professional career, I noticed that people of color received quite different treatment from the criminal justice system. Before I knew to use the term "reentry," I recognized the difficulties that individuals in my community faced as they tried to reintegrate into the neighborhoods they had been forced to leave. After law school, I chose to return home to work in the San Francisco Bay area; I settled in the east bay, in the very community where I had been reared. I spent a decade working as a public defender in that community. As a resident, I sought to be active in the social, cultural, and political fabric of the community. I saw no conflict between my community involvement and my role as a public defender, and I viewed my practice and my concern for the community as fundamentally linked. By the time I began practicing criminal law, drugs, drug cases, and drug probation and parole were the primary driving force in the criminal justice system. We knew so little about how to address drug problems that when someone tested positive for drug use, judges simply sentenced them to prison. There was little data on the process of recovery from drug addiction. Court actors considered relapse nothing more than volitional conduct on the part of probationers and parolees who were making conscious decisions to use drugs. Later, of course, we learned the error of that perception: research and experience taught us that relapse is a part of recovery and that graduated supportive sanctions rather than custody were the appropriate responses to recovering addicts.

Years after becoming a law professor, as a participant in criminal justice meetings and in conducting Socratic dialogues with judges, often I heard them say, "Oh, I have learned so much about relapse and recovery. I remember when I used to send someone to prison for one dirty test." Strikingly, as we developed our knowledge base, we did not go back and adjust sentences or sentencing schemes to compensate for our new knowledge. Rather, the criminal justice players and policy makers simply sat back idly and let a generation of young men and women, most often persons of color, sit needlessly and uselessly behind bars. Too often, those men and women received no treatment, vocational training, or education. As the decades of the 1980s and 1990s passed, I continued my community involvement and activism. Slowly, the political discourse began to include and embrace broader notions of punishment and community corrections. But reconnecting with the community is difficult for recently released individuals. We never stopped to think that limiting access to education and vocational training would make reentry so terribly challenging.

At the same time, no one focused on the fact that employers habitually discriminated in hiring ex-offenders. Moreover, by limiting access to drug treatment both inside and outside of prison, we did not recognize that the temptation ex-offenders faced upon release was a recipe for disaster. We spent so much time trying to fend off the incredibly long and harsh prison sentences that we lost sight of how our clients were being transformed in prison. The civil rights of probationers and parolees were so limited that as the 1990s began and the politicians' lightly camouflaged use of racial imagery became the norm, we didn't anticipate the long-term negative consequences of the policies that were developing.

Racial imagery, mixed with police practices and racial profiling, transformed our society. The confluence of pervasive media images, popular culture, and our nation's history has led us to an almost unconscious acceptance of racial stereotyping and a deep-seated fear of people of color. Socially, politically, and culturally we continue to remain two societies—one White and one of color. A collision course of race, and the presumptions about crime, and the tacit acceptance of police misconduct began a chain of events whose effects and implications we are only now beginning to feel.

In communities of color—the African American community in particular—there are certain social and cultural "norms" that don't exist in the White community. My father-in-law, a world-renowned jazz pianist, jazz educator, and television personality is as prepared to be stopped and harassed by the police as my twenty-something, college-educated nephews. It is understood that law enforcement will act differently toward men—and increasingly women—of color than toward all others.

As a law professor I have observed, analyzed, and taught the cases that present an illusory world, absent race, that serves as the construct and foundation of the bulk of United States Supreme Court decisions regarding the conduct of police officers in immigrant, poor, and of-color communities. In traffic stops, pretextual justifications for race-based behavior are no longer frowned upon but instead lauded as good police work. Although superficially addressed in election years and occasionally given media attention, racially charged differences continue to be seen in discretionary decision making. Numerous studies have brought race to the surface in various aspects of the decision making that occurs throughout the criminal justice system. In arrests, charging, plea bargaining, and sentencing we see people of color treated differently than their White counterparts. The criminal justice system, although based in large part on the need for the public to believe in its even-handedness, is replete with evidence to the contrary.

In jury trials, where a cross-section of the entire community is supposed to be included, the courts have allowed for the exclusion of people of color with little more than "plausible excuses" from the prosecutors using peremptory challenges. In both state and federal court trials, it is not unusual for judges to ask potential jurors of color if they can be fair and impartial in cases where the defendants were also people of color (of the same race) without considering the atmosphere this creates in a courtroom: the question itself presumes same-race bias and plants a seed of distrust. The Supreme Court continues to demonstrate insensitivity to the courtroom racial dynamics that allow prosecutors to use virtually any excuse to dismiss same-race jurors.

We continue to allow wide disparities in sentencing, and we now are beginning to see the result of decisions made in the past two decades.

Reentry, the reintegration of ex-offenders back into their communities, has been the concern of parole agents, parole boards, those concerned with corrections policy, and, of course, ex-offenders, their families, and the communities to which they return. In its latest incarnation reentry became the concern of Attorney General Janet Reno and her then–National Institute of Justice director (and now the president of John Jay College in New York City), Jeremy Travis. They, along with some forward-looking researchers and some concerned community activists at the time, were the proverbial "canary in the coal mine" or, in more modern terminology, an "early warning system." Reno and Travis focused the lens of government and think tanks on the provocative question, What happens to individuals as they leave custody? They began to direct the resources and energy of government toward the question of reentry. Foundations, states, nonprofits, and local communities all began to identify the successful reintegration of large numbers of individuals from prison and jail as central to the survival of many neighborhoods.

In recognition of the bold steps that Attorney General Reno and Jeremy Travis took to reignite the discussion of reentry, I now add my voice to the debate. Reentry, race, and politics are intimately intertwined and will remain so unless those of us who have seen the impact of our inaction speak of its devastating consequences. In this book I begin each chapter with an anecdote as an attempt to illustrate the individual and personal consequences of our reentry policy. The first chapter is an overview of the effects of race and stigma. Even without using the lens of the criminal justice system, it is easy to see that we in this country have not resolved some of the fundamental conflicts in our notions of equality and the ways in which use of discretion continues to be corrupted by stereotyping and racial bias. In chapter 2, I try to identify the central ways in which the media and politics have contributed to and exacerbated the problem.

In addition to the increased media coverage of race, crime, and parolees in the 1990s was the simplification of the description of the problem. The notion that crime fighting is simple was articulated by a number of commentators proffering that "[t]here's no secret to fighting crime," suggesting that the only things needing to be done were to "hire more police, build more prisons, abolish parole, stop winking at juvenile criminals, severely enforce public-nuisance laws, permit self-defense for the law-abiding and put deliberate murderers to death."[7] Simplistic notions highlighted by the media only led to simplistic policy decisions on the part of legislators. The effects of these longer, harsher sentences were to reduce programming in prisons and create additional obstacles to reentry.

In the third chapter of the book, I look at how women have become the new fodder for the mass incarceration effort. Although some of the most important criminal justice research completed in the last two decades has brought our attention to the disproportionate representation of men of color in prison, it has largely ignored the fact that women of color are being arrested, charged, and incarcerated at alarming rates. Part of this chapter also examines the consequences to children and other aspects of community cohesion that are affected by this phenomenon.

The next three chapters of the book sketch out some of the fundamental needs of ex-offenders upon release: housing, health care, and employment. These chapters also focus on the ways in which segregation, policy decisions, and bias conspire to make reentry particularly difficult for people of color given the current socioeconomic and political realities in this country. Those chapters attempt to paint a picture of what an offender must overcome to attempt to reintegrate into his or her community.

In the final three substantive chapters I look at governmental responses to reentry. After an unfair, political, and media-driven attack on the entire parole profession, in response to which the industry has tried to reinvent itself, parole officers have moved from having once been the primary source for referrals to employment and social services to fulfilling a more surveillance-oriented law enforcement adjunct role. However, in recent years we are beginning to see some retreat from this enforcement focus as more officers rediscover the importance of corrections and parole participating in community justice efforts.

These chapters also explore the complicated and ill-conceived "tough on crime" politics that have created a web of collateral consequences to incarceration that further hinder the reentry of ex-offenders. Individuals who have been arrested and incarcerated have become the pariahs who continue to be denied many of the fundamental rights of citizenship despite having paid their debt to society. Seemingly no consequence is too harsh for consideration as an obstacle to reentry.

Finally, in these chapters on government's response to reentry, I analyze the use of courts in the reintegration of ex-felons into their communities. Building on the well-researched and well-documented success of drug courts, new specialized "treatment courts" have emerged as the most recent cure-all for criminal justice problems. Notwithstanding the fact that there is little research to validate the claims that courts can correct the range of ills they purport to address, politicians and policy makers have promoted the use of courts principally because courts provide them with a degree of political cover. By providing services under the supervision of the courts, they gain a means of coercion, a way to force individual compliance. So, reentry courts have begun to appear. For communities of color, where social services have been cut over the last two decades, we are seeing a reemergence of these services, though provided in coordination with and at the added expense of the criminal justice system.

I do not want this book to be reduced to a simple racial critique of criminal justice policy mistakes that are made in the name of being "tough on crime." Rather, it is my hope to underscore the way race and bad policy have constructed seemingly insurmountable reentry barriers. In the concluding chapter I challenge the notion that the so-called crime problem must be cast as a race problem. As a nation we have the will to make the necessary course correction, to provide an opportunity for people who have paid their debt to society and only seek an equal chance to become full citizens again.

1

Reentry, Race, and Stigma

A young man's life went off track early. Among other crimes, he raped and robbed a young woman in her home. The crimes cost him sixteen years in prison, which was time he certainly had earned. Released, he returned home and for three years tried to piece together a life for himself and to raise a family. At thirty-seven years of age, it might be said that the man, Lane Mikaloff, was redeeming himself and was finally doing precisely what society demanded of him.

Shortly after he returned home, however, Mikaloff learned from the sheriff's office that as a registered sex offender, he could no longer live in the house to which he had returned. It was located too close to a school. Living there would violate a state law prohibiting convicted sex offenders from residing within one thousand feet of a school.

Society expected Mikaloff to embark on a path of personal redemption. At a minimum, this meant that Mikaloff should support himself and live as a productive member of his community. The grand promise behind the criminal justice process is that once an individual pays his or her debt to society, he or she can reintegrate into society. But, as Mikaloff learned, society erects barriers to that reintegration.

Mikaloff was a sex offender, which means that he fell into the class of criminals least likely to garner any sympathy. Yet, even those individuals who have engaged in the worst deeds can and often do genuinely renounce their criminal paths. Perhaps then they deserve an opportunity to outlive their pasts and to overcome the stigma of a criminal record.[1]

The last two decades of the twentieth century witnessed an unprecedented increase in the number of people incarcerated in the United States. By 2001, approximately two million men and women resided in state and federal prisons and jails.[2] Although other communities of color suffered the effects of this increased incarceration (as described later in this work), this dramatic rise in incarceration had a particularly catastrophic impact on African American communities. African Americans represent roughly 13 percent of the general U.S. population. But African American men and women made up 46.3 percent of those imprisoned in state and federal jurisdictions by 2000.[3] Young men and women of color were literally swept into the criminal justice system at alarming rates, a development that often deprived families and communities of the precise individuals who, under the right circumstances, would have been the more productive members of the communities.

But the numbers only reveal part of the story. To see the story in its entirety, we must examine the various threads that create the criminal justice storyline. The communications vehicle for the story involves political rhetoric and media coverage. Indeed, the combined result of political and media coverage of race and crime has been to stoke the hysteria around crime and the responses to it.[4] The negative labeling and narratives that surround criminal justice involvement have created significant hurdles that make it difficult for individuals caught up in the system to repay and move past their debt to society. Stigmas that attach to criminal convictions have impaired the ability of formerly incarcerated individuals to reintegrate into society after even a successful completion of a sentence. When race is added to the mix, it becomes clear that these "collateral consequences" of conviction have had at once a disparate and a devastating impact on communities of color.

Explanations for the radically unequal incarceration rates between white offenders and people of color abound. One particularly potent argument attributes the disparities to the high concentration of law enforcement resources in communities of color generally and in the African American community in particular. In the 1980s and 1990s, the federal government waged the War on Drugs. This war created incentives for law enforcement to target open-air drug markets in low-income communities and, in the process, to turn its considerable attention to communities of color. There were a number of reasons why law enforcement concentrated its resources there. First, the federal government provided substantial amounts of funding to local law enforcement for the creation of drug task forces. These groups of officers often worked in conjunction with federal law enforcement agencies such as the Drug Enforcement Agency (DEA), Alcohol, Tobacco, and Firearms (ATF), and in some instances immigration officials. These task forces focused almost exclusively on Asian, Black, and Latino communities. Some of the focus on transportation hubs led to the use of "drug courier profiles,"[5] which again tended to target people of color. Second, in addition to the increase in state and federal funding, local police also found considerable political support for their work. While politicians inside the Black community voiced concerns about protections against unreasonable searches and seizures under the Fourth Amendment, politicians outside of that community increasingly simplified their message and encouraged harsh enforcement tactics to stop the migration of crime into the suburbs. Finally, the media's tendency to flood the airwaves in both the news and crime dramas with faces of color as the perpetrators of crime fueled the public belief that crime ran rampant in communities of color and that law enforcement's targeting efforts were logical. The effect of these enforcement decisions was that communities of color became the focal point of attention and effort. As a consequence, the arrest rate and imprisonment of African American and Latino men soared.[6]

The policies of the War on Drugs focused more on supply-side enforcement against low-level dealers in inner-city areas than on those higher up in the chain, who were importing drugs and laundering money. While those involved at the top of the drug chain tended to be White, they rarely appeared in criminal courts facing drug or conspiracy charges. A significant amount of the racial disparity we see even today can trace its roots to those policies.[7] In addition, the adoption and implementation of the Federal Sentencing Guidelines, which impose a 100-to-1 sentencing disparity between crack cocaine and powder cocaine, coupled with a federal law enforcement focus on crack offenses, contributed significantly to racial sentencing disparity.[8] Again, since crack cocaine tended to be sold in low-income communities at a lower price point, the choice to focus enforcement on crack led to greater arrests of people of color.

The enforcement double standard that the War on Drugs reflected and drove was just one example of the sort of structural inequalities that characterize the U.S. criminal justice system. Crime control today continues to concentrate primarily in the inner city.[9] Aggressive policing targeting communities of color is augmented by harsh mandatory sentences that combine to have a particularly pernicious effect in these communities.[10] But these enforcement policies simply flow from structural inequities embedded in the system.[11] While some make the empty argument that we can remedy all of the ills in the criminal justice arena by simply eliminating explicit and intentional racism,[12] the real culprit is the double standard on which the criminal justice system depends and thrives: the choice to target particular communities and to turn a blind eye toward the same crimes committed in affluent communities.[13] The Sentencing Project's first report on the status of Black men in the criminal justice system, noting the disproportionate involvement of African American men in the system, opened the country's eyes to the dramatic disparities in the justice system.[14] Some data suggests a correlation between stereotypes about young men and issues of enforcement. A more in-depth view of this very difficult problem recognizes that the research involved in addressing racial disparities in offending, arrests, and incarceration requires more study.[15]

Others, though, point to different reasons for racial disparities in the criminal justice system. Some argue that the racial imbalance exists because of a disproportionate involvement in the commission of crimes that breaks down along racial lines. These commentators contend that African Americans are overrepresented in the prison population because they engage in more criminal activity. This view attempts to justify any criticism of racial inequity by suggesting that the "representation of Blacks in the criminal justice system is relative to their representation among the population of criminal wrongdoers."[16] Conservative commentators have asserted that because African Americans commit more crime, they should be detained and arrested more often than Whites.[17] And as a seemingly logical extension of this argument, they contend that profiles that enable police officers to identify who is likely to commit a crime ought to include race as an element. Therefore, police should be able to consider race as a factor in making the decision to stop, question, or arrest a suspect.

But such arguments conveniently ignore empirical evidence that contradicts their premise. Let's take drugs as an example. African Americans do not use drugs any more than Whites.[18] Whites, however, are incarcerated at substantially lower rates than people of color.[19] If the rate of criminal activity were really the differentiating factor, then one would expect roughly equal percentages of White offenders and people of color in criminal courts for drug offenses. But that is not the case. The face of the arrestee and convicted drug user tends to be a face of color. When presented with statistics that suggest consistent drug-use rates, some amend the argument to account for this discrepancy. They suggest that Whites are simply more discreet in that they commit the crime within the confines of their homes instead of on public streets. As a corollary to this argument, others then suggest that one of the reasons why crime, such as drug usage, is committed openly in communities of color is that these communities tolerate crime, treating the commission of crimes as a rite of passage for young men of color. Despite the lack of evidence to support such claims, these views have gained surprising traction in the public debate about crime.

The media may be partly to blame for the general acceptance of this view. Media depictions historically have powerfully influenced the development of public opinion, and have provided a launching pad for public policy. Indeed, the coverage of a criminal case or a victim's story often leads to the introduction of legislation in the name of a victim. Media coverage of crime has often led people to believe that crime rates, violent crime, or drug crime was on the increase even when the reverse was true.

In the mid-1980s, crack cocaine exploded onto the streets and into the national media.[20] The media described crack as a "demon" drug that posed dangers that differentiated it from any other drug: it was highly potent, was instantly addictive, and encouraged systemic violence, they claimed, even though these claims would later prove false.[21] By the end of 1986, the major daily and weekly news magazines had presented the nation with more than one thousand stories in which crack figured prominently.[22] Network television coverage mirrored the print media. The intensive coverage included CBS's "48 Hours on Crack Street," a prime-time presentation that was one of the highest-rated documentaries in television history.[23] The media stories emphasized certain supposed features of the crack cocaine story: that the high addiction rate of the drug caused users to commit crimes to support their habits and that youths were being lured into the crack-selling business. Most importantly, the stories focused on the violence associated with attempts to control crack distribution networks. Finally, the stories had a significant racial edge.

A systematic study[24] of drug war coverage in the *New York Times, USA Today,* the *Washington Post, Time,* and *Newsweek* from the late '80s and early '90s revealed that the print media consistently identified African Americans as the "enemies" that the drug war intended to target. Network television was no different. In a study of network television news in 1990 and 1991,[25] it was shown that reporters regularly stressed the theme of "us against them" in news stories, with the "us" referring to White middle-class Americans and the demonized other being typically reserved for African Americans and a few corrupted White individuals.[26] In addition to the images on the covers of newspapers and leading the evening news, the War on Drugs generally and crack cocaine in particular allowed the media to link drugs with race, and African Americans with deviance.[27] This focus on race and crime fed the public's fears and helped to embed the impression that most dangerous criminals were people of color. *Newsweek* boldly declared the threat that White Americans secretly feared: "Crack ha[d] captured the ghetto" and was "inching its way into the suburbs."[28] The media exacerbated White concern by warning of the potential for crack to seep out of the inner city and into their neighborhoods.[29] By 1986, the media had labeled crack the most dangerous drug and had decried the outbreak of a national "crack epidemic."[30]

At the same time, popular culture adopted the images of people of color as drug dealers and leaders of violent criminal drug syndicates. Prime-time television featured an increasing number of police shows with drug themes and people of color in the role of kingpin or petty criminal. This attached a certain stigma to all people of color. Because of the profound segregation in housing patterns in this country, research suggests that opinions about people of color held by Whites are often based upon images on television.[31] Dorothy Roberts argues that the dominant society is not appalled at the racial disparities in arrests and prison sentences because they believe that African American people are dangerous.[32] The media portrays the drug problem as one that primarily exists in communities of color, and the racial disparities in the prison system are viewed, if noticed at all, as reflecting reality rather than reflecting overenforcement or discrimination. The media's barrage of coverage and images of urban youths involved in drug dealing, coupled with high-profile events such as the death of the Boston Celtics basketball team's number one college draft pick in 1986, Len Bias, caused politicians to enter the fray.[33]

Politicians came into the criminal justice debate riding the "tough on crime" bandwagon. They used images that the media had provided. They focused on urban youth, with thinly veiled racial attacks. Using terms like "super-predators," both Democratic and Republican politicians used front-page and television evening news stories to support their political agendas. Politicians focused on a number of areas, but drug laws and drug convictions were the primary targets. According to the Sentencing Project, one in three Black men between the ages of twenty and twenty-nine is under correctional supervision or control, and approximately 14 percent of Black men have lost their right to vote due to felony convictions.[34] These crusades created a range of unrelated sanctions, such as the mandatory suspension of the driver's license of anyone convicted of a drug offense (even if no car was involved in the crime), but not of rapists, robbers, or murderers. This not only seems illogical but further exemplifies the unbalanced focus on drugs. Politicians also embraced mandatory minimum sentencing for drug offenders, adding to the incarceration explosion that took place in the late 1980s and early 1990s.

A. The Politics of Race, Crime, and Reentry

The media's intense focus on race and crime and its interpretation of the "tough on crime" electoral messages of the 1980s and 1990s helped forge a new political direction for the country.[35] This direction focused on increasingly punitive sanctions for people of color. A number of researchers have examined the mass media's role in creating and fueling the focus on crime and the ensuing response of overincarceration,[36] and a number of leading theorists, including David Garland, have grappled with the process by which this punitive approach has crept into popular and political language.[37] Particularly during the Reagan/Bush administrations, crime and crime control became the political capital through which politicians assumed and maintained electoral power. When this political focus was coupled with media attention on state and local crime issues, the public became willing and vocal supporters of policies that provided some semblance of controlling the crime problem. The expansion of imprisonment became a primary vehicle to accomplish that, especially at the federal level.[38]

The rush to embrace crime control as a model occurred as the public clamored for answers to the recurring crime problem and as the perception grew that nothing could be done to change the behavior of offenders. Research in the 1970s began to suggest that rehabilitation was limited in its effectiveness as a treatment for addressing criminal behavior. Although first used in relation to prison-based treatment, this research was later used to characterize probation, parole, and other aspects of the criminal justice system.[39] Increasingly, sanctions focused on prison as the primary punishment for drug offenses.[40] In the directional shift toward custody, we find the seeds for the current crisis in reentry. The 1980s marked the declaration of the War on Drugs and its intensification.[41] In fear of being perceived as soft on crime, politicians moved to increase penalties, incarceration, and collateral sanctions with little or no research as to the long-term consequences of these policies.[42]

Until the 1970s, the focus of criminal justice intervention seemed to be rehabilitation. But in the '70s, an array of news stories, features, and research followed up on Robert Martinson's suggestion in 1974 that "nothing works" in penal rehabilitation efforts.[43] This sparked a major retreat from rehabilitation and treatment in prison settings, both in policy work and by therapists themselves. Although recent studies suggest that prison-based treatment can be effective, we have not witnessed an expansion of substance-abuse services.[44] The constant barrage by the media of stories detailing—sometimes graphically—the crimes committed by ex-felons fueled the public perception that the crime problem was spiraling dangerously out of control. This intense coverage by the media and conservative public officials led to the ratcheting up of enforcement policies. Criminologist Jonathan Simon has suggested that "governing through crime," a process by which policy makers substitute punitive crime-control rhetoric for substantive governance, accounts in large part for the fundamental shift in penal practices.[45]

The 1988 presidential election witnessed Republican propaganda focusing on Willie Horton to call the nation's attention to race and parole. The Bush campaign used Willie Horton, who had committed murder and rape while on work furlough, both to characterize opponent Michael Dukakis as soft on crime and simultaneously to capitalize on the threat, allegedly posed by Black males generally, that had been steadily cemented in the public mind by a decade of media spin.[46] More specifically, the campaign centered on Black parolees and work release, furloughs, and other programs aiding in the reentry of all ex-offenders.[47] The political force and persuasiveness of the images, however, paralyzed those who might otherwise have taken a more principled position.[48] There was no opposition to this particular issue in the campaign.

The primary political fallout from the combined media and political blitzkrieg of the 1980s was the creation of the Federal Sentencing Guidelines and an array of state mandatory minimum sentences for drug offenses. In 1986, Congress created the Federal Sentencing Guidelines, essentially a sentencing grid that maintained a dramatic sentencing differential between crack and powder cocaine. Powder cocaine was widely viewed as the drug of choice for Whites, while crack was demonized and largely associated with people of color in urban communities.[49] This sentencing disparity was reinforced in 1988, as legislators on the state and federal level defended it by alleging that crack is more addictive and produces a stronger, more debilitating high than powder cocaine. Despite the vehemence of their arguments, science did not support their claims—the pharmacology of the two drugs is identical.[50] The real difference in these drugs relates to relative cost and accessibility. Because crack costs significantly less than powder cocaine, it became more widely accessible; crack does allow for a faster, higher absorption than snorted powder cocaine, so it might seem like a more powerful drug even though it is not.

In the same way liberal politicians and commentators were slow to respond to the racist use of the Willie Horton imagery, they were slow to recognize the racially disparate impact of the crack/powder-cocaine sentencing scheme. Their inaction may have been partly due to fear of being portrayed as "soft on crime."[51] "Crack" became a code word for "Black drug use" and was accompanied by images of violence and lawlessness. This, in turn, became a rallying cry for many conservative politicians.

The focus on crack also refocused law enforcement policies. Because crack was sold in open-air markets or readily identifiable "crack houses" and the extremely high penalties for small amounts made convictions or guilty pleas easier, local, state, and federal law enforcement efforts almost single-mindedly focused their efforts on crack. In addition to the focus on other collateral sanctions, such as loss of housing, food stamps, or the inability to apply for a wide variety of occupations unrelated to the crime, politicians also embraced mandatory minimum sentencing for drug offenders. This added to the incarceration explosion that took place in the late 1980s and early 1990s. Although the nation experienced increases in many serious crimes, between 1985 and 1995 the number of drug offenders sent to prison increased 478 percent as compared to 119 percent for all other crimes.[52] Incarceration became the primary focus of the drug war. Although much of the War on Drugs was fought at the local level, the pattern of large numbers of prosecutions followed by extensive incarceration was evident in the federal system as well. Federal drug prosecutions increased by close to 100 percent from 1982 to 1988, while prosecutions for other crimes rose only 4 percent.[53]

In 1994, U.S. District Judge Clyde Cahill found the 100-to-1 disparity between sentences for crack cocaine and powder cocaine to be unconstitutional. The case was significant in that Judge Cahill openly called the guidelines "racially biased legislation."[54] He went on to identify the reason for the drafting of the legislation, writing that panic based on media reports designed to incite "racial fears" was the catalyst for generating this policy.[55] The Eighth Circuit Court of Appeals reversed Judge Cahill and chastised him for questioning the racial animus of the legislation.[56] In one of the most significant academic contributions to the crack-versus-powder equal-protection debate, David Sklansky points out that the rhetoric surrounding the passage of the 1986 statute, with Congress stating that "big shouldered Trinidadians . . . [and] bands of young Black men . . . peddling crack near unsuspecting White retirees," suggested a racial animus in its intent.[57] Sklansky further points out that in the Eighth Circuit reversal of Judge Cahill's decision, the appellate court reasoned that Congress did not have "racial animus, but racial consciousness that the problem in the inner cities was about to explode into the White parts of the country."[58]

As the Federal Sentencing Guidelines were implemented there were outcries from virtually every sector. Politicians, state and federal judges, lawyers, and even two United States Supreme Court justices have called for the review of the discrepancy between crack and powder cocaine. A number of those challenging the disparity have pointed to the obvious racial impact of the sentencing scheme. The challenges have taken the form of legal complaints alleging a lack of equal protection under the law, as well as challenges on policy grounds. Before his election, in response to a question about the sentencing disparity, George W. Bush stated, "[I]t ought to be addressed by making sure the powder cocaine and the crack cocaine penalties are the same. I don't believe we ought to be discriminatory."[59] Ultimately, not only did Bush's administration refuse to proffer legislation leveling out the penalties for crack and powder cocaine, but President Bush's deputy attorney general also told the United States Sentencing Commission that "[t]he current federal policy and guidelines for sentencing crack cocaine offenses are appropriate" and that crack "traffickers should be subject to significantly higher penalties than traffickers of like amounts of powder [cocaine]."[60] Again, despite a lack of scientific data, many continued to allege that crack is a more potent form of the drug. Others pointed to the violence associated with crack trafficking—but this is a distracting issue, because the Federal Sentencing Guidelines have existing means to address the use of firearms in the commission of criminal offenses.

But there have been more vociferous criticisms. In November 2003, United States Supreme Court Justice Anthony Kennedy gave a speech at the American Bar Association annual meeting criticizing these sentencing disparities.[61] In a speech at the Harvard Kennedy School of Government, Supreme Court Justice Stephen Breyer also criticized mandatory minimum sentences.[62] Notwithstanding all of the criticism and the pointing to racial disparities in creating, enacting, and enforcing the sentencing guidelines, little has been done to address the issue. And so we have continued to overincarcerate people of color for drug offenses.

Very little political support has come to communities of color subjected to overincarceration, the collateral consequences, and the accompanying policies. The nation might have looked for leadership from seemingly liberal, of-color, or other politicians elected on platforms suggesting a fairer shake for people of color, but that has not been the case.[63] In fact, the impact of sweeping huge numbers of young African American, Asian, and Latino men and women into the criminal justice system was the creation of a political vacuum. Removing young people who may have been eligible to vote from a position where they could exercise that right effectively silenced their voices and neutralized any political capital that they might have had. The wide gap between the middle class and the "permanent poor" increased and the War on Drugs only helped to widen the cultural, political, and representational divide.

Throughout the decades of the 1980s and 1990s politicians of color largely remained mute in the national debate on drugs and crime. When the War on Drugs was at its rhetorical height, conservative and Republican politicians had cornered the market on tough-on-crime positions. Liberal and mainstream Democratic politicians often did not (and still do not) have adequate responses to this rhetoric. Politicians, who routinely asked for impact studies on environmental legislation, never required in-depth examinations of the impact of criminal justice legislation. Instead, the sanctions became more draconian, and collateral consequences increased unchecked for decades. In many communities, the victims of crime were people of color as often as the alleged perpetrators of crime were, further complicating things for politicians of color. Even toward the end of the 1990s, as the crime rates gradually inched downward and the crack epidemic began to subside, drug arrests and prison populations continued to rise.[64] In the face of continued repression in communities of color under the guise of implementing the nation's drug laws, political leaders remained relatively silent.[65]

These get-tough policies in the 1980s and early 1990s reflected the racial demographic changes that occurred in America's cities between the 1960s and the 1980s—the emergence of a Black underclass living in concentrated poverty. Previously, the effects of inner-city life created a narrative that enabled sociologists and the popular media to describe the environment within low-income communities as encouraging a "culture of poverty" or a deviant subculture in which poor people sought out, enjoyed, and perpetuated destructive lifestyles.[66] This narrative suggested that African Americans were primed to populate this permanent underclass. About 40 percent of African Americans exist at or below the margin of regular employment, minimal income, and personal security.[67] Contact by affluent Whites with people of different races or those in low-income communities comes through personally experiencing crime, passing through blighted communities, or having limited contact with people working in the service economy—cleaning people, delivery persons, security guards. Occasionally, the contact is a direct experience of crime. But more often interracial experiences come through stories related by friends or family or on a more regular basis through the daily news reports of crime, drugs, and violence that appear in the newspapers or on the nightly televised news.

The majority of Americans have had their views of this underclass shaped by a lack of personal interaction with individuals of a different race and by the fear of crime leaving the urban ghettoes and invading the suburbs. Andrew Hacker, in his book *Two Nations,* points out that "few White Americans feel any obligation to make any sacrifices on behalf of the nation's principal minority."[68] Many in this country call for a tougher stand toward what is seen as the misbehavior of many Blacks.[69] The lack of contact[70] between Whites and most persons of color has made it virtually impossible to break down the large and diverse racial stereotypes promulgated in the media and in politics.[71] Consequently, much of the political and policy debate describes poor and of-color communities as undeserving and responsible for their conditions.[72]

The permanence of this underclass has been reinforced by a lack of "economic optimism" even in times of great financial prosperity for the balance of the country. The economic boom years of the 1990s largely passed unnoticed in communities of color. Job growth generally has occurred in the suburbs and in sectors of the economy that require levels of education beyond that possessed by many urban minority workers, because of the economic and racial changes in the population of urban areas in the last few decades.[73] This has led to the existence of an environment of concentrated poverty and racial, social, cultural, and political isolation.[74] This concentration of poverty results in negative policy decisions.[75] When we consider the already monumental obstacles associated with race, along with the profound burdens that society then adds to the status of the formerly incarcerated, what results is a permanent stigma that affixes itself to an entire generation of people of color. The net effect has been that communities of color in many areas of this country have been sentenced to generational poverty and can expect continued isolation for the foreseeable future.

In the wake of the terrorist attacks of September 11, 2001, a new national focus on terrorism, paired with very little political dissent, encouraged a justice policy that virtually endorsed the unrelenting assault on civil liberties, especially in communities of color. In a society already struggling with stereotypes involving race and crime,[76] attaching this incredible stigma to a large portion of the population by way of collateral consequences of felony conviction may push us toward the brink of developing a "permanent underclass."[77]

The next section takes a closer look at how we form stereotypes and allow them to govern our perceptions and choices. The impact of stereotypes is palpable in our approach to reentry.

B. Stigma

A criminal conviction by itself creates significant obstacles to finding legal employment by interrupting employment, limiting the development of job skills, and discouraging potential employers from hiring those with a criminal history.[78] It also undermines the social connections necessary to maintain stable job opportunities.[79] When ex-offenders return from prison they often lack the education and skills needed to compete in the labor market, and the stigma of criminal conviction makes employers extra wary of hiring them. Where an occupational license is required, ex-offenders are often legally barred from obtaining jobs.

Where the particular job that an ex-offender seeks is not one that requires a license, the ex-offender frequently finds that employers will not interview, let alone hire, someone who has been convicted of a crime. Many employers fear those convicted of crimes or believe that ex-offenders will not be reliable employees. Other employers are concerned about hiring applicants with a known criminal past because of the risk of negligent hiring liability for insurers and other employees. The labels attached to ex-offender status as well as the negative connotations often result in a self-fulfilling prophecy that ex-offenders cannot successfully reintegrate into society.[80]

Ex-offenders of color carry a particularly strong stigma as they attempt to become contributing members of their communities. Some researchers have suggested that the damage of ex-offender stigma permanently impairs the earning capacity of people of color.[81] The stigma begins early, and teenagers who are incarcerated have very little chance of obtaining a steady employment pattern in life.[82] The stigma of ex-convict status also significantly affects families of ex-offenders.[83] In addition to the damage a criminal conviction inflicts on the individual and the family,[84] researchers have also concluded that removing large numbers of residents who engage in both legal work and crime constitutes a significant loss to local economies.[85] When we pause to consider this country's economic boom in the 1980s and '90s, we rarely notice the number of young men of color who dropped out of the economy and into prison or onto the unemployment rolls.[86]

Most would concede that addressing issues of stigma is essential to planning for prisoner reentry. However, the extent to which the stigma of a criminal conviction, race, and bias interact makes this a particularly onerous task. A recent study sent matched pairs of young Black and White men to apply for entry-level job openings; a criminal record had a greater adverse impact on Black applicants than White applicants. Even more disturbing and quite telling of the problem's intractability, White applicants with criminal records were more likely to receive callbacks from employers than Blacks with no criminal history.[87]

The stigma of race and its relationship to crime may provide us with significant insights into how we should think about reentry. In my own work I have described the ways in which race and suspicion intersect, particularly in the context of Fourth Amendment protections against police searches and detentions of suspects.[88]

Social scientists and cognitive psychologists have studied the manner in which people make sense of themselves and others. This process of categorization enables us to organize and make decisions about information with less time and effort than we would require confronting behavior and events anew each time. It is the process of grouping of information into smaller, more manageable bits of information that achieves the efficiency of human cognitive organization.[89] Categories become a set of characteristics treated as if they were, for the purposes at hand, similar or capable of being substituted for each other.

Clustering information into categories leads inevitably to some prejudgment based upon our perceptions of those groupings. Stereotypes have been defined as the "general inclination to place a person in categories according to some easily and quickly identifiable characteristic such as age, sex, ethnic membership, nationality, or occupation, and then to attribute to him qualities believed to be typical of members of that category."[90] Schemas are best described as the preconceptions that define category members.[91] A schema is a piece of knowledge that represents an "averaging" of specific items or events.[92]

The research of cognitive psychologists suggests that negative stereotypes about other races and ethnicities can develop early in our lives and become deeply rooted in our minds.[93] The interrelationship among self-identity, social identity, and racial beliefs is so complex that a person's beliefs about different races, once developed, are highly resistant to change. Of course, stereotypes about groups tend not be any more accurate than any other type of generalization[94] because they represent oversimplification of complexities.[95] But we tend to rely on them and, at times, to be prejudiced by them in making complex discretionary decisions.

Not all categories lead to intractable stereotypes. Some categories are held tentatively and the individual remains open to information that is inconsistent with the stereotypical category. Nonetheless, in most instances, categories stubbornly resist change.[96] Moreover, in the case of racial and ethnic stereotyping, "people tend to hold to prejudgments even in the face of much contradictory evidence."[97] Cognitive psychologists further explain that learning processes are facilitated by the development of schemas—mental constructs that facilitate the processing of new, unfamiliar stimuli by comparing them to familiar ones and drawing conclusions about the new based on what the person knows about the familiar.[98] All of this creates certain strong perceptions about race and behavior.

Individuals tend to make judgments about people using their learned categories as contexts for making such judgments. These judgments are often interpreted to coincide with the prevailing schema.[99] When a criminal conviction is added, the tendency to stereotype becomes overwhelming. Given the images in the media, the news, and popular culture—which often portray people of color as dangerous criminals—it is not hard to imagine why an individual would make presumptions about someone applying for a job or seeking housing. Because prejudice based on race is a difficult issue to parse, legislative and administrative protections that limit the types of permissible background inquiries tend to be less than effective.

Assumptions about the criminality of African Americans are widespread.[100] The number of race-related judgments that a particular individual will make is determined by intrapersonal factors, including social identity,[101] myths about "legitimate racial differences,"[102] and self-esteem maintenance.[103] Jody Armour cites a 1990 study suggesting that over 56 percent of Americans perceive Blacks as prone to violence.[104] Moreover, while other ethnic minorities are also stereotyped as crime prone, the stereotype of African American criminality tends to be bolstered by the media. Consumer discrimination research vividly describes the extent to which African Americans are targeted by the commercial retail industry for surveillance on the assumption that they are more likely to be engaged in criminality.[105]

These same beliefs about criminality and dangerousness do not exist with white-collar criminals—who are predominantly not people of color. The term "white-collar crime" was coined by Edwin H. Sutherland, and the definition has as much to do with class as it does with crime because of the particular forms economic inequality have taken in the United States.[106] Sutherland himself suggested that the stigma associated with a white-collar criminal is much diminished as compared to that associated with other criminal conduct.[107] Although a wide range of conduct seems to fall into the white-collar category,[108] and a range of harms is included, the criminal stigma does not attach as quickly and white-collar offenders are often well assisted in their reentry into society.

Commentators rarely question whether white-collar offenders should immediately return to their communities, even when their conduct may have done far more harm than so-called street crime. Defendants of color from inner-city communities are most often presumed to be prison bound even before conviction; their eventual reentry is more often impeded by all of the players in the criminal justice system. From the prosecutor who charges, plea bargains, and recommends prison to the probation officer who compiles the probation report, the entire process is stacked against the person of color's rehabilition and reentry. In addition to the criminal justice participants, the defendant charged with a street crime must also overcome immense obstacles, such as employment bans, education-grant ineligibility, and denial of housing and social welfare benefits.

Non-White defendants sentenced by judges of a different race and/or ethnicity are frequently used as opportunities for exemplification. Judges in these circumstances objectify the defendant and focus more on the crime in making the sentencing decision than on the circumstances that led to the crime. The exact opposite happens when the defendant is a white-collar defendant, and even more often when the defendant is of the same race as the judge. In those instances, the court is willing to examine a wider range of factors in making sentencing decisions. White-collar criminals have often been described by judges as some of the most difficult offenders to sentence.[109] Judges describe the need to "look past the crime," to look at the defendant's "whole life and his place in society."[110] This becomes easier when race is not an issue, as is often the case in white-collar sentencing. In those settings race does not carry the negative impact that it does in other (nonviolent) sentencing. Arguably, this wider range of factors and alternatives should be considered in all cases. This is instructive as we contemplate the issues surrounding reentry.

In the white-collar scenario a number of alternative punishments have been explored. Some suggest shaming is enough of a punishment for white-collar criminals. Judges are willing to impose the least punitive sentence because judges are willing to believe that less drastic steps will have a significant impact on white-collar offenders. The negative impact of a loss of social status, when the defendant is upper middle class, is given great weight in the sentencing process. The notion that incarceration is "too far a fall from grace" to be fair is presumed before sentencing.

Defendants of color are not generally given the same benefits of social status as White defendants, even if they have never been incarcerated or committed a violent offense. In the instance of a first-time offender of color in a drug case, we rarely hear that shaming would be appropriate. Some argue that white-collar crimes involve situations where victims are hard to identify and harm is difficult to quantify. In addition, the "rationing of corrections space" also becomes a factor when white-collar criminals are to be sentenced. In cases involving nonviolent offenders that are of a different class, race, or ethnicity than the sentencing judge, officials seem more apt to suggest building more prisons than to suggest rationing existing beds.

Judges and prosecutors are more willing to take into account the circumstances of white-collar defendants' lives than those of defendants who have had access to far fewer opportunities, perhaps because they can see themselves in the face of the offender. One need only look to the treasurer of Enron, Lea Fastow. In a case involving six felony counts, prosecutors sought to enforce a plea bargain wherein Ms. Fastow could serve a sentence of five months in custody and five months at home caring for her children.[111] This would allow her to stagger her sentence with her husband's sentence.[112] The judge hearing the case refused to be bound by the deal, given the severity of the charges. The judge indicated that he would probably impose a sentence of ten to sixteen months.[113] Prosecutors seeking to placate Ms. Fastow dismissed all six felony counts and allowed her to plead to a misdemeanor, prompting one commentator to describe the deal as "indicting someone for bank robbery and knocking it down to spitting on the sidewalk."[114]

Prosecutor assistance in the Fastow case is the type of assistance that defendants need in order to prepare for release and formal reintegration into their communities. Cases involving defendants of color in nonviolent criminal conduct rarely see this type of cooperation, which raises some fundamental questions about how the court system treats white-collar defendants as opposed to indigent defendants. There is a not-so-subtle, implied notion that white-collar defendants have "more to lose" and therefore should be treated differently.

2

Media Influence on Public Perceptions of Prison Life

In the aftermath of Hurricane Katrina, two news photo-graphs ricocheted around the Internet and set off a debate about race and the news media. The first photo, taken by Dave Martin, an Associ-ated Press photographer in New Orleans, shows a young Black man wading through water that has risen to his chest. He is clutching a case of soda and pulling a floating bag. The caption provided by the AP says he has just been "looting a grocery store." The second photo, also from New Orleans, was taken by Chris Graythen for Getty Images and dis-tributed by Agence France-Presse. It shows a White couple up to their chests in the same murky water. The woman is holding some bags of food. This caption says they are shown "after finding bread and soda from a local grocery store." Both photos turned up on Yahoo News, which posts automatic feeds of articles and photos from wire services. Soon after, the rapper Kanye West ignored the teleprompter during NBC's live broadcast of "A Concert for Hurricane Relief," using the opportunity to lambast President Bush and criticize the press. "I hate the way they portray us in the media," he said. "You see a Black family, it says they're looting. You see a White family, it says they're looking for food."[1]

Many people have had no direct contact or experience with the criminal justice system, so their information about criminal justice comes exclu-sively from second-hand reporting, entertainment, and other representa-tions in the media. This fact has important implications for public per-ceptions of law enforcement agencies, the courts and prisons, offenders, and victims. Several studies have shown that television programming greatly exaggerates the amount and frequency of violent crime relative to property crime.[2] Both news and entertainment media consistently portray a more violent and dangerous view of our world than exists in reality.

The media's dramatic effect on shaping perceptions of reality is clear.[3] One study has correlated the amount of media coverage on a particular correctional topic with public knowledge of and interest in the same subject. In Florida, polling information revealed that the general public perceived overcrowding of prison facilities as the most pressing correctional problem, and a content analysis of Florida news media showed "overcrowding" to be the most frequently reported correctional issue.[4] There was, in fact, no real problem of overcrowding in Florida prisons at the time, but media coverage and emphasis informed and shaped public perception despite the reality of the situation.[5]

So-called reality programs sometimes integrate actual footage and dramatic reenactments of the real-life adventures of police officers, suspects, emergency medical personnel, and everyday citizens performing heroic feats.[6] Popular crime dramas focus primarily on violent offenders, perhaps for dramatic effect. One is left with the clear impression that criminal activity is typically random or results from individual pathology rather than larger social ills such as poverty, racism, and unemployment.[7] And much as we see in the local news, the entertainment industry quite regularly depicts the crime problem along racial lines, with a disproportionate number of White officers compared to White offenders, and a disproportionate number of minority offenders compared to minority officers.[8] Obviously, the script writers and producers of these crime dramas have no interest in presenting—and are under no obligation to offer—a balanced viewpoint. So, it is not unusual to view the events that these shows depict from the perspective of either law enforcement officials or prosecutors.[9] Viewers are left with the impression that the police operate efficiently and always solve their cases. These distorted images may combine to skew viewers' perceptions of the crime problem in the United States. And these distortions become particularly problematic when we consider how they serve to stereotype people of color.

The popular media's portrayal of our corrections system tends to focus on violence, corruption, and a severe degree of disorganization. Nightly news coverage and investigative stories represent the media's effort to provide more in-depth coverage of the lives of inmates and the problems they encounter. But, more often, the public builds its perception of prison life from the entertainment media. Television programs such as *Prison Break* and *Oz* and popular movies such as *The Shawshank Redemption* often purport to give the public an insider's view of the daily lives of inmates.[10] Millions of people watch these forms of entertainment; the influence upon the public imagination cannot be discounted.[11] But, the public is unaware of this impact. In a self-reporting survey, many people underestimated the role of entertainment in the creation or reinforcement of their own subconscious assumptions, especially in comparison to the impact of explicitly "informative" news programming.[12]

A. News Coverage of Prisons and Offenders

The news media continues to have a significant impact on the development of public policy in the related areas of prisons, crime, and delinquency. Crime coverage in the news media plays an important agenda-setting role, as well as influencing public perceptions about the incidence and severity of antisocial behavior.[13] By looking at the percentage of stories and their content, we can begin to glean patterns that may explain policy as well as public opinion.

A content analysis of 206 *New York Times* articles relating to corrections published between 1992 and 1995 found that more stories focused on institutional violence and riots than any other issue, at 40 percent.[14] Interestingly, the second most reported were stories on correctional programs and rehabilitation (34 percent), followed by health care (17 percent), followed by stories about tough-on-crime policies (16 percent).[15] Content analysis found that the majority of sources quoted by the *New York Times* were government officials voicing support for the government's position on a particular issue.[16] In the case of institutional violence, the articles focused almost entirely on particular violent events, rather than on policy debate.[17]

Articles on institutional violence often took the form of investigative reporting, a method almost entirely absent from other articles on correctional issues.[18] As for the prevalence of articles on rehabilitation, the authors of the content analysis use this result to suggest that, "contrary to the claims of some correctional pundits, the issue of rehabilitation is far from dead."[19] The statistical content analysis at least suggests that the bulk of the stories on corrections—and indirectly on those who inhabit prisons—focused on violence. This is more than a confirmation of the "if it bleeds, it leads" mantra. Rather, this speaks to the difficulty in developing a constituency and support for reentry. It also highlights the focus on government sources for quotes. If the public sees that the primary "in-depth, newsworthy stories" from prison are full of violence, then the news contributes to the notion that prisons are violent places filled with people who cannot easily be reintegrated.

Electronic media have been equally as focused on violent crime. Researchers have documented the media's predilection for stories of criminal violence against another person.[20] A survey of local television news in Los Angeles revealed that crime coverage was overwhelmingly focused on violent crime rather than property nonviolent crime and that where the race of the offender was recorded, nearly 70 percent were non-White males.[21] A similar study of local news in Chicago confirmed that television images were not only violent but also disproportionately focused on incidents involving perpetrators who were people of color.[22] People tend to forget, ignore, or miss altogether distinctions in crime news, which is a further means of developing false impressions. In watching and reading the news, the average viewer tends to think of a person who kills after being released from prison for a lesser—or less violent—offense simply as another murderer who was released too early. This assumption ignores altogether that he was released as someone who had committed a lesser crime and had never committed murder. Thus, news accounts of murders committed by persons who have previously served prison terms for other crimes, or by persons who were charged with first-degree murder but convicted of lesser offenses and later paroled, may contribute to the false impression that convicted first-degree murderers are back on the streets far sooner than they actually are. Of course, such selective ignorance makes these stories more consonant with myths of crime and punishment.

There is no question that the public is deeply concerned about crime; however, the average citizen actually knows very little about rates of incarceration, who is being incarcerated, and how much time they serve. This information is not part of the media coverage on crime; that coverage is episodic, not analytical. Nonetheless, Julian Roberts and Loretta Stalans have conducted a number of studies that seem to indicate that the majority of the public in the United States, the United Kingdom, Canada, and Australia share the view that sentences imposed on adults are too lenient.[23] In 1996, polls conducted by the National Opinion Research Center reported that 67 percent of those surveyed thought that the nation spent too little on stemming the rising rate of crime,[24] while 78 percent said that the courts in their area did not deal harshly enough with criminals.[25] Elected officials have responded to public concern about crime with an easily explained, superficially appealing strategy that does not provide an effective response to that concern. Simplistic terms and limited sentencing discretion proffered by elected officials are not limited to violent crime (which the public is largely focused on) but tend to catch large numbers of property and drug offenders in their indiscriminate nets as well.

B. Entertainment Media

In thinking critically and analytically about policies and attitudes regarding offenders, ex-offenders, reentry, and race, it is helpful—if not necessary—to examine the entertainment media. Movies, in their two-hour format, provide an opportunity to transport the viewer to a world wholly divorced from his or her own daily experiences. This medium taps into emotions and transmits messages about the prison and post-prison experiences. At its best, entertainment media can educate the public to a side of life that is normally concealed to the average person. At its worst, it can caricature, stereotype, and titillate with little concern about the accuracy of its portrayals. What follows is a closer look at a few examples.

1. *The Shawshank Redemption*

Although not initially a huge hit upon its release in 1994, *The Shawshank Redemption* became enormously successful through video rental and sales.[26] In the Internet Movie Database list of the top 250 movies of all time, as voted by users, *Shawshank* rates as number two—trailing only the original *Godfather*, and easily eclipsing in popularity such iconic films as *Star Wars* and *Casablanca*.[27] *The Shawshank Redemption* (Castle Rock Entertainment, 1994) is based on "Rita Hayworth and the Shawshank Redemption," a novella that Stephen King published in a collection called *Different Seasons*.[28]

Shawshank combines two genres: escape fantasy and prison movie. Although stylistically and thematically, the film sets itself apart from other prison movies, it does employ classic prison movie devices, including corrupt prison authorities, unchecked inmate violence, and sexual assault. The lead character, Andy, played by Tim Robbins, must endure the repeated experience of homosexual rape at the hands of the "Sisters," men who represent the perceived brutal side of prison life. The ultimate message is that the prison experience is so brutal and entrenched that no one can truly be rehabilitated.

The prison librarian, Brooks, has lived in an institutional setting for so long that not only has he adjusted to it, but he cannot survive outside its walls. Consequently, when he is released and reenters society without the support of people he knows and the familiarity of the structured environment in which he had lived for so long, he cannot cope and hangs himself.

Finally, the third key inmate character is the old-timer, Red (played by Morgan Freeman). He is African American and seamlessly manages to navigate the racial conflicts and the politics of the prison. Through his friendship with the White character, Andy, he moves beyond the loneliness and despair that he too experiences upon release. He violates parole to follow clues to hidden money Andy has put away, and he is magically transported to Mexico to live out his days with his buddy.[29] It is only through the extraordinary intervention of Andy, culminating in an utterly mythologized ending where the two friends meet on some nameless, featureless beach in Mexico, that Red can actually be redeemed. This is not unlike other prison films that require the intervention of some metaphysical force for any type of lasting reintegration to take place.

The film never posits anything other than a broadly cast, allegorical reentry or redemption, rather than the specific example of an ex-offender successfully reintegrating into society.[30] Consider the recurring parole hearing scenes, which serve as markers of Red's slow progress into hard-bitten wisdom. As film critic Roger Ebert characterized it in his review, "in his first appeal [Red] tries to convince the board he's been rehabilitated. In the second, he just goes through the motions. In the third, he rejects the whole notion of rehabilitation, and somehow in doing so he sets his spirit free, and the board releases him."[31] Finally, at least one reviewer picked up on the trope of prison as a "school" for crime, as Janet Maslin takes note of Andy's successful new career as the prison financial consultant offering shady advice to the warden and his guards.[32]

In the twentieth-century prison depicted in *Shawshank*, the concept of reformation had practically disappeared. For the most part, penitentiaries like Shawshank are seen as serving a purely custodial function—as a warehouse for the convicted. This warehousing prison philosophy reemerged in the 1980s and 1990s and has remained part of our prison landscape.

The ultimate messages of *Shawshank* are threefold. First, prison is brutal and numbing and most inmates cannot make it through the experience once they have been exposed to this illogical and meaningless place. Second, prison becomes so debilitating that its members lose their ability to function in the external world. As sentences become longer, we have old-timers like Abraham who cleaned Wakefield prison long after his sentence is completed, and Brooks, who is unable to function outside the prison. Finally, the only way to prevent the inevitable destruction of spirit is to escape the confines of society. Redemption is ultimately linked to escape, not reintegration.

Television provides an opportunity to reach more individuals than can be reached in movie theaters. Cable takes characters and storylines that were once deemed too intense, too explicit, and too violent for television and puts them in late-evening slots. Cable tends to take more chances and devotes more time to character development, while at the same time still seeking the dramatic content to move the story and the viewer.

2. *Oz*

The HBO hit series *Oz*, which ran for six seasons between 1997 and 2003, depicted daily prison life as brutal and chaotic. One reporter wrote, "mention *Oz* to those who have seen it and many will squirm at its soap-operatic tales of scheming, divided loyalties and unfortunate consequences, namely shankings, rapes and beatings."[33] The aim of the show, as expressed by the writer/producer Tom Fontana, was to create a realistic representation of prison life, and "not to entertain people."[34] His notion of what "real prison life" looked like suggested that "it lets you know there's a part of society out there that you don't want any contact with."[35] Unfortunately, it also led viewers to conclude that they didn't want any contact with the people in prison—while they are inside or, presumably, once they are released.

Because the prison is perceived as a brutal, inhumane place and prisoners as its unflinchingly evil inhabitants, *Oz* only served to confirm viewers' notions of prison life. As it turns out, viewers were both entertained by the program and convinced of the "deeper truths" mined by *Oz*. A sampling of viewer comments[36] regarding the show reveals that much of its appeal derives, in fact, from the assumption that it depicts prison life "unflinchingly"—i.e., as it really is. "Dark, dark drama about life in prison. If you want to scare kids straight, make them watch *Oz*; if that does not turn their life around nothing will."[37] The unchallenged assumption that the drama and violence as shown in *Oz* and other television and movie dramas constitutes an accurate portrayal has led individuals to form inaccurate beliefs about prison and what prison and reentry policy should look like.

C. What the Public Thinks It Knows

Generally speaking, the public knows little of correctional institutions, especially compared to its knowledge of other law enforcement agencies.[38] This is not surprising given that prisons are closed spaces, and most people have never had reason to be inside a prison in any capacity.[39] Also, the lack of knowledge about prisons is not new. According to a study conducted forty years ago in the United States, researchers found that "people are generally ignorant of [prison] programs."[40]

Although the public also holds gross misconceptions about other criminal justice issues, such as the rate of crime, "perhaps the area reflecting the greatest degree of misunderstanding and misinformation is institutional corrections."[41] While one might expect that the general public would only pay attention to corrections issues if it had a direct experience with them, one might also expect that our most educated citizens would have more than a superficial understanding of institutions that constitute part of the enforcement of the social contract. In a survey of undergraduate college students, respondents were asked to estimate the prevalence of antisocial behavior in prisons. Students were asked to estimate (1) the number of inmates killed by inmates in prison; (2) the number of correctional officers killed by inmates; and (3) the number of male sexual assaults in prison. The results show that all students, even those majoring in criminal justice, vastly overestimated the frequency of these events.

- Inmates killed by inmates. Of all undergraduate students, 64.5 percent thought that more than four hundred inmates were killed by other inmates on a yearly basis. In 2002, according to the *Corrections Compendium*, the actual number of inmates killed was seventeen.[42]

- Corrections officers killed by inmates. Most college students (39.2 percent) thought that between ten and ninety-nine corrections officers were killed by inmates. A full 25.3 percent thought more than four hundred were killed. In 2002, a total of one corrections officer was actually killed by an inmate.[43]

Given our knowledge of the frequency with which the news and entertainment media focus on these types of images in programming, this study strongly suggests that this media focus influences beliefs. Even when individuals have access to better-quality information, the influence of media images seems compelling.

D. Public Attitudes toward Incarceration

The myths and stereotypes that drive public opinion about prison enable elected officials to operate publicly without a factual basis for their policy goals. Moreover, there is rarely an impact study completed in advance of policy enactment to establish the impact on the community, the victim, or the offender. The perhaps predicable result of this behavior has been the erection of vast, inconsistent, and often illogical barriers to housing, employment, voting, and almost every other manifestation of community reintegration.

1. Prison as an "Easy Life"

Although the public overestimates the occurrence of violence and sexual assault in prisons, paradoxically, it also sees prison life as one of idleness and even leisure. This could be partially explained by stories in the news that tend to dwell on the amenities to which prisoners have access.[44] For example, 90 percent of respondents to a survey in Florida believe that inmates are housed in air-conditioned facilities, but for the vast majority of prisoners this is not the case.[45] A poll by Doble Research Associates found that two-thirds of the public believe that prison inmates don't work.[46] Another poll found that 60 percent of the public believes that inmates sit around playing cards or watching television all day.[47] A recent survey in the United States found that six of ten respondents agreed with the statement, "criminals don't mind being sent to prison."[48]

These are interesting but, upon reflection, perhaps not surprising results. In addition to the "dehumanizing" images of prison life, one sees a parallel narrative of the undeserving inmate: sitting around, lifting weights in the yard, getting three square meals a day purchased by our tax dollars. Although the perception that prison life is brutally hard somewhat contradicts the perception that prison life is "easy," both narratives serve legitimizing functions. If rehabilitative effort for the dehumanized inmate is hopeless, then rehabilitative effort on account of idle inmates is undeserved.

This image of prison time as easy time begins to suggest that, not unlike the welfare recipient, working America is paying for these individuals to live off the dole.[49] Conservative politicians attempting to create a tough-on-crime image by taking something away from the incarcerated are the primary beneficiaries. Inmates looking for educational or vocational training and corrections officers who see the benefit of good prison programming tend to be on the losing end of these political maneuvers.

2. Prisons as a Training Ground for Future Criminals

The public also believes that the prison experience increases criminality in inmates. According to Doble Associates survey data, nearly 50 percent of respondents agreed with the statement, "prisons are really schools for criminals that turn new inmates into hardened criminals."[50] Another survey by Doble Associates found that two-thirds of respondents believe that prisoners become more dangerous by the time they leave prison.[51] As a result, the public holds pessimistic views about the rate of recidivism among prisoners. In Florida, 58 percent of respondents believed that by serving time, inmates released would be more likely to commit crimes than before they went to prison.[52] In fact, only 18 percent of ex-offenders were reconvicted of another crime within two years of release, according to Florida statistics.[53]

This image of prisoners becoming more dangerous as they leave prison is a narrative developed by those who seek to depict prison as a place where no constructive learning can take place. It comes from popular culture's notion of the evil con artist, rapist, robber, or murderer who will continue to ply his trade behind bars. Conservative politicians angling for longer sentences and corrections workers seeking to describe a workplace in need of more (and higher-paid) individuals combine to promote this notion. Inmates in need of vocational and educational training as well as recently released parolees are injured by this depiction.

E. Prisoners Get Out Too Early

Another image often manufactured for policy reasons and rhetorical flair is that of prisoners "getting out too early." As mentioned earlier, there is some evidence that a widely held and strongly felt sentiment exists that murderers get back on the streets too soon.[54] Some studies confirm a pervasive public mistrust of the criminal justice system, which is especially manifest in perceptions that convicted criminals spend too little time in prison.[55] Media crime coverage helps to support the illusion of early release by what it chooses to report and ignore.[56]

News accounts of murderers released to rape or kill again are surely effective in confirming the impression of predatory criminals being released too soon. The Willie Horton story cited earlier is perhaps the most striking example.[57] It succinctly illustrates both selective media coverage as well as "tough-on-crime" political posturing in the electoral process.

This image has always been used by those seeking to build reputations on law and order by talking of generic "criminals" not being punished enough and the courts being too lenient. Willie Horton was actually on work release—and not on parole or finished with his sentence, as often represented. The length of sentences of incarceration has actually increased over the last two decades, and sentenced prisoners tend to serve longer portions of their sentence in most states. Parole has decreased—there is less potential for a prisoner to get out "too early."

Politicians and others seeking to build reputations on law and order as well as those opposed to training and work-release–type programs for offenders all attack any form of furlough for those charged with a crime. The notion of early release and "putting communities in danger" is also a characterization that serves the media well, allowing another level of drama.

F. Race and the Media

Media descriptions of offenders tend to make reentry a difficult policy initiative to champion. Shorthand descriptions of crimes and perpetrators, often engaging animal metaphors, create hostility and fear. Front-page articles of crime and victimization often get politicians to call for sympathetic laws in the name of a victim rather than spurring them to focus on the root causes of the crime. The media uses the same shorthand to link race with poverty and crime in ways that caricature offenders of color and characterize them as particularly unworthy of our compassion or assistance.

The 1980s and 1990s saw a shift in the way poverty, public political dissent, and crime were characterized in print and electronic media as well as in political circles. After the riots of the late 1960s and civil unrest in the 1970s, conservative politicians recast the political unrest as an issue of "law and order" rather than of human rights and social justice. At the same time, new "coded" terminology was employed to recast public welfare as an issue of race. Increasingly, White America found itself hostile to public welfare. This stemmed in large part from the erroneous perception, often bolstered by media coverage, that most welfare recipients are Black. This also led to the conclusion of many that Blacks evince less commitment to the work ethic.

The United States Supreme Court decision *Bakke v. California Board of Regents* and the line of cases about affirmative action that it spawned have also influenced the national debate on race. Media coverage and depictions of "worthy Whites" being denied jobs and admission to college or graduate school because of "less worthy" Blacks and other people of color have each contributed to the impression that deserving Whites were being displaced by "unqualified" Blacks. Indeed, the double impact of media portrayals of poor African Americans as criminals and middle-class African Americans as unworthy (due to affirmative action) spurred public debate. Indeed, it became commonplace for politicians to voice concerns about "welfare queens" and "lazy, shiftless" prisoners as a way of rousing public anger and rallying public support for particularly draconian—and not necessarily effective—crime policies. Conservative politics and backlashes against civil rights gained ground and mainstream support.

The obvious shift from support and encouragement to attacks on—

and distrust for—people of color seeking higher education, seeking employment, and seeking to support their children in difficult economic conditions laid the groundwork for public opinion to demonize those individuals with criminal convictions. Politicians soon capitalized on the prevailing sentiments that people of color tended to be dangerous, unworthy of rehabilitation. The country was well on its way toward turning young men of color, particularly those who came from low-income communities, into an underclass. By the end of the 1980s, the assumption that Black men were dangerous had soaked deeply into America's consciousness, powerfully sustained by the steady flow of news coverage depicting Black men under arrest, in court, and incarcerated.[58] This strategy incited racial prejudices rather than concerns about crime and fostered great resistance to public policy efforts to reduce racial inequality.[59]

The ability of the poor to adjust to social and economic disadvantage increased as the prosperity of the 1990s increased. As a result, the poor and less fortunate became alien to the well-to-do. The economic and criminal justice policies that resulted were focused increasingly on punishing the poor and people of color, and attempted to discredit social explanations of problematic behavior. This culminated in the vast array of zero-tolerance policies that emerged from the "broken windows" theory. The research, advanced by two criminologists, posited the theory that broken windows left unaddressed in a community would invite criminal conduct.

Policy makers, at a loss for answers in dealing with increasing homelessness, embedded poverty, and increasing petty crime, jumped on the theory and began treating manifestations of poverty as crime. Communities upset with graffiti, prostitution, and public drug use and the nuisance crimes that accompany these activities supported increased enforcement over social programs. As a result, the criminal justice infrastructure exploded. Community policing and community prosecution—programs that had initially come into being to be more sensitive to community needs—morphed into misdemeanor and petty crime enforcement. Community courts of all types sprang up. Many of these courts were modeled after drug courts, though they lacked the same rigorous empirical support for success, and were financed by the federal government and applauded by local communities. In some part, lack of services or treatment for the homeless and drug addicted increased the frustration of communities; the new criminal justice focus on enforcement and incarceration for petty crimes with some treatment available seemed to the public a more palatable approach.

Local television news and fictional programming as well as reality police shows substantially exaggerate the crime problem in the United States. Typically, law enforcement is shown in a somewhat flattering light on most programming, and crime and the circumstances of criminal conduct are not contextualized for the viewer. The result is the overwhelming impression that "these are just bad people." Employment, housing, education, and opportunity are rarely, if ever, mentioned in descriptions of the commission of crimes or the investigation, trial, and sentencing of television suspects, defendants, and ex-offenders. The media not only contributes to the perception that ex-offenders cannot ever integrate into society; it also has profound effects on how race is perceived. Offenders are disproportionately shown as people of color and often in the role of violent psychopath or gang leader.

In addition to lack of context, there is a stereotyping of roles (also called "typification") when it comes to the race of characters. Although some studies suggest that the actual number of minority offenders is less than that of White offenders, on television the percentage of minorities shown as offenders compared to those shown in other roles is much higher than with White characters. Consequently, it is not enough to know the content of television programming; it is also important to examine the consequences of viewing this content. The media's perpetuation of racial stereotypes of the typical offender may not only be a function of African Americans being shown more frequently as offenders than in other roles; rather, it may include the way viewers process this information about race in making comparisons to their own knowledge (or assumed knowledge) about certain races.

G. What People Think They Know about Other Races

There is a good bit of research on the knowledge lens through which people develop opinions and strongly held beliefs. This "ordinary knowledge" is often hard to contradict even in light of specialized knowledge to the contrary produced by social science professionals.[60] Ordinary knowledge is derived from many sources that most citizens would find difficult to identify. When consistent with ordinary knowledge, specialized findings of social science tend to enhance the validity of ordinary knowledge. However, when specialized findings are inconsistent with ordinary knowledge, they are generally ignored or dismissed as unreliable or irrelevant.[61]

The media news coverage of crime through a racialized lens has had a pronounced effect on the way Americans view people of color generally and African Americans in particular. Media portrayals of violent crime, especially visual images, are dominated by pictures of African Americans. The *Washington Post* reported that even when the racial identity of a criminal is not pictured on television, two-thirds of those who think that the perpetrator was shown believe that he was Black.[62] This presents a very seductive picture in the minds of all Americans that Blacks are the primary perpetrators of crime, even when statistics objectively defy that picture. In situations when crime and race are linked, the crime is generally reported as involving violence—most particularly murder, robbery, and rape. This creates and solidifies in the mind of the American public the myth that Blacks are more often the worst criminals.[63] This stereotype must surely cause excessive fear and create certain unwarranted beliefs about people of color. In circumstances where Whites have African American friends, the strength of the stereotype, reinforced by negative media portrayals, results in the belief that their Black friends are the exception to the "rule."[64]

H. Impact of News Media on Public Policy

Crime coverage plays an agenda-setting role, and has a significant influence on the public's perceptions of frequency and behavior. News media play a number of roles in the criminal justice debate and policy agenda that ultimately affect offender reentry. News coverage influences the public by "priming" certain perceptions through its coverage of an issue.[65] Additionally, media coverage has systematically distorted reality by overreporting violent crime and by focusing on the race of the perpetrators in the coverage of violent crime.[66]

One of the ways in which the news media functions in an agenda-setting role is in the way it fosters public misperception, especially as public opinion relates to crime rates, the rates at which parolees become repeat offenders, and the nature and severity of punishment that the legal system metes out.[67] Increasingly, people rely primarily on the media to get their information regarding what percentage of people on welfare use it as an alternative to seeking a job, the proportion of ex-mental patients who commit crimes, and which minority groups have criminal tendencies. These media messages are often very distorted or incorrect. Examination of media reporting on crime shows that the race of minority offenders, especially for violent crimes, is often disproportionately reported.[68]

One of the prime examples of the media's influence on public policy can be seen in its description of the intersection of poverty and crime, both of which are portrayed as primarily an inner-city problem affecting people of color. Blacks are often shown not only as poor but also as overrepresented in the juvenile justice system. The public's understanding of youth crime is shaped in large part by the media's portrayal of disproportionate minority involvement. Meda Chesney-Lind, among others, has identified the common media practice of demonizing young women of color. Contemporary news accounts of young African American and Latino girls usually show them as gang members, despite the fact that there is little evidence to suggest any significant increase in female gang membership or involvement.[69] These media distortions of juvenile crime, perpetrator race, and juvenile violence dramatically affect public consumer perception.

Media reports identified violent juvenile crime on the increase in the 1980s and 1990s. Lori Dorfman, director of the Berkley Media Studies Group, and Vincent Shiraldi, president of the Justice Policy Institute, coauthored a report entitled "Off Balance: Youth, Race, and Crime in the News."[70] That report discussed the impact of the media on the perceptions of youth violence. The authors examined more than one hundred studies of news content featuring youth and crime.[71] The studies provided overwhelming evidence that news coverage of crime—especially violent crime—is out of proportion to its occurrence, distorts the proportion of crime committed by youth, and overrepresents perpetrators of color while underrepresenting victims of color. Acts of violence are pushed to the foreground despite occurring relatively infrequently.[72] The end result is a change in public opinion and a corresponding change in public policy.

Some authors have argued convincingly that the popular and political link between serious juvenile crime and race has had a primary effect on the increasingly punitive focus of juvenile justice policy nationwide.[73] Much of this coverage has caused the public to lose faith in treatment as a component of the juvenile justice system, just as it lost faith in rehabilitation in adult prisons. The juvenile court is also often portrayed as ineffectual and lenient, without any real effort to analyze, or cover, the working of the court in any systematic fashion. The description of youths of color as predators, thugs, and gangsters has successfully ramped up political efforts to streamline these youths into the adult criminal justice system and ultimately into prison. National and political divisions about race enabled conservative Republican politicians to advocate particular crime and welfare policies for electoral advantage. During this period, news media coverage put a Black face on youth crime, and political campaigns to get "tough on crime" and on youth violence turned juveniles into symbols of race and crime.[74]

I. Conclusions

In thinking about potential remedies for media depictions of race, poverty, and crime, one can easily become pessimistic about any hope of progress because the negative images of people of color are so deeply ingrained in our social fabric. Indeed, Derrick Bell's notion of the "permanence of racism" in American culture has an uneasy ring of truth, notwithstanding the fact that there are some small, identifiable examples of progress.

In the entertainment industry, there are a few glimmers of hope. At one time, the number of movie directors who were people of color was so small as to make these directors a novelty. While their numbers are nowhere near what they should be, many directors of color are more established and now have the opportunity to paint pictures of characters of color that are less stereotypical and refreshingly different from historical representations. Taking people of color, particularly African American actors, out of the stereotypical roles of pimps, prostitutes, drug dealers, and police informants also helps. The African American media purchasing dollar is very strong. Advertising aimed at people of color during sporting events, targeted television programs, and movies confirms this fact. Movies that focus on audiences of color do well at the box office. In the future, coordinated efforts to lobby movie companies to create more balanced scripts, taking people of color and putting them in different situations, will continue this positive trend. Urging news writers, producers, and outlets to focus on the quantity and quality of their coverage in communities of color will also help in developing more accurate portrayals of what is actually going on in these communities.

Unfortunately, none of these remedies is totally satisfying. If you live in, work in, or are concerned with communities of color, it seems there is little hope that current policies will change in the near future. Journalists, television and movie writers, producers, and corporate advertisers have no vested interest in turning from their established operating procedures. There is no constituency to influence them, no government incentive to lure them toward the truth.

3

Women
The Afterthought in Reentry Planning

*LaDonna Cissell is a single mother of three who grew up on
the east side of Indianapolis. She became pregnant with her first child at
fourteen and never completed school. She was incarcerated after cash-
ing a series of counterfeit checks worth about forty-five hundred dollars. Sometimes she cashed as many as four a day, spending the money
on clothing, meals, and cars. Her crimes were nonviolent. Nationally,
about 50 percent of the total crimes committed by women are nonviolent. Cissell describes her time in custody as the "worst six months of
my life." She points out that her mother did not want to bring her children to see her while she was locked up and that the separation was
hard on both her and her children. Her experience is not unlike that of
many women who interact with the criminal justice system.*[1]

Women have unique experiences arriving in, getting through, and recovering from the criminal justice experience. Women continue to be the
fastest-growing segment of the U.S. prison population, and they bring a
unique set of problems into the criminal justice system. According to a
Rocky Mountain News story on women in recovery:

> Women are more likely than men to be addicted to more than one
> mood altering substance, and many addicted women report that they
> began using drugs after a specific traumatic event in their lives. Among
> women problem drug users, 35% report major depressive episodes vs.
> 9% of other women. Women represent 43% of clients in methampheta-
> mine treatment, 40% of clients in cocaine treatment, 34% of those in
> heroin treatment and 26% of those in marijuana treatment. Moreover,
> about 80% of Miracle's women have some kind of mental illness.
> Nearly all of them have been victims of abuse, sexual, physical, emo-
> tional, much of it in childhood. Many women do not seek treatment for

fear of losing custody of their children. Treatment is complicated by the need for child care, transportation and financial assistance.[2]

LaDonna Cissell's story, noted at the beginning of this chaper, is not unlike many contemporary stories of women attempting to complete the difficult task of reentry.

Even a cursory examination of the hurdles that women typically encounter—both in prison and upon release—reveals the limitations of a penal system built to house male offenders. To the extent that policy makers have focused on prison programming or reentry planning, they have generally relegated issues faced by women to the margins. Women have entered prison with a wide range of problems and related needs but have been the beneficiaries of few meaningful interventions. At the point of release, it is not uncommon for women leaving prison suffering from disabilities to find out that their condition is often more acute due to a lack of focused attention. When we add to that common foundation a frequent lack of support to ease the transition back into their communities, it is no surprise that reentry for women has been as much a dismal failure as for their male counterparts.

A common misperception may begin to explain this phenomenon. Conventional wisdom suggests that criminal conduct of women constitutes such a small proportion of crimes that it need not garner much attention. Compared to men, women do represent a smaller percentage of individuals reentering communities from prison and jail. However, their numbers are rising at a much higher rate than those of men. This steady climb in the number of women offenders can be attributed to a host of factors. Some have suggested that women are engaging in increasingly more serious criminal conduct that more often exposes them to prison terms.[3] Others counter that women have not become more criminally active; instead, they have simply been caught up in the fervor to sweep more people into the criminal justice system.[4] A range of arrest policies for everything from domestic violence to drugs is one reason why more women are coming to the attention of criminal justice officials. Competing explanations aside, the number of women in U.S. prisons has "quintupled since 1980."[5]

One phenomenon I have observed in the massive overincarceration of women in the last two decades is the casting of a wider law enforcement net. In my experience and observations, women have been incarcerated more often for nonviolent, drug-related or drug-involved crimes (i.e., crimes committed to obtain resources for drugs or allegedly done in concert with male offenders where the woman is marginally—if at all—involved in criminal conduct). From the law enforcement standpoint, arresting and charging these women offers prosecutors an improved chance to prove the case against other individuals charged in the case. By turning the woman into a cooperating witness, prosecutors strengthen their case against the more serious male offender. In the mind of many in law enforcement, these women deserve no special consideration. Those who have children are perceived as bad parents who should not be raising children. Consequently, there is no hesitation to plunge them into the criminal justice system.

The profile of the average woman in custody is a woman of color in her early thirties with more than one child under the age of eighteen. She is in custody on a drug or property offense and was unemployed or underemployed when she was sentenced. Of course, not all women in custody fit this profile. However, statistically, women are more often incarcerated for nonviolent property or drug crimes. Although some of these trends are beginning to shift, we need only look to some of the policy decisions made in the last two decades of the twentieth century to explore the reasons women are finding themselves in custody in unprecedented numbers.

A. The Impact on Women of More Retributive Criminal Justice Policies

It is ironic that the 1980s and the 1990s, periods of profound economic growth in this country, should also mark the most dramatic increase in imprisonment rates for women. This much-heralded economic boom principally benefited upper- and middle-class Americans with virtually no uplifting effect on economically subordinated communities. In 1993 approximately 16.9 percent of this country's female population was living below the poverty line.[6] In addition to the women below the poverty line, children did not fare well during this country's bull market. Over eleven million children lived in poverty in the year 2000.[7] The net effect of the boom was a widening gap between the wealthy and poor in this country.

The progress of women of color, in particular, in moving out of poverty lagged behind that of other population groups. The economic upsurge in America was fueled in part by a dramatic rise in high-tech and skilled work opportunities. Women of color did not typically benefit from increases in this sector of the economy. These women had not been trained for these jobs, so upward mobility was limited. The very nature of the tech boom meant a reduction in available unskilled jobs. Race and gender affect women's ability to secure one of the limited number of unskilled jobs, resulting in unemployment and underemployment. This leads to loss of earnings, which can exacerbate feelings of insecurity when a woman cannot provide for herself and her family.

At the same time that women of color were finding less success in the job market, they were more frequently coming to the attention of the criminal justice system. During the ten-year period after the passage of mandatory drug-sentencing laws, the number of women in prison rose by 888 percent.[8] Previously, women who faced incarceration had been those involved in what were described as "gendered" crimes: assaulting or killing an abusive partner, robbing a client during prostitution, engaging in violent offenses as a "lookout" or other minor player. In contrast, during the 1980s and 1990s, women—and particularly women of color—faced sentences of incarceration for a wide range of drug-related crimes.

Between 1986 and 1991, this country witnessed an exponential rise in the number of women in prisons for these offenses. The number of African American women incarcerated for drug-related crimes rose 828 percent, far exceeding the increase for White women, which was 241 percent.[9] The number of Latinas in prison for drug crimes rose 328 percent.[10] Two-thirds of women parolees are now women of color, with close to half having been imprisoned following drug convictions. Prison classification instruments identify the overwhelming majority of female inmates as low-risk inmates, and yet they often endure lengthy prison sentences.

The principal criminal justice policy that led to unprecedented numbers of women being locked away was the War on Drugs. The strategies used to wage this war represented a fundamental shift in law enforcement policy. The rise of potent forms of cocaine was perceived by many as contributing to increased addiction and corresponding social disorder. Later, the advent of crack cocaine and the violence that often attended the fierce competition for profits in the drug trade sent shock waves through the general public. Increasingly, the public clamored for policies that would restore order and remove the problem from sight. Police departments, armed with this mandate, deployed a wide range of forces to attack and shut down open-air drug markets located principally in inner-city neighborhoods. Massive arrests took place, sweeping large numbers of drug users and low-level drug sellers into the justice system.

Although much of this activity was confined to poorer neighborhoods in the nation's central cities, media attention escalated the public's fear of rampant violence around every corner. When the average White American raised questions about the causes of the rise in crime in the nation, news coverage provided a ready, if not entirely accurate, answer. The violence associated with open-air drug markets involved young Black men, and the media was able to put a face on crime for much of America. More often than not, that face was of a young man of color. The baggy pants, jewelry, and pagers became the trademarks of this younger generation. However, rather than being perceived as manifestations of teenage rebellion, these differently clad young men became the image of danger and intimidation in the minds of many. These powerful images of "feral" young men would ultimately fuel a retributive political movement in the criminal justice system. Ironically, the policy decisions that emerged from this period would strike its most severe blow on an unintended target: young women of color.

Prior to 1980, the number of women in state and federal custody was much smaller. Indeed, female offenders often received more favorable sentences than male offenders. A number of studies have attributed this pattern of lighter sentencing based on gender to a combination of chivalrous and/or paternalistic attitudes toward women. Many of the judges were older men who did not see prison as an appropriate place for any woman. These judges were, at times, more receptive to arguments that imprisoning women would have far-reaching consequences—particularly where the woman was the primary caregiver in a family with small children. Because courts had more sentencing discretion, they could differentiate between violent and nonviolent offenders and could, therefore, show some leniency to women.

Research suggests that judges tended not to exercise this discretion as frequently in cases involving women of color. Rather, law enforcement officials and judges reserved this favorable discretion for middle- and upper-class women who tended to conform to their gender stereotypes.[11] Although on its face this notion of chivalry or paternalism in sentencing had a positive impact on women, this stereotyping also negatively affected women in a number of ways. Women whose criminal conduct violated the decision makers' gender-stereotypical assumptions about the "proper" roles for women were often treated more harshly than their male counterparts with similar charges. Some studies have pointed to longer sentences for women in assault or child-abandonment cases, in part because this conduct was deemed to be decidedly unfeminine or nonmaternal.[12] In one case, for example, an Alameda County California superior court openly admitted sentencing women convicted of narcotics possession to jail as an alternative to drug treatment because he believed treatment programs did not work. He also claimed that jail was the only place where pregnant women would have no access to drugs and would have access to the prenatal care he thought appropriate.[13]

As described above, the wide disparities in the sentences issued in criminal cases throughout the 1980s resulted in the Sentencing Reform Act of 1984, which instituted the Federal Sentencing Guidelines. Included in the guidelines submitted to Congress were policy statements that provide that an offender's age, physical condition, mental or emotional condition, and family and community ties are not "ordinarily relevant" in decisions to depart from the guidelines. The phrase "ordinarily relevant" made it clear that these factors may be relevant only in extraordinary cases. In contrast, gender, like race, national origin, and socioeconomic status, is never relevant. In seeking to balance the scales of justice, the Sentencing Commission and Congress essentially defined the norm as a male norm. Women, who were overwhelmingly single parents (roughly 81 percent of all single parents are women),[14] witnessed the elimination of family ties as a relevant component of the sentencing framework. The guidelines ultimately limited judges' ability to depart downward from a recommended sentence for a single mother. So, the Federal Sentencing Guidelines—and an increasing number of states that chose to adopt similar sentencing schemes—dealt a dramatic blow to women.

The War on Drugs also provided the impetus for more extensive use of prosecutorial tools such as conspiracy statutes. Once reserved for use in unraveling organized crime schemes associated with the Mafia, conspiracy statutes became the favored tool to fight the local drug trade on the state and federal level. The power of the conspiracy statutes was that they eased prosecution of all coconspirators—from the alleged kingpin to the least influential members of the group. Conspiracy, coupled with a relaxation of the rules of evidence in criminal trials, paved the way for megatrials involving allegations of drug sales in which less evidence could lead to a criminal conviction. One consequence of this powerful tool was that women in relationships with men who were charged under conspiracy laws often found themselves caught up in the criminal justice net largely because of a personal relationship.

Adrian Nicole LeBlanc brings this fact to life in the pages of her important book *Random Family*, which chronicles the life of a number of women, including Jessica, who served a ten-year federal sentence for conspiracy. In the cases she describes, LeBlanc helps us see that these young women were often only marginally involved in the actual drug trade.[15] Too often, these women were trapped in abusive relationships in which their criminal activity occurred in the context of a relationship where they had little or no control. These women often had become involved in a relationship with an abusive partner and would experience considerable difficulty escaping that situation. For psychological and often economic reasons, the woman did not see an alternative and simply stayed in the abusive relationship despite the danger. If the abusive partner happened to sell drugs, for example, it was likely that the woman would have been aware of this activity, which technically made her a knowing coconspirator. However, the gap between having knowledge of illegal activity and having control over the choice to engage in this conduct is typically quite wide. Still, if the government charged her partner with drug conspiracy, she often faced charges as a coconspirator. Her knowledge of his illegal activity would often be enough for prosecutors to charge her, for a jury to convict her, and for a judge to sentence her to a mandatory prison term.[16] One particular example of this that received considerable attention was the case of Kemba Smith. Before being pardoned by President Clinton, Kemba Smith was sentenced to twenty-four years in prison as a first-time offender.[17] The prosecution conceded that Ms. Smith never handled, used, or sold drugs, but she was still subjected to full prosecution simply because of her relationship with an alleged drug dealer.[18] Thus, growing numbers of women ended up in prisons across the country. African American women were incarcerated in numbers disproportionate to their representation in the population.[19]

Much like their male counterparts, women often entered prison with a range of needs. However, the programs, facilities, and services available to women prisoners in this country's dual prison system were inferior in number and quality to those offered to men. Complicating matters, the needs of women prisoners were, in many ways, unique to women. Unfortunately, prison facilities typically had not been designed with women in mind. Thus, programming in these facilities did not pay particular attention to health or mental health issues as they might affect women, did not specifically seek to address the cluster of legal and emotional issues related to the custody of minor children, and did not focus on helping these women develop or sharpen skills that they might need to become gainfully employed upon release.

Even those features of prisons intended to address the perceived different needs of women ultimately had significant negative consequences. For example, women still tend to be placed in prisons located in rural settings, which are thought to be less harsh and psychically jarring for women than the concrete walls of an urban prison or jail. But placement in remote areas often means that women are housed at considerable distances from their families and friends. Particularly for women of color, whose families most often need to rely on public transportation, these remote locations present insurmountable distances. The lack of proximity increases the difficulty of maintaining ties and often leads to greater social dislocation. Women's prisons also tend to be smaller in size and population. While in theory smaller prisons may signal greater safety, they also tend to receive less funding and less attention because so few people are housed there. Thus, women tend to have access to a more limited range of programs than are often available to men in larger prison settings.

Further complicating this picture is the lack of attention being paid to the reentry needs of women now being released in record numbers. Policy makers have begun to consider the steps that government should address during the massive release of ex-offenders. But they still have not seriously considered differences for women in their planning. At a minimum, prison officials and reentry planners should consider health issues that women prisoners present as they attempt to gain a better understanding of their needs.

B. Developing a More Complete Picture of Women's Unique Health Issues

Medical research has only recently focused on women's health issues as an area of study distinct from men's medical concerns. So perhaps it is not so surprising that prison and reentry policy makers have barely begun to recognize, let alone meet, the unique health needs of female prisoners and the formerly incarcerated in communities. Given the overwhelming numbers of women with serious health problems in custody, prison and reentry planners can no longer afford to ignore their needs. In fact, the numbers are startling. For example, women in prison are now more likely than men to be infected with HIV: 3.4 percent of female inmates are HIV positive compared to 2.1 percent of male inmates.[20] The HIV infection rates among females are predominantly related to injecting drugs, crack use, and prostitution for drugs, which should give prison planners a starting point for counseling. Along with higher rates of HIV infection, women are at greater risk for sexually transmitted diseases that can have long-term implications for their overall health. Many women in prison also suffer from tuberculosis and various strains of hepatitis.

Apart from these chronic illnesses, women often have other health needs that go unattended as well. The Kaiser Family Foundation published information from its comprehensive 2001 Women's Health Survey.[21] In that important study, disparities in access to health care and the ability to receive treatment and services for women of color were detailed.[22] One conclusion drawn from this literature suggests that if the physical problems women face as they are admitted to prison are not addressed while they are there, the problems are compounded when they are released into poor, urban communities.

According to the *Women's Health Data Book*,[23] nonfinancial factors —including the availability of needed health services in communities, transportation, child care, and the lack of culturally specific services— all combine with other factors to deprive low-income women of adequate health services. Lack of education, single-parent status, and access to—as well as utilization of—preventive health care services also play a significant role in the provision of health services to women of color.[24] In addition to physical health problems, a number of studies suggest that women in custody also have higher rates of depression and other mental health problems.[25] Often these mental health issues have not been diagnosed or treated. Women of color in custody are often victims of sexual and physical abuse. According to the United States Department of Justice, more than 50 percent of women in jail report that they have been the victims of physical or sexual abuse in the past, compared with 10 percent of men.[26] Without intervention, these women are likely to return to their abusive relationships upon release.

Health problems can have a ripple effect in reentry planning and implementation. For women leaving prison with health problems, managing to engage in the behavior expected of a parolee may be difficult. They may experience difficulty keeping parole appointments. Quite obviously, health and mental health problems that remain unaddressed can interfere with anyone's ability to obtain and maintain a job. When we add physical and mental health issues to the often overwhelming stress associated with regaining custody of children that they may have lost as a result of incarceration, the picture for women is even more troubling. It is this combination of health needs and the pressures of parental roles that weighs most heavily on the women ex-offenders and often guides their choices upon release—a factor too often ignored in examinations of the problems posed by reentry.

C. The Challenge of Motherhood behind Bars

Perhaps the most significant factor distinguishing women from their male counterparts relates to responsibility for their children. The average woman in prison had physical custody of a child before her incarceration. In the United States, approximately 2.1 percent of all children under the age of eighteen have parents in state or federal prison.[27] This means that 1.5 million children are affected by the lack of any coherent reentry policy. The majority of mothers currently incarcerated were the sole caretakers for their children prior to incarceration. Generally, when a father goes to prison the mother keeps the family intact. However, a number of studies show that when a mother enters prison, the father often does not remain involved in the caretaking of the children. One study of state prisoners in the late 1980s found that 67.5 percent of the women had minor children as compared with only 54.4 percent of males.[28] In 1986, "76% of women prisoners were mothers and nine out of ten of them had children younger than eighteen."[29] While "some children live with a relative during their mother's incarceration, many enter the foster care system because no family member is available to care for them."[30] So for many women in custody or returning from incarceration the greatest challenge is reestablishing a relationship with their children. This fact has profound implications for women's reentry programming.

One of the most punitive and detrimental effects of incarcerating women is the physical separation of mothers from children. There are few women's prisons throughout the country. States generally have one or two women's facilities, while the federal government maintains and operates relatively few institutions exclusively for women serving federal sentences.[31] The limited number of institutions often means that women will be sent far away from their home communities and may often be housed in a separate state. A common side effect of this housing pattern is that women receive fewer visits from their children and family than men. Maintaining parental ties becomes all the more difficult. Children are often left to the care of the mother's relatives or in the state's foster care system when women are incarcerated. Consequently, women are often dependent on others to establish contact with their children. Women prisoners often must become accustomed to a lack of contact with their children.

As one would expect, the toll of this separation on mothers can be quite severe. Mothers commonly suffer from overwhelming anxiety and concern for their children. In many instances, the anxiety springs from the uncertainty of their children's living situation. Mothers in custody have often made only temporary arrangements for their children. This instability of care arrangements becomes a continuing source of stress. Mothers in custody routinely report being overwhelmed by feelings of helplessness and hopelessness, which undoubtedly contribute to the higher incidences of clinical depression among women prisoners. This emotional and mental health toll can adversely affect the physical well-being of these women as well. Whatever the manifestation, the tremendous emotional burden that women carry is only complicated by the realization that they may ultimately lose custody of their children as they struggle to make sense of the legal system.

Physical and emotional separation from their mothers can cause severe emotional damage in children. Constancy and continuity of relationships, especially in the mother-child relationship, is essential for a child's normal development during different life stages. Interruptions in those relationships can have a lasting impact on the child's ability to bond with others. To the extent that infants and toddlers change—and must adjust to new—caretakers, they will often experience setbacks in their emotional development. Attachments, particularly at younger ages, are critical, and yet the imprisonment of their mothers often means that they will not have the benefit of constant, uninterrupted presence and attention from a familiar adult. When infants and young children find themselves abandoned by a parent, or shuffled between relatives, they may suffer separation distress and anxiety that will have long-term implications for their mental health.

The stress experienced by single mothers may be the most acute. They often risk termination of their parental rights simply due to the fact of their incarceration. A significant number of state prisoners find that following their admission to prison a court will place their children in the legal custody of others—often through the foster care system. In many instances these children enter the foster care system because no family member is available to care for them. When children are placed in the foster care system, the chances for permanent separation of mother and child become greater because it is more likely that a court will terminate the mother's parental rights. Typically, once this has occurred, the mother will lose all rights related to her children and her children will be eligible for adoption—often without her knowledge or consent. Not only is there no guarantee that all the children awaiting adoption will be placed in adoptive homes, "but adoption does nothing to address the needs of poor families who are most at risk of involvement in the child welfare system."[32] This policy has a two-fold effect: it burdens the biological parents and simultaneously puts the children at risk of being cast into the system of child welfare. This happens with the greatest frequency to children of color.[33]

There are a number of reasons why an incarcerated mother has an increased chance of losing permanent custody once the state places her children in the foster care system. First, the state may have specific laws aimed at terminating the rights of parents who "voluntarily abandon their children." These laws do not adequately differentiate between physical abandonment in the traditional sense and involuntary "abandonment" as a result of incarceration. Second, despite language in many state statutes that mandates efforts toward reunifying families, incarcerated mothers rarely reap the benefits of such services. Child welfare workers and foster parents are often reluctant to facilitate visitation between children and incarcerated parents because they believe parental contact is harmful to the children, or they blame the parents for the children's problems. Third, foster care is the first step in most jurisdictions toward a permanent termination of parental rights. "Twenty-five states have 'termination of parental rights' or adoptive statutes specifically for incarcerated parents, which makes the permanent loss of a child a stark reality."[34] Although the language of most statutes indicates that a state cannot terminate a parent's right to custody of her child solely on the basis of incarceration, this prohibition tends to be honored in the breach. Some states have demonstrated a willingness to speed up termination proceedings in situations involving an incarcerated parent.

Of course, certain offenses might themselves render the offenders unfit parents. A conviction for extreme acts of domestic violence against the child or the other parent, for example, might provide sufficient grounds for terminating parental rights. But in most cases, both incarcerated parents and children have an interest in preserving their bond. In *Santosky v. Kramer,* the U.S. Supreme Court acknowledged this, finding that parents' liberty interest in maintaining a relationship with their children applies equally to incarcerated mothers and fathers. The Court reasoned,

> The fundamental liberty interest of natural parents in the care, custody, and management of their child does not evaporate simply because they have not been model parents or have lost temporary custody of their child to the State. Even when blood relationships are strained, parents retain a vital interest in preventing the irretrievable destruction of their family life. If anything, persons faced with forced dissolution of their parental rights have a more critical need for procedural protections than do those resisting state intervention into ongoing family life.[35]

The Court further explained that, to terminate a parental right, courts should adhere to a standard of proof requiring a showing of "clear and convincing" evidence that the parent is unfit. In choosing this standard of proof, the Court may have been concerned about the conscious and unconscious influence of cultural or class bias in these decisions. The parents most likely to be subject to removal of their children and termination of all parental rights are often the poor, the uneducated, or members of minority groups. So, the Court may have intended the heightened standard to serve as a check against such biases.

However, the standard of proof may not be up to this considerable task. As indicated earlier, many of the women serving prison terms have been incarcerated after drug convictions. Drug dependency among this population has often contributed to involvement in the criminal justice system. Rather than seeing drug usage as a medical or public health problem, American society tends to regard it as a criminal problem. And Americans tend to reserve their most severe criticism for female drug users.[36] They label drug-dependent women as, at best, neglectful parents and, at worst, abusive. While drug dependency can lead to both neglect and abuse, it does not inexorably lead to such problems. However, the perception that drug usage and abuse go hand in hand may influence decision makers in custody cases. So, many incarcerated mothers lose custody of their children for unstated assumptions that may have little bearing on whether they are actually capable or can become capable parents.

In addition to establishing the standard of proof, the Supreme Court has also broadened the factors that courts should assess in determining whether a parent is to be stripped of her parental rights. The Court directed lower courts to consider the nature of the relationship between parent and child as well as the degree to which the incarcerated parent has benefited from rehabilitation in prison. However, because many state statutes and an abundance of cases allow physical separation to serve as grounds for termination, the incarcerated mother often cannot overcome this burden since separation is likely during the period of incarceration. Although incarceration typically cannot be the sole reason for terminating parental rights, it is still more likely that a court will find that an imprisoned parent, as opposed to the average parent, meets the statutory criteria leading to the termination of her rights.

A better option is for the court to examine parenting and reentry as two sides of the same coin. Parents and parental rights as a legal matter should be viewed in light of the reentry plan for the parent. Parenting classes, treatment regimens for the parent, and educational and vocational training should all be a part of the equation when courts are determining the status of parental rights. This is, of course, assuming that the crime for which the parent is in custody is not a crime committed against the child. In that circumstance, one might use a different equation.

Adoption is another concern for incarcerated mothers. This scenario typically arises when the father has custody of the child and marries or remarries. It is common for the new spouse to adopt the child. In addition, a foster parent may wish to adopt the child currently within her custody. All states have statutes outlining the procedures and circumstances of the type of adoption that can take place without the consent of one parent. Furthermore, the 1981 Federal Adoption Assistance and Child Welfare Act allows a child to be adopted by a foster parent if the child does not live with his or her mother for a year. As is the case with termination of parental rights proceedings, adoption will completely sever the relationship between the incarcerated mother and her child. Many critics of this adoption policy argue that because the law so heavily emphasizes adoption, adequate resources are not directed to support services for biological families who want to maintain their parental rights. Therefore, "these families are not given a sufficient opportunity to be reunified."[37]

If the mother manages to retain parental rights during her incarceration, her first priority upon release is likely to be the fight for custody of her children. Given the obstacles, the fight can be overwhelming. In making the custody determination, family courts will consider whether the mother is able to provide financial support and housing for children upon release. Because vocational and educational training in women's prisons tends to be severely limited, women ex-offenders often lack the marketable skills that might enable them to obtain the sort of employment that a court would be likely to approve. Then, federal welfare laws reduce their access to benefits that might provide transitional support as they seek employment. Complicating all of this is the fact that adoption laws have begun to reduce the amount of time that parents have to reunite with their children before permanently losing custody.[38] One year after Congress passed the welfare reform law, it enacted the Adoption and Safe Families Act of 1997 (ASFA).[39] This act allows states to begin termination of parental rights if a child has been in foster care fifteen of the last twenty-two months. So women ex-offenders find themselves in a race against time to overcome significant obstacles as they attempt to regain custody of their children.

To the extent that government and the courts are serious about easing the burden of women exiting jail and prison, dispensation must be made for custodial parents reentering communities, looking for work, and attempting to provide for their children. The added burden of simultaneously trying to reestablish themselves after incarceration and having to fight for custody significantly hampers reentry and imposes incredible stresses on the parent.

D. Welfare

In addition to restrictions on housing, some formerly incarcerated individuals are barred from receiving federal and state welfare benefits.

These are especially devastating collateral consequences for some populations, such as offenders who are parents. The denial of welfare benefits, including Temporary Assistance for Needy Families (TANF),[40] presents particular problems for formerly incarcerated parents. For many women, their inability to gain access to food stamps and public housing either makes it impossible to reunite with their children or prevents them from creating a suitable living environment. These benefits—often in the form of food stamps, Social Security Insurance, or Medicaid benefits—are barred in certain circumstances under the federal Personal Responsibility and Work Opportunity Reconciliation Act of 1996. Section 115 of PRWORA denies both TANF and federally funded food stamps to any individual convicted of a felony involving "the possession, use or distribution of a controlled substance." The federal welfare statute not only requires states to deny TANF benefits and food stamps to anyone who has been convicted of a drug felony, but it also requires state welfare systems to review state and federal penal records systems.

Congress passed the lifetime ban on benefits for individuals with felony drug convictions after a total of two minutes of debate in the Senate, and no debate at all in the House of Representatives. States may opt out of the ban, but to do so the state legislature must vote affirmatively, in state legislation passed after the effective date of the federal bill, to provide benefits to those individuals. Although thirty-six states[41] have eliminated or modified the ban in order to reduce recidivism, ensure that drug and alcohol treatment services remain available, encourage family reunification, and support individuals in recovery, the ban remains in full effect in fifteen states. The deprivation of social and welfare rights has further marginalized some ex-offenders.

E. A Gendered Approach to Reentry

Much of what recently released individuals encounter upon returning to their communities can be anticipated and addressed. The standard approach has been to make ex-offenders fend for themselves with little or no support or guidance. Critical to unraveling the tangle of issues facing those being released is open acknowledgment that there are common difficulties. A logical second step involves mapping a reentry path for ex-offenders to follow, given those difficulties. Issues of gender and geography also bear consideration in developing strategies to address the morass of reentry problems. Planning reintegration for women, especially in communities of color, should involve consideration of some of the profound cultural barriers placed in the path of these women. Given the large number of incarcerated women of color, particularly African American women, one of the central issues of reentry is how these women are accepted back into their communities. Because African American men have, for generations, been overincarcerated, there is a basic acceptance that Black men will have some interaction with law enforcement. But prior to the current cycle of increased female incarceration, Black women simply were not imprisoned as often as men. Those who were incarcerated were viewed as outside the norm or the mainstream. As these incarceration rates changed, that information did not make its way into Black communities. The result has been that women are less readily accepted back into their communities. Regina Austin describes the aggressive or antisocial behavior of Black male lawbreakers as functioning within accepted mainstream gender roles.[42] Women, on the other hand, do not enjoy this cultural acceptance. Indeed, women who return home from prison are often viewed as acting outside of accepted gender and racial roles.

F. Programming for Women and Reentry

Although women's needs are different in very central ways, the majority of corrections and pre-release programming still reflects an absence of the information and the policy direction that a truly gendered approach might take. Some long-time, well-informed commentators, such as Myrna Raeder, Judith Resnick, and Judge Patricia Wald have all suggested that corrections officials can and should rethink the approach to providing programming for women. Obviously this programming should acknowledge that women bring a different set of needs and programming challenges in preparing for reentry and should research those needs and challenges. Programming should reflect those instances of success that have been supported by evidence. Evidence-based programming provides the most certainty and optimism for the future of reentry planning.

Programming for women has traditionally provided fewer opportunities for women than for men. In the 1970s, first men and then women in prison responded by launching a wave of litigation targeted at state correctional systems. In a series of class action suits, women prisoners claimed that their rights had been violated under the Fifth, Eighth, and especially the Fourteenth Amendments to the U.S. Constitution. A number of these suits focused on incarcerated women's access to basic education, vocational training, work, medical care, and legal assistance. A series of favorable court rulings led to an initial expansion in the range of programming available to women in prison; subsequent cutbacks in spending on prison programs and services, however, have reversed many of these changes. For example, a larger proportion of women than men participated in all levels of educational programming (adult basic, secondary, and college) and had work assignments. However, the nature of prison work remained gender typed. Women were disproportionately involved in janitorial work, kitchen work, and cosmetology, whereas men were overrepresented in farm, forestry, maintenance, and repair. Pay levels also varied by gender, with men being paid more often than women for their prison work.

The most pressing needs for women preparing for reentry are lack of vocational training, history of drug abuse, and tenuous family situations. While studies show that vocational training is an important aspect of reducing recidivism rates for all offenders, female offenders are more likely than their male counterparts to be lacking in such training. Most women beginning a prison sentence have little job experience and few marketable skills. Inside the prison walls, the same woman is far less likely than a male inmate to receive training that will improve her former situation. Much of the relevant case law arising from female inmates relates to claims of disparate treatment in educational programming and vocational training. The number of cases in this area reflects the need for those women who commit crimes to be equipped to function productively outside the prison walls.

Kentucky and Virginia are two excellent cases in point. In Kentucky, female prisoners were denied access to many vocational, educational, and training programs that were available to male prisoners.[43] The programs that were made available to the female prisoners were inferior in quality to the corresponding programs at the male institutions.[44] In the Kentucky case the court held that the differential treatment between male and female prisoners was unrelated to any important government objective, and therefore violated fundamental notions of fairness embedded in the Constitution and expressed in the Equal Protection Clause.[45] The court went on to hold that the Equal Protection Clause requires parity, not identical treatment, for female prisoners in the area of jobs, vocational education, and training.[46]

Lack of access to vocational training and prison-industry work inhibits an inmate's adjustment to incarceration and post-release success. Inmates in vocational programs are less likely to commit crimes after release.[47] While this is true for both male and female inmates, women prisoners have an even greater need for employment training than their male counterparts. Women tend to enter prison with less work experience and fewer skills than men. More than half of all female inmates were unemployed at the time of their arrest. When released, women are more likely to have a family to support. Of women with children, 85 percent plan to live with their children after release compared to 52 percent of men.[48]

G. Women, Community Corrections, and Reentry

Some recent successes have posed the question of where we should place our reentry dollars. The correctional system has historically been male dominated. Not only are the structure of prison settings, the rules, the operating procedures, and the treatment programs largely based on the needs of males, but research studying the effectiveness of programs is also based on male subjects. Correctional systems often assign male inmates to programs on the basis of the individual needs of the offender, the severity of the crime, and their assessment of the security risk posed by the offender. There are compelling reasons why reentry programming for female offenders, as opposed to male offenders, should be a priority. First, women tend to be imprisoned for far fewer violent offenses. Nonviolent offenders should face less community resistance and might more easily gain access to, and benefit from, reentry programming connected to community-based programs. Given that communities should share the desire to keep families intact, programming that would include contact with children and assistance with parenting responsibilities would seem to make sense. Second, because women have fewer job skills than their male counterparts, programming that would teach and increase marketable skills would seem an obvious priority. Of course, the fact that women struggle with addiction at a higher rate than men would seem to require a regimen of drug treatment and related physical and mental health care to enable women to function at work and at home.

Because female offenders pose less of a security risk than their male counterparts given the nature of their offenses, correctional systems have a legal and moral obligation to design, develop, and institute programs that meet the special needs of female offenders. All of these arguments could be utilized in a gender-neutral fashion: nonviolent offenders who are primary caregivers, drug dependent, and poorly trained should have priority for community-based sentencing.

Community programs allow women offenders more opportunities to visit with their children, and sometimes to remain with them, while serving their sentences. Participation in job training, school, or work is encouraged or required by alternative programs while prison programming rarely provides women with truly marketable skills. Prison facilities that house female offenders are few in number. Most states within the United States maintain only one facility to house female inmates. Thus, most female offenders are not assigned to facilities based on their individual rehabilitative or treatment needs, or on issues of security or the severity of the offense committed, but on the basis of their gender.

Often, because of the nature of crimes committed by females, the community is not at high risk if female offenders are allowed to serve their time in community-based programs. These programs reduce the overall cost to taxpayers by consolidating the cost of imprisonment and foster care into one placement for both the mothers and the children. The most beneficial feature is that because the mother stays with her children while serving her sentence, there is less disruption to the family. As a result, the mother-child separation that inevitably comes in a prison term is avoided. Finally, in jurisdictions where there is only one facility to house women, individuals with different classifications must be housed together; minimum-risk female offenders are treated in the same manner as maximum-risk female offenders.

Community-based programs suit female offenders' diverse needs and reduce recidivism. Alternative sanctions should take into account the circumstances that generally characterize the lives of incarcerated women: primary care for children, the type and level of offenses, drug use, and the degree to which there is a history of surviving domestic violence. One significant alternative sanction for women rests with community corrections. Here women can often maintain their status as mothers and primary caretakers, allowing them (as nonviolent female offenders) to be confined in smaller community-based facilities and to remain with their children. Programs targeting parenthood is of the greatest service for female offenders. Community correction facilities provide a much more child-friendly setting as well as intensive supervision. Although some observers view these as a form of "lesser punishment," the truth is that we can provide a unique facility with the potential to offer real preparation for parenting and reentry.

H. Conclusions

Visitation between an incarcerated mother and her children is a critical component of a reunification program. One commentator stated that visitation is the most important factor for successful reunification. In addition, family visitation increases the likelihood of successful reunification upon release from prison. One example of a successful program preparing women to reconnect with family is at the Bedford Hills Correctional Facility for Women in New York.[49] Bedford Hills has implemented a unique visitation program for incarcerated mothers and their children. The facility operates a Parenting Center that "helps mothers maintain contact with their children and arranges visits."[50] The facility houses a Children's Center that has a visiting area designated exclusively for mothers and children. Bedford Hills also provides parenting programs for the mothers, including education on child rearing and health issues. Mothers also learn how to work with the child welfare system to improve their chances of reunification.

While most prisons allow visitation between an incarcerated mother and her children, problems remain. For example, more than half of the mothers incarcerated in state prisons nationwide reported that they have never had a visit with their children.[51] Because of the distance between women's prisons and the places where the children of these inmates are living, visits are hampered by transportation costs, and are often exhausting for the child. In addition, prisons often have rules restricting contact visits. Where "no contact" rules exist, visits are conducted through plastic or glass partitions and telephones must be used to communicate. These prohibitions on touching intensify feelings of separation for the mother and her children. Additional problems inhibit visitation between an incarcerated mother and her children. For example, some facilities require permission for visitation, which is used as a behavioral control mechanism. Thus, it is not uncommon for children to travel a long distance only to be denied visitation because their mother committed an infraction after permission was granted for the visit.

The incarceration of women in the United States has been notorious for creating fewer educational and vocational training opportunities. First, very few of the female correctional facilities nationwide have vocational training programs, and in general there are a limited number of work programs for female offenders. Second, the services provided to female inmates are problematic in that the vocational training programs for women provide skills that are not in demand in the outside job market—and so do not provide a livable wage. Without a useable skill set and the development of soft skills, such as being able to arrive at work on time consistently, dress appropriately for the occupation, and communicate with coworkers, the risk of reoffending remains high. Vocational and educational training for incarcerated women enables them to obtain jobs that provide a living wage, thus allowing them to be actively involved in raising their children.

Where correctional programming does provide women with work programs, they are often limited to domestic work, hairdressing, typing, sewing, and nurse's aide work. Explanations for these differences claim that the relatively small female prison population makes providing better services cost prohibitive. Another argument focuses on the incentives in the correctional system. It essentially suggests that spending money to rehabilitate women in custody is less cost efficient because women are not as dangerous to society upon release as men.[52] A related argument proffered by prison authorities is that men are more likely to riot over inadequate prison conditions. This policy response not only denies women prison programming but also exacerbates women's powerlessness.

When we look at prospects for reentry, a terribly disconcerting picture for the future of women inmates emerges. When one combines the lack of programming with the continued increase in the number of women entering the state and federal prison system and the lack of vocational and educational preparation, very little is being done on the policy level to reduce recidivism rates and prepare women to become active members of their community upon return. "The average woman beginning her prison sentence has little job experience and few marketable skills. Most women who did work before their incarceration did so in lower paying, low skilled, traditionally perceived gendered jobs: service, clerical, and sales positions."[53] Inside the prison walls, the same woman is far less likely than a male inmate to receive training that will improve her former situation.

Much of the litigation around programming for women arises out of the equal protection area and women making claims of disparate treatment in educational programming and vocational training. The court challenges use men's programming as the example of the types of services that should be provided for women. However, this searching for equality of programming may not reap the desired benefits when we more closely examine women's needs. Women should not be denied programs, such as child-rearing and prenatal-care programs, just because the programs are not offered for or demanded by men. A woman's needs and preferences should be considered when programs and services are designed. The effective pursuit of these goals will sometimes require different programs for women.

In addition to the problem of the average female inmate's lack of marketable skills, many of those same women suffer from various forms and stages of drug addiction. Much of the increase in the general prison population in recent years, as noted above, is a result of increasing rates of drug abuse by both men and women, as well as the accompanying legislative action to combat that abuse. Notwithstanding that women are more likely than men to be incarcerated as a result of a drug offense, little is being done to ensure that women in prison have access to drug treatment. Just as providing vocational training helps former inmates succeed upon release, treating the offender's drug addiction also improves recidivism rates.

4

Reentry and Housing

In her illuminating article in Time *magazine, Amanda Ripley described Jean Sanders, who was released from prison after serving seven years for stealing a car while under the influence of drugs. One of his first challenges was to find a place to live. Unable to live with his mother, he spent his first six months' worth of nights in a homeless shelter. Shelter life brought with it the usual police sweeps and interrogations. Within a five-block radius of the shelter were three crack houses, which also brought the temptation of relapse. Several buses of parolees would release their charges to the shelter. Parolees would be forced to ignore one of the explicit conditions of parole: not to associate with individuals with criminal backgrounds. Some studies suggest that 30 to 50 percent of parolees are homeless. Unlike that of most parolees, Sanders's story had a happy ending. He found a job and a room, and despite a brief relapse, the story ended with Jean Sanders still on parole.[1]*

A. Housing as a Basic Need

Ex-offenders' first priority upon release is to find suitable housing. But "suitable" is quite obviously defined differently depending on one's vantage point. If one were to ask a representative of the criminal justice system—a parole officer or a member of law enforcement—to define the term, one would probably elicit responses that involved some combination of verifiable address where the parole office could locate the parolee, conduct spot checks, and monitor whether the ex-offender was conforming to the conditions of parole. Indeed, locating housing and maintaining an address is often a condition of parole. So housing takes on a more administrative aspect, offering the justice system some ability to track and perhaps control the ex-offender's activities.

But "suitable" housing from the ex-offender's perspective would probably have a more personal and profound meaning. The term not only holds all of the promise that the word "home" might imply for anyone needing shelter, but it also creates a critical foundational link to other steps in the reintegration process. A place to live that is secure and consistent provides the stability necessary to adjust to living outside of confinement. It perhaps might even offer a haven from the challenges of coping with the other demands of reentry—reunification of family, physical and mental health treatment, and connecting to a community. Permanent housing allows the formerly incarcerated to become a part of the community to which they are returning. Perhaps as importantly, a stable address offers the ex-offender a necessary base of operations in obtaining critical services. Stable housing is particularly important in the process of gaining employment. Employers need to be able to reach a potential employee, and having an address allows the ex-offender to receive communications that can link him or her to a job opportunity.

But as basic as the need for housing may be, it is often one of the most confounding of obstacles that the ex-offender will encounter when he or she leaves prison. First, inmates may expect that families will welcome them home and offer them a place to live even if the offer is necessarily temporary—until the ex-offender can get back on his or her feet. But more often than not, families are reluctant simply to open their homes to the ex-offender. Many of those individuals caught up in the criminal justice system in the last decade suffered from drug addiction that either directly or indirectly led to their imprisonment. As described in the previous chapter, that addiction may have caused significant stress within the family unit. Families that have addressed issues of addiction are often forced to make difficult choices about their living space. In the African American community, addiction to crack cocaine has shaped familial relationships in unique ways. In his groundbreaking work *Streetwise,* Elijah Anderson describes the phenomenon:

> When addicts deplete their resources, they go to those closest to them, drawing them into their schemes for getting high. The process may go something like this: Unable to fully appreciate what is happening, the family may put up with the person for a while. They come to realize that the person is on drugs, though at first this may be hard to believe. But reality sets in, and family members begin to accept the fact of addiction as they put together the person's past actions and repeated, increasingly desperate demands for money. . . . Eventually the addict

begins to "mess up" in various ways, taking furniture from the house, perhaps a lamp, a toaster, or anything of value. Despite stories about thefts and burglaries, the others can see through these tales. The evicted young woman or man may then gravitate to the home of a sympathetic relative or friend and be allowed to stay awhile, but the backsliding repeats itself.[2]

Although some of the behaviors described above vary with the type of drugs or alcohol to which the individual is addicted, the result is generally the same. The family, particularly the family of color, makes the "tough love" decision to protect the rest of the family and bans the addicted individual from living in the household. Once the addict leaves prison, if the family home is unavailable, then the ex-offender may face substantial hurdles finding a place that will accept him or her. When this problem is coupled with the dramatic patterns of segregation, the options are limited for those with drug convictions returning from prison to communities of color.

When the family opts to allow the ex-offender to reside in the family home, the decision may cause unexpected tensions. Families that allow parolees to live with them are subject to searches at any time of the day or night as a condition of most parole grants. This can lead to unwanted disruptions that increase tensions in the household.[3] Added to already strained relationships, these unannounced intrusions can raise old tensions and cause new eruptions. In addition, the choice to add another person to a household may create tremendous economic burdens. If the ex-offender has not secured a job, he or she is simply another mouth to feed. Moreover, to obtain employment, the ex-offender, like any other prospective employee, may incur certain expenses to prepare to find a job. The ex-offender may need to purchase suitable clothes to make a good impression on an employer; may need transportation money to follow up on job leads; or may simply need some money to survive. These added—and sometimes unwelcome—costs can make the choice to return home and reside there unacceptable, which can then force recently released individuals to gravitate toward shelters or other temporary housing.

But shelters and transient housing options are fraught with problems. According to Flavin and Rosenthal, "homeless shelters are not ideal placements for offenders upon release from prison for a number of reasons, including the likelihood that an individual will come into contact with people who engage in crime or illicit drug use. Other problems associated with temporary housing include the stress of not having privacy or a secure space to store one's belongings."[4] Shelters also present a variety of safety issues. Some shelters also bar residents from remaining in the shelter during the daylight hours, thus presenting problems of time management for ex-offenders.

In much of the literature discussing offender reentry, a stable living environment ranks as one of the primary necessities upon release. This is due largely to the number of ex-offenders being released to inner-city communities where housing options are already very limited for low-income residents. When one adds the overlay of race, additional factors of discrimination come into play. Without access to stable housing, a large number of ex-offenders become homeless. Despite the booming economy of the 1990s, researchers estimate that on any night the national population of homeless people exceeds seven hundred thousand. That number is merely a brief glance at the number of homeless on a single day; indeed, it may be misleading.[5] Estimates of the number of individuals who are homeless vary widely; however, it is well documented that the number of people who are homeless for some period during the course of a year exceeds one million.[6] Millions more remain on the brink of losing permanent housing.[7] Incarceration and criminalization may temporarily serve to lessen the visibility of homelessness. The obvious affordable-housing crunch that has arisen as a result of the burgeoning need for housing for the poor has only worsened an already tight housing market. For ex-offenders of color, the problem is compounded by the intersection of poverty and residential segregation.

B. Impact of Concentrated Poverty

Increased poverty, as well as decreased political support for public housing, has led to a high demand for public housing that is largely unmet. The relatively modest increases in the number of vouchers for housing and in units of housing provided have not come close to meeting the need for affordable housing units. Between 1970 and 1995, the number of low-income renters increased 70 percent, but the total number of units available to low-income renters fell.[8] In addition to a declining number of units available, public housing remains segregated by race. Almost two-thirds of public housing residents are African Americans.[9]

Today's public housing residents are some of the poorest in history; the median income for a household in public housing is $5,850, about 19 percent of the national median income.[10] This poverty is disproportionately borne by people of color—especially Latinos and African Americans.[11] The disparity between the groups varies regionally, but there is no urban area where the Black poverty rate is less than or equal to the poverty rate for Whites.[12]

The intersection of poverty and segregation is amplified nationally. Poverty and race intersect most dramatically in public housing. Racial minorities living in public housing are even more likely than Whites to earn extremely low incomes. Consequently, the effects of poverty in public housing are especially acute for African Americans who reside there. Black public housing residents live in neighborhoods populated by large concentrations of poor African Americans; this is markedly different than for Whites living in public housing.[13] The average African American household living in family public housing resides in a project that is 85 percent Black and 8 percent White, with 80 percent of tenants below the poverty level.[14] The neighborhoods surrounding the developments in which typical African American public housing families live are similar: the census tract is 68 percent Black, 25 percent White, and 47 percent below the poverty level.[15] Because of discrimination patterns in public housing, very low-income people of color have been concentrated in specific urban areas.[16] The situation for White-dominated public housing offers a stark contrast. In general, Whites in public housing live in conditions that seem to realize "the promise of decent, safe, and sanitary housing."[17]

According to Douglas S. Massey and Nancy A. Denton, African Americans are more racially segregated than any other group.[18] They label this segregation "hyper-segregation." Massey and Denton divide hyper-segregation into five components: unevenness (Blacks over- or underrepresented in neighborhoods); isolation (Blacks rarely share neighborhoods with Whites); clustering (Blacks form one large, contiguous enclave); concentration (Blacks live in a very small area or settle sparsely throughout an urban environ); and centralized (Blacks live in a spatially focused area around an urban core or along its periphery).[19] Massey and Denton point out that the structural factor underlying the construction of the Black ghetto is White racial prejudice—a racially discriminatory attitude that finds support in existing institutional mechanisms.[20] Black Americans in these metropolitan areas live in densely packed neighborhoods that are focused around an urban or urban-like center. Because of appearance, Puerto Ricans are often considered African Americans by many Americans and consequently, they face similar discriminatory treatment in the real estate market.[21] They often "resemble the Black poor in the proportion of female-headed families, welfare recipients, and central city residents."[22] It is not difficult to understand that the intersection of poverty and race, coupled with the segregated housing patterns in this country, lead to extremely limited housing resources for people of color.[23]

Public housing as it currently exists in the United States began with the passage of the United States Housing Act of 1937.[24] Housing shortages as well as lack of quality housing became much more intense in the late nineteenth and early twentieth centuries.[25] Congress found that private initiatives alone would not ameliorate substandard housing.[26] As a result, Congress declared that the federal government must intervene and encourage local government to construct acceptable housing for low-income people.[27] In response to overwhelming need during the Great Depression, the federal government seized land and built more than twenty thousand units of rental housing through the Housing Division of the Public Works Administration (PWA).[28] In 1935, however, federal courts held that the PWA had exceeded its power of eminent domain; this in turn delayed the government's first attempt at building large-scale public housing.[29]

By 1949, the federal government found a way to build public housing. Congress passed a housing act that articulated a goal of providing a suitable living environment for every American family.[30] Segregation was the law of the land and housing units were created separately for Blacks and Whites.[31] During the 1950s public support for the public housing program began to wane and Congress failed to appropriate sufficient money to achieve its target of constructing 810,000 units.[32] Post–World War II America also witnessed the migration of African Americans from the South to northern cities, leaving what had been primarily agricultural jobs for manufacturing jobs.[33]

Public housing now served a different mandate. It shifted from its original goal of being "suitable housing" for America's middle class to becoming homes for primarily low-income and Black households.[34] As the income of public housing residents plummeted and the age of public housing projects increased, the rents charged by public housing authorities (PHAs) to cover operating expenses became increasingly burdensome. Increasingly, maintenance and security began to falter.[35] Although tenant rents were to pay operation and maintenance costs, deficiencies in this area plagued the program from the start. As poor tenants continued to have limited ability to pay escalating rents, the public housing program's funding structure has led to its fiscal instability.[36] Tenants themselves, particularly the large number of tenants of color, began to feel the effects of both dilapidated properties and substandard housing units. Lawrence Vale, a professor of urban studies and planning at the Massachusetts Institute of Technology who has written extensively about the design and history of public housing, suggests that public housing renters feel the impact of living at the bottom of the architectural pile not merely from the shame of association with visibly deteriorating structures and exclusion from the world of those who live in more acceptable housing but also from internalization of the architectural stigma: "layers of stigma blend and merge into a single image of the *undeserving poor.*"[37] Public housing by the late 1960s and early 1970s had developed a reputation (and some would argue a reality) of being substandard facilities. By the mid-1980s public housing projects were occupied primarily by people of color; 1986 Public Housing Authority data indicated that "60% of all families in public housing are headed by Blacks and an additional 24% by Hispanics."[38] Later, public housing would become a political football of both the Democratic and Republican parties.[39]

Profound increases in poverty have led to an extremely high demand for public housing. Even as incomes have increased overall through the end of the last century, by the end of the 1990s over thirty-four million people lived in poverty.[40] Extreme poverty became concentrated in the inner cities, the same place where housing is in great demand, and the same place where large numbers of ex-offenders return to seek housing.[41] This has resulted in an increased need for housing units and unexpected competition between different groups of individuals vying for limited public housing resources. Nationally, there are over nine hundred thousand families on waiting lists for public housing units, and about 1.4 million waiting for housing subsidies.[42] The average time spent waiting for a housing voucher exceeds two years.[43] The wait is even greater in areas with large public housing authorities; on average, an applicant will wait five years in Chicago, eight years in New York, and ten years in Los Angeles.[44]

As public housing and other resources have become progressively more limited, the political leadership in this country increasingly blames the poor for the conditions they face. It has become a standard political trope to suggest that poor people are responsible for their own fate and that it is a reflection of their own failings that they are poor. As part of this new, harsh philosophy, policy makers have made explicit their intention to provide affordable housing only to those deemed the "deserving poor."[45] Coupled with this shift in terminology has come a change in identification of the poor. Politicians coined the phrase "welfare queen" and focused the lens of poverty on the African American community.[46] The obvious intent was to create code words to invoke stereotypes of race and prejudice while at the same time attacking some of the neediest in our society.[47] Notwithstanding this nation's social, economic, and political debt to redress harm to people of color, the rhetorical and policy damage had been done. Instead of pursuing a housing policy that put forth the notion that every human being has a right to a home—not just shelter—at an affordable cost or, in the case of the destitute, no cost at all,[48] communities and individuals have been pitted against each other.

Of all the federally supported programs, public housing in particular became a favorite target of politicians. Congress cut the Department of Housing and Urban Development (HUD) budget by over one-quarter in fiscal year 1996.[49] Access to housing became more of a competitive enterprise as a result of continued budget cuts and an increase of pressure on public housing, shelters, and other low-income residences. The population in need of housing was virtually the same population that makes up the prison population in the United States.[50] For parolees and particularly parolees of color who have been a large part of the War-on-Drugs incarceration boom, housing is the most important need and most difficult to find. And as people of color are released from prison, they inevitably return to those communities where the housing stock is exceptionally limited. Moreover, policy changes in the last decade involving HUD have made finding housing extremely difficult for ex-offenders.

C. Government-Sanctioned Exclusion of Offenders from Housing: Crime and Safety in Public Housing

By the end of the twentieth century we as a nation had come to recognize that public housing was both segregated and dangerous. In his 1994 testimony to the House of Representatives Committee on Banking,

Finance, and Community Affairs, Secretary Henry Cisneros described his observations of the Robert Taylor Homes in Chicago, where residents were forced to

- walk with their children through automatic weapons fire between buildings held by opposing gang members;
- prevent their children from going outside to play because playgrounds were littered with bullets, used hypodermic needles, and used condoms;
- cower behind darkened windows in their own living rooms as bullets made holes on walls or in windows.

Chicago, New York, Washington, D.C., Boston, Detroit and every other major city in the United States has some form of public housing. By the end of the 1980s these housing projects had become very dangerous places. Tenants began to clamor for some help from city, state, and federal officials. Some residents were willing to go so far as signing open-ended "consent-to-search" clauses, giving police carte blanche to search their apartments. Most of the crime appeared to be drug related, and the violence involved turf battles. Congress responded with legislation focused on drug dealing.

In 1990, Congress made housing exceedingly difficult for ex-offenders to secure. Congress enacted the Anti–Drug Abuse Act to respond to increasing rates of crime and violence in public housing projects. The Anti–Drug Abuse Act required public housing authorities, who received federal funds or assistance, to include a lease provision that policy makers believed would help to eliminate such activity. Specifically, the act called for lease provisions that would make criminal activity of a tenant, guest, or person under the tenant's control an express basis for eviction. In 1990, the Cranston-Gonzalez National Affordable Housing Act reiterated the policy that housing authorities were not to tolerate any drug or violent criminal activity.

The Cranston-Gonzalez Act stated that "criminal activity that threatens the health, welfare, safety or right to peaceful enjoyment of the premises" would be grounds for termination of the lease. Accelerated administrative grievance procedures for the eviction of criminal tenants were added. This policy expanded the rights of public housing authorities to review tenant files and conduct criminal background screening of prospective tenants. Applicants for federally subsidized housing would have to face more scrutiny and restrictions in their efforts to secure public housing. Directives from the highest levels of government made clear that public housing would be the new battleground for the fight against crime and drugs.

In his 1996 State of the Union address, then-President Bill Clinton stated that "[f]rom now on, the rule for residents who commit crime and peddle drugs should be one strike and you're out."[51] The Department of Housing and Urban Development accordingly issued "One Strike and You're Out Screening and Eviction Guidelines for Public Housing Authorities," outlining the statutory language for housing authorities to adopt. This policy required public housing authorities to screen and evict tenants for drug-related or "safety-threatening" behavior. Once Congress enacted this legislation, public housing authorities began to include lease provisions that made any allegations of drug or violent criminal activity sufficient cause for termination of the tenancy. Interestingly, the language of these provisions did not limit the activity to the premises. So an individual who allegedly engaged in this activity, regardless of its proximity to—or distance from—the public housing project, could face eviction.

More troubling still, the legislation had a broad reach. The tenant could face removal from public housing even if he or she were not the alleged criminal. The lease provisions applied to "any criminal activity that threatens the health, safety, or right to peaceful enjoyment of the premises by other tenants or any drug related criminal activity on or off such premises, engaged in by a public housing tenant, any member of the tenant's household, or any guest or other person under the tenant's control."[52] Criminal activity engaged in by a guest or someone assumed to be under the tenant's control would constitute adequate grounds for termination of the tenancy. Furthermore, criminal activity by any of these persons does not have to occur on the leased premise. The public housing authority can thus hold a tenant strictly liable for criminal activity by a guest or invitee allegedly committed away from the residence, even if the tenant does not know about the activity. The penalty for the tenant is the loss of public housing. This deals another blow to family structures, community networks, and prisoners reentering society by encouraging tenants of public housing to avoid the reentrant—to shun those who were coming home.

D. Department of Housing and Urban Development v. Rucker

Pearlie Rucker was a sixty-three-year-old woman who had lived in public housing for approximately thirteen years. She was living in Oakland Housing Authority (OHA) housing with her mentally disabled daughter, two grandchildren, and one great-grandchild.[53] Rucker's daughter was found in possession of cocaine three blocks away from their apartment. Pearlie Rucker was not aware of her daughter's drug use.[54] Pearlie Rucker was only one of the tenants whom the OHA sought to evict. OHA brought eviction proceedings against Willie Lee and Barbara Hill, each living with a grandson.[55] Lee was seventy-one years old at the time of the proceeding and had lived in public housing for twenty-five years; Hill was sixty-three years old and had lived in public housing for thirty years. The grandsons living with the Hills were caught smoking marijuana together in the parking lot outside the apartment complex. Neither Lee nor Hill had any knowledge of this activity.[56] The fourth tenant involved in the case was Herman Walker, a partially paralyzed former minister who had lived in public housing for eight years.[57] Walker had a healthcare worker assigned to him, and he was evicted when persons other than himself and his caretaker were found in the apartment, along with drugs and drug paraphernalia. Three of the four named respondents were grandparents living with grandchildren.[58] Pearlie Rucker's household included a great-grandchild.[59]

In *Department of Housing & Urban Dev. v. Rucker*, 533 U.S. 125 (2002), the OHA moved to evict all of these tenants based on a claim that they were in violation of the new "One Strike" policy established by the Clinton administration. In Rucker's case, her daughter, Gelinda, was also a resident of her apartment, and was mentally disabled and addicted to alcohol.[60] In light of Gelinda's prior treatment for alcohol abuse, Rucker described her practice of searching her daughter's room periodically for evidence of drugs or alcohol.[61] Rucker stated that she had no indication from these searches that her daughter was using drugs or alcohol.[62] Gelinda was observed drinking with an open container three blocks from the complex.[63] A search of her person revealed cocaine and a crack pipe; she was arrested and charged with possession.[64]

Herman Walker, the disabled resident,[65] was partially paralyzed on the left side, walked with difficulty, needed a cane, and periodically used bottled oxygen; all of these factors were described in court papers.[66] He could not live on his own and required the services of a home healthcare worker.[67] The home healthcare worker that was assigned to him at the time of the eviction proceeding was a woman named Eleanor Randle.[68] On three separate occasions, OHA police found persons other than either Walker or his caregiver, Randle, in the apartment and found drugs or drug paraphernalia in the apartment or in one of the individual's possession.[69]

HUD v. Rucker arose when Rucker, Lee, Hill, and Walker each sought permanently to enjoin their evictions in the United States District Court for the Northern District of California. The district court ruled in favor of the tenants, holding that they had raised serious questions about HUD's interpretation of section 1437d as allowing for strict liability evictions. Strict liability evictions would mean that the government could simply prove the act of possession of the drugs without needing to establish the tenant's knowledge of that act. An en banc panel of the Ninth Circuit affirmed the district court by a seven to four vote. The court based its final opinion on textual interpretation and an analysis of congressional intent. The Ninth Circuit articulated significant doubts about the constitutionality of the government's interpretation. The court stated, "[P]enalizing conduct that involves no intentional wrongdoing by an individual can run afoul of the Due Process Clause."[70] The Court's reasoning was, in part, that public housing tenants have a property interest in their tenancy, and that HUD's notion of strict liability would permit tenants to be deprived of their property interest without any relationship to the alleged individual wrongdoing.[71]

The Supreme Court unanimously reversed the opinion of the United States Court of Appeals for the Ninth Circuit. The Court stated that HUD was well within its rights to act as a landlord and invoke a clause in a lease to which respondents have agreed and which Congress has expressly required."[72] The Court also held that the statute does not lead to absurd results because the statute does not require the eviction of any tenant who violates the lease provision. Rather, the statute gives the discretion to the local public housing authorities, who are in the best position to take into account the "level of drug or criminal activity."[73] The Court rejected the notion of an "innocent owner defense," stating in its decision that Congress could have inserted language providing for this type of defense if it had wanted to do so.

The results of this decision were twofold. First, it eliminated the primary substantive and procedural defenses to eviction in allegation-of-criminal-conduct cases. Second, it created an environment that allowed public housing authorities to act with impunity in their decisions to evict and to prescreen those with criminal records to keep them from obtaining public housing. After "One Strike" and *Rucker,* public housing typically is in effect not an option for individuals returning to communities from prison. Federal housing policies permit and, in many instances, require PHAs, Section 8 providers, and other federally assisted housing programs to deny housing to individuals who have previously engaged in certain criminal conduct.[74] If the terms of the act do not require that housing authorities deny a lease to an ex-offender, the housing authorities retain discretion to do so. And, if the ex-offender chooses to move in with family or friends already living in public housing, that decision can put the entire family at risk of eviction. The Legal Action Center, based in New York City and Washington, D.C., has provided one of the most comprehensive surveys of the range of collateral consequences faced by ex-offenders. In their publication regarding public housing, they note that, in addition to the clauses that allow for ineligibility based on drug-related criminal convictions or other convictions,[75] federal regulations grant discretion to PHAs to prohibit admission to public housing of all "criminally involved" individuals. When these restrictions are combined with the lack of available public housing stock, the formerly incarcerated are essentially per se excluded from this important public benefit. Effectively eliminating ex-offenders from access to public housing, policy makers have increased the likelihood that, upon release from prison, ex-offenders will join the ranks of the homeless.

E. Homelessness

Just as in the development of the image of the welfare queen, the conservative policy maker and media collaboration actively fostered the notion of the homeless skid-row bum.[76] Approaches to homelessness rarely focus on factors such as policy decisions to decrease government programs for low-income housing initiated during the Reagan administration, the rise in unemployment, poverty, the decrease in public assistance programs, changing demographics, urban renewal, or the deinstitutionalization policies of the late 1970s and early 1980s (which closed mental health hospitals around the country). Rather, the focus has overwhelmingly been on the homeless themselves.[77] The factors listed above have resulted in a decrease in the supply of housing and an increase in the number of persons needing access to housing assistance.[78] Because private landlords often do not want to rent to ex-offenders—particularly to ex-offenders of color—many of these individuals ultimately find themselves on the street, unless family members who do not reside in public housing are able to take them in.[79] Policy makers have been slow to respond to this need, on the rationale that felons should be banned from public housing altogether. The notion of "exiling" a criminal may carry with it certain political appeal; however, in reality it simply sets in motion a set of consequences that imposes costs upon all of us. Preventing someone who has served time from obtaining public housing and doing nothing to assist in the reentry process will force that individual into the ranks of the homeless or send him or her back to the easy money of the criminal underworld.[80]

Prisons generally do not offer pre-release housing assistance. In fact, many facilities do not even confirm the address provided by the prospective parolee prior to release.[81] Where pre-release assistance is provided, housing is not usually one of the services that corrections can or will assist the inmate in locating.[82] The overwhelming majority of the offender population is left to fend for itself in obtaining housing and employment upon release.[83] Adequate housing is often a key factor in determining whether an individual will reoffend.[84] Stable housing is necessary for an ex-offender to reintegrate and become a lawful and productive member of society.[85] But the large numbers of individuals in need of housing and the lack of affordable housing in the areas where ex-offenders are returning, coupled with a variety of discriminatory policies, set the stage for increased risk of homelessness.

Remedies for the ex-offender side of the homeless problem lie first of all with the government response. Government can and should recognize this threat to communities already brimming with poverty and in need of housing resources. The logical response would be to loosen the restrictions on public housing resources for formerly incarcerated individuals.[86] Instead, the government response more often than not has been to criminalize homelessness.

Cities, under the guise of protecting residents against crime, controlling threats to public health and sanitation, and trying to attract business and tourism, have declared war on the homeless.[87] In cities known for tourism but with significant numbers of homeless and inadequate affordable housing—such as New York City and San Francisco—we have seen particularly harsh policies against the homeless through aggressive enforcement of "quality of life" measures.[88] These policies reflect hostility against rather than concern for, or compassion toward, more visible homeless activities like aggressive panhandling and sleeping in public parks.[89] This move toward law enforcement as a replacement for social services is most prevalent in areas that do not provide sufficient resources for their homeless populations.[90] Ultimately, we are seeing increasing numbers of ex-offenders become homeless, even though they have paid their debt to society and want only to have a reasonable opportunity to succeed. By denying them housing and allowing them to join the ranks of the homeless, then incarcerating them for doing so, we create a society worthy of the pages of Charles Dickens.

By moving housing, mental health treatment, literacy programs, and other necessary social services into the criminal justice system, policy makers have virtually guaranteed a return to an approach of combating the social problems of poverty through criminal sanctions and of increasing the discretion given to local law enforcement officials. Coupled with the free hand that has come with fears about terrorism, law enforcement today can ignore civil liberties that were in the forefront merely a few years back.

F. Unacknowledged Discrimination in the Private Housing Market

It is well established that discrimination in public and private housing violates the law. One week after the assassination of Martin Luther King, Jr., Congress passed the Fair Housing Act, Title VIII of the Civil Rights Act of 1968.[91] The act was amended in 1988 and now stands as the principle vehicle used to launch claims against instances of housing discrimination.[92] In addition, in *Jones v. Alfred H. Mayer Co.*[93] the United States Supreme Court held that the Thirteenth Amendment and a provision of the Civil Rights Act of 1866[94] prohibit governmental discrimination, as well as private discrimination, in housing. Notwithstanding the clear legal bar to housing discrimination, residential segregation continues unabated in this country. In addressing the problem of reentry and housing most critics focus on public housing, the inherent difficulties in lack of housing stock, and federal, state, and local prohi-

bitions against ex-offenders. However, one obstacle that is virtually ignored in discussions about reentry is that of the private rental market.
Although financial resources come into play, widespread discrimination
in housing has been tolerated for decades.[95] Since many ex-offenders
will not receive governmentally subsidized housing, private, unsubsi-
dized housing may present the only opportunity for social integration of
these ex-offenders.[96] As a result, discrimination based on race, ethnicity,
and ex-offender status must be addressed.

A number of instances of housing discrimination documented by
solid empirical evidence continue to surface.[97] Housing discrimination
creates a uniquely damaging harm. The consequence of allowing this
insidious form of bias to persist creates a range of deeply rooted social
problems. Because this nation has allowed poverty to be so closely
linked to housing, if discrimination and segregation are allowed to persist, poverty will inevitably deepen and become more persistent within
a large share of the Black community, crime and drugs will become
more firmly rooted, and social institutions will fragment further under
the weight of deteriorating conditions. With continued separation of
the races, racial inequality will continue, racial prejudices will be reinforced, and hostility toward people of color will increase, making the
problems of racial justice and equal opportunity even more insoluble.
Housing affects access to good schools, exposure to clean and safe environmental conditions, and access to employment.[98]

The clearest evidence of discrimination comes from audits of practices in the rental and sale of residential properties. A 1979 study concluded that Blacks are more likely to be excluded from renting or buy-
ing in certain residential areas, are more likely to be given quotations of
higher prices and rents, and are frequently directed to areas already
densely populated by Blacks.[99] A decade later, HUD sponsored a second
national testing study, the Housing Discrimination Study. In that study,
3,745 tests were conducted in twenty-five metropolitan areas to track
the frequency of discrimination experienced by African Americans and
Latinos in the sales and rental markets.[100] The test concluded that discrimination in the rental markets continues. One study concluded that
over half of the African Americans seeking housing experienced some
form of discrimination in rental markets.[101] A similar result was also reported from Latino testers.[102] One author describes the effects of continued housing discrimination: "[R]ace discrimination plays an impor-

tant role contributing to high levels of racial segregation in the City and inferior neighborhoods and housing conditions for racial and ethnic minorities."[103]

According to a study based on 2000 census results, in the thirty metropolitan areas containing a majority of all Blacks in the United States, 65 percent of Blacks would have to move to achieve a uniform racial composition across the metropolitan area.[104] As a result of continuing segregation, the average African American in a number of cities lives in a census tract that is about two-thirds Black, indicating a relatively low probability of contact with Whites.[105] The corresponding effects implicate schools; because most K-12 schools draw their students from local neighborhoods, they are equally segregated. Approximately one-third of Black students attend schools in which less than 10 percent of the students are White.[106] In large states such as New York, Michigan, Illinois, and California, less than 25 percent of the average Black student's classmates are White.[107] Notwithstanding the *Brown v. Board of Education*[108] decision, racial segregation in the schools has been increasing in almost every state, even during the 1990s.[109]

Employment is also affected by the segregated housing patterns described above. Employers located outside Black neighborhoods and beyond the reach of public transportation are significantly less likely to hire Black employees.[110] An examination of White-owned firms located in Black neighborhoods reveals that one-third of these still have no employees of color.[111] One survey of jobs found that half of all job titles were occupied by Whites only, and one-quarter of Blacks worked in jobs to which only Blacks were assigned.[112] No one would argue that these segregated work patterns were based solely on segregated residential patterns; however, the two practices complement one another.[113]

G. Lack of Enforcement

Discrimination in the private market is similarly made illegal by Title VIII of the Civil Rights Act of 1968, commonly referred to as the Fair Housing Act,[114] which prohibits discrimination by most home sellers and landlords.[115] The original Fair Housing Act was ineffective due in part to its structural inadequacies with regard to enforcement.[116] Originally, the attorney general was authorized to initiate enforcement actions.[117] However, for the most part, the protection and preservation of fair housing rights was the domain of the injured party.[118] Even after the 1988 amendment, which supposedly bolstered enforcement capabilities, discrimination remained.[119] Lack of significant enforcement of fair housing laws in the face of strong discrimination, coupled with the advent of housing vouchers and certificate programs, tends to resegregate integrated neighborhoods. Zoning to block minority housing, and discrimination in federally supervised mortgage-lending institutions, along with the notion that most Americans feel little obligation to allow people of color access to the housing market, all add to the nation's poor record on providing housing for some sectors of the population.[120]

Perhaps the most glaring problem with the enforcement of laws against private housing discrimination is the extent to which discretionary enforcement decisions are politically motivated. One only needs to take a glance at the number of prosecutions brought by Democratic administrations versus Republican administrations.[121] People of color generally, African Americans particularly, and ex-offenders of color specifically, do not have the political resources to instigate wide-ranging enforcement against private housing discrimination that might lead to industry-wide change. As a result, private landlords continue widespread discrimination in the lease, rental, and sales of property to people of color and ex-offenders.

As to housing more generally, until we begin to focus our policies and resources on providing safe and adequate housing to ex-offenders, we will continue to see the problems associated with lack of housing, including high unemployment, poor education, and high recidivism rates. This problem must be addressed through legal means, for example, through stricter enforcement of the Fair Housing Act resulting from cases brought by private plaintiffs, as well as through large-scale policy changes focused on increasing available housing stock, and through administrative rules that allow adequate housing for ex-offenders.

H. Conclusions

There is a dearth of available housing for all low-income individuals. When we add the heavy burden of a conviction, the housing dilemma becomes all the more acute. Given the confluence of factors that operate against the returning ex-offender in his or her search for housing, no single remedy will suffice. But a necessary prerequisite to alleviating this problem is making the commitment to recognize that it exists and should not persist.

Some of the answers to the housing dilemma rest in the control of government authorities. Prior to release, it is imperative that corrections officials and agencies in communities collaborate to verify that those being released from custody will not be subjected to homelessness immediately upon release. Government housing authorities, in conjunction with corrections departments, may need to find ways to provide transitional housing for recently released ex-offenders as a short-term solution. Housing at the point of release enhances the ex-offender's ability to gain access to other reentry services and to facilitate his or her reintegration into a community. Jobs, treatment, and connections to family and community are dependent on an individual's ability to maintain a safe and stable housing situation. But even this limited step has met with considerable resistance at the federal level, and governments have consistently failed to make any significant progress on this issue.[122]

Still, the need to provide housing for individuals who have paid their debt to society is clearly linked to their ability to transition into productive members of their communities. With the large number of drug-related offenses, we see many individuals returning from custody struggling with addiction. Even in the most ideal circumstances, their path is difficult. However, homelessness only exacerbates the problem. In fact, lack of housing alone operates as a predictor for recidivism.[123] Many treatment professionals argue that without stable housing, relapse is almost certain.[124]

It is certainly in the interest of government to work to remove barriers to housing. While government officials cannot mandate that private landowners rent housing to ex-offenders, they can create incentives that might make the activity more attractive financially. So, for example, local, state, and federal governments should mandate set-asides for all new housing developments in their jurisdictions. These set-asides should be accompanied by tax subsidies.

But perhaps where the government has the most leverage and, as importantly, the greatest opportunity to relieve some of the housing pressures that recently released individuals experience involves public housing. Although the United States Supreme Court in the *Rucker* case held that public housing authorities have the discretion to evict the formerly incarcerated, this need not be the result. Currently, public housing authorities receive points if they establish procedures to evict those with criminal histories.[125] The net effect of empowering housing authorities to evict individuals not engaged in—or even having knowledge of—the criminal conduct of those visiting or living in their apartment is that families are separated and ex-offenders often lose the ability to establish a stable lifeline. If the government were to create a system of incentives that led public housing authorities to attempt to keep families intact and to exercise discretion that might allow the formerly incarcerated to establish ties with their nuclear families, then perhaps the housing dilemma could become a little less onerous.

The incentive system might follow this process. Congress could design and implement legislation that requires the Public Housing Assessment System to award points only for evictions of criminal conduct that takes place on public housing authority property and spaces within a limited proximity. In addition, points should also be awarded to the successful reunification of families in public housing. In appropriate circumstances, probationary agreements should be worked out with the relevant tenants. PHAs should be required to develop and administer discretionary guidelines when it comes to the consideration of past criminal conduct. Sunset provisions that wash out convictions over time and other mitigating factors should create a presumption that families will be reunified when individuals are released from custody.

One final option that might help us alleviate the difficulty of housing for formerly incarcerated individuals would be to enact and enforce municipal human rights ordinances that prohibit public and private discrimination in housing based on formerly incarcerated status. If such ordinances also included provisions for attorneys' fees to be paid by the losing party, the civil justice system might be engaged in a way that might encourage private and public landlords to refrain from discrimination on this basis.

5

Reentry and Health Care

"Mr. T.P. suffers from schizophrenia for which he was diagnosed at an early age. On August 15, 2000, Mr. T.P. was released from the D.C. Jail after being granted parole. His mother had been aware of his impending release date and was in regular communication with his case manager at the D.C. Jail. On the day before his pending release, the case manager assured his mother that he would be released on the morning of August 15, 2000. Having heard the horrible stories of prisoners being released in the middle of the night, the mother repeatedly asked for assurance that T.P. would be released the next morning when she could pick him up. The case manager again assured her that she could pick him up the next morning. However, when the case manager ended her workday, personnel in the records office noticed his release date and began the process of releasing Mr. T.P. Despite all assurances to his mother, the jail released T.P. at 1:00 A.M., and no one bothered to notify his family of his release. He was given $2.50 for carfare, but did not know where to go. He wandered through the streets of D.C. in his prison jumpsuit until he came to a neighborhood that was familiar to him. He was found by his mother's in-laws. He was sitting on the porch two doors down from where these relatives lived. The relatives called his mother and notified her that he was there. They gave him a pair of jeans, a tee shirt and took him home. It is truly a mystery how he was able to recall the neighborhood of his relatives when this was his first release after serving nineteen years in prison. Though he had been on psychotropic medication throughout his entire incarceration he was also released without any supply of medication. T.P.'s mother and father called D.C. Superior Court, the Office of Parole Supervision, and worked hard to stabilize T.P. and to place him in the Spring Road Mental Health Clinic where he reported daily while living at home. Due to the collaborative efforts of his parole officer, psychiatrist, and caseworker, T.P. was successfully in the community for nearly a year until

he was arrested by the U.S. Marshal Service for violating the conditions of his parole. He allegedly submitted one urine sample that tested positive for marijuana. Both of his parents, his caseworker and a psychiatrist attended and testified at his parole revocation hearing. His psychiatrist testified that he was working with T.P. teaching him to be more assertive. T.P. expressed his concern that the neighborhood in which he had to walk after leaving the Spring Road Clinic everyday to go home was a drug infested area and the guys would often ask him to participate in smoking marijuana. The hearing examiner revoked his parole, but, convinced that further incarceration was not necessary, scheduled a release date of November 2, 2001.

This, however, is not the end of the story. The U.S. Parole Commission has recently determined that T.P. could not be released because his case manager had submitted insufficient release planning information. Mr. T.P. remains housed at the D.C. Jail."[1]

People enter prison with a variety of health problems, and, once they are housed in prison settings, a disturbingly high percentage of individuals contract an illness or develop ongoing health problems. The law mandates a duty of care to ensure that inmates receive treatment while in custody. But that care is eliminated virtually immediately upon release from custody. Most of the health problems, identified in prison and often prior to incarceration, are severe and, if left untreated, can obviously lead to more serious health issues. But these pervasive health issues present an often unrecognized problem: they pose substantial hurdles to reentry. Recently released individuals with acute physical and mental health needs find it difficult to obtain housing, to find and maintain employment, and to live crime-free lives. Generally, people in need of health services are left on their own to patch together services that might help address their particular health problem. However, the challenge for recently released individuals becomes all the more difficult as they attempt to locate comprehensive health services in low-income communities that are already experiencing a dearth of such services. Indeed, the health problems that exist behind prison walls are likely to persist once the individual leaves prison and will disproportionately affect people of color in low-income communities in this country.

A. What Happens in Prison: A Duty to Provide Care

In 1976, the United States Supreme Court mandated a standard of care for all incarcerated individuals. In *Estelle v. Gamble*,[2] a Texas inmate filed a complaint pursuant to 42 U.S.C. § 1983 alleging that his prison's failure to provide adequate medical care subjected him to "cruel and unusual punishment" in violation of the Eighth Amendment. Gamble's medical issues began when he sustained an injury while performing a prison work assignment.[3] Although he attempted to work after sustaining the injury, working aggravated it. Prison officials allowed him to go to the unit hospital.[4] Medical professionals diagnosed his problem as a "strained back," and they prescribed some period of rest.[5] But his medical difficulties continued for several months and began to include chest pains and irregular cardiac rhythm. These symptoms led to additional hospitalization and medication.[6] Later, Gamble once again began experiencing chest pains and requested the opportunity to meet with the prison doctor. Prison officials refused his requests for two days. That refusal to honor his request led to the filing of the initial complaint.[7]

In *Estelle v. Gamble*, the Court articulated and established the government's obligation to provide medical care for incarcerated individuals who would otherwise have no means to supply medical care for themselves.[8] The Court opined that "[it] is but just that the public be required to care for the prisoner, who cannot by reason of the deprivation of his liberty, care for himself."[9] The Court determined that 42 U.S.C. §1983 and Eighth Amendment principles required that the government provide medical care and announced that "deliberate indifference to serious medical needs of prisoners" would form the standard for civil suits brought under 42 U.S.C. §1983.[10] The Court ruled that the deliberate-indifference standard applied both to prison doctors and to prison guards.[11] The Court explained that "indifference is manifested by prison doctors in their response to the prisoner's needs or by prison guards in intentionally denying or delaying access to medical care or intentionally interfering with the treatment once prescribed."[12] The denial of medical care, when shown as "deliberate indifference to serious medical needs of prisoners constitutes the 'unnecessary and wanton infliction of pain,' proscribed by the Eighth Amendment."[13]

The Court further refined the principles articulated in *Estelle v. Gamble* in 1991. In *Wilson v. Seiter*,[14] the Supreme Court extended the deliberate-indifference standard to conditions of confinement.[15] In so doing, the Court developed a two-part test for determining deliberate indifference.[16] First, the prisoner must demonstrate an objective component: he must show a "sufficiently serious" deprivation. Second, the inmate must establish a subjective component: he must show that the prison official had a "sufficiently culpable state of mind" that demonstrated deliberate indifference to the prisoner's safety.[17] Building on the *Wilson* decision, three years later the Court decided *Farmer v. Brennan,*[18] where it further fleshed out the *Wilson* test. *Farmer* held that the second part of that test created a subjective standard of deliberate indifference.[19] The Court found that liability of the prison official cannot be established unless (1) "the official knows of, and disregards, an excessive risk to inmate heath or safety; (2) the official [is] aware of facts from which the inference could be drawn that a substantial risk of serious harm exists; and (3) [the official draws] the inference."[20]

Following on the heels of *Estelle v. Gamble,* federal courts have also indicated that the government must provide mental health treatment to incarcerated individuals who require such services. Although the Supreme Court has never explicitly stated that mental illnesses are medical illnesses, courts consistently interpret medical care to encompass mental health care.[21]

Despite the mandate, increasing numbers of individuals suffering from severe mental illness end up in jails and prisons, without access to appropriate treatment. In fact, too often the reason that they have come into contact with the criminal justice system in the first instance is related to their mental illness. The inability to conform their conduct to societal norms—due to their illness or the lack of treatment—means that individuals will engage in often minor antisocial or disruptive behavior that brings them to the attention of law enforcement and the court system.[22] Perhaps the best evidence of this assertion is that the largest numbers of persons being treated for serious mental illness are not in hospitals, but in the three largest jails: Rikers Island (New York City), the Cook County Jail (Chicago), and the Los Angeles County Jail (Los Angeles).[23] Some studies on the population of persons with mental illness in both the state and federal prison systems put the number at approximately 283,000.[24]

Mental health treatment in the context of prison is vital, but it also has significant implications for reentry. We know that many seriously mentally ill persons simply cannot thrive, or even survive, in their communities without individualized help. Many individuals either live in the shadows of the community or are ejected from it. Without access to treatment in prison and after, these individuals will almost inevitably rotate back into the criminal justice system.

B. Substance Abuse

Similar concerns surface when we consider the problem of substance abuse. Studies estimate that approximately 60 percent of people arrested in major cities in the United States used drugs at the time of arrest.[25] Nearly 70 percent of state prisoners and over half of federal prisoners suffer with problems related to drug addiction or alcoholism.[26] Moreover, a Bureau of Justice Statistics study revealed that over 75 percent of the surveyed state prison inmates used illicit drugs, and more than half reported using drugs within the month prior to committing the crime for which they were incarcerated.[27] Although the *Estelle* decision did not directly address drug and alcohol treatment, it led to a general improvement in the response to inmates' medical problems, including substance abuse and addiction.

Some studies suggest that drug abuse treatment is a significant factor in reducing recidivism.[28] Although few would dispute the fact that treatment is a critical component in the rehabilitative process, very few inmates actually receive drug treatment.[29] The roots of this problem can be traced to the early 1970s. At that time, a number of well-publicized studies openly challenged the idea that prisoners could be rehabilitated. The substance abuse treatment field was still in its infancy, and with the exception of methadone maintenance for heroin addiction, few treatment programs existed that could provide data validating the claim that treatment could be effective in changing the behavior of imprisoned addicts and substance abusers. Soon after, the increased media attention on crime and drugs and the hyperbolic political rhetoric that followed in the 1980s and early 1990s encouraged policy makers and legislators to implement increasingly punitive policies against criminals and prisoners.[30] Studies indicate that more than 31 percent of federal inmates require some level of substance abuse treatment, and a staggering 74–85 percent of state inmates are in need of treatment.[31] Although empirical evidence proves the effectiveness of prison-based treatment, substance abuse services have not expanded.[32]

Not surprisingly, correctional departments offer a wide range of explanations for their failure to provide treatment. Budgetary constraints, lack of available counselors, lack of space, too few volunteers, and limited inmate interest are the principal reasons that prison officials cite for not offering such treatment.[33] In addition to "external reasons," correctional departments also blame the failures of prison-based treatment on the frequent transfer of inmates to other prison facilities.[34] Transfers certainly interfere with the continuity of treatment that meaningful drug intervention would seem to require.[35] But whatever the reason, prisons and jails are simply not furnishing offenders with the type of pre-release substance abuse treatment that might facilitate their transition back into the community.

Without access to education, job training, or substance abuse treatment, individuals attempting reentry must rely upon parole agents and other service providers in the community to help them address these critical issues. The burden of addressing the wide range of competing system demands of parole office appointments, drug treatment, employment, medical/psychiatric care, and other services is placed solely on the ex-offender. While these demands pose difficulties for all ex-offenders, the ones who are also battling substance-abuse-related problems can become overwhelmed. In exercising judgment about which issue to address first, some may understandably choose to address the most pressing need (such as housing or employment) and neglect other needs. The result is often a failed attempt at reentry. Increasingly, studies have begun to highlight the large number of reincarcerations for technical violations, such as missed parole appointments or failed drug or alcohol tests. Overall, during 1995, 200,972 probationers and 110,802 parolees were incarcerated for violations of their probation or parole conditions —many involving positive drug tests.[36]

C. Common Types of Problems

When we stop to examine the health issues that find their way into prisons and jails and back into the communities to which recently released individuals will return, we see a few common, disturbing trends. Tuberculosis, hepatitis C, and HIV tend to affect growing numbers of inmates housed in our jails and prisons. Indeed, the numbers far exceed those in the general public. More virulent strains of some of these illnesses have begun to surface within prisons and, in some instances, have infected broader populations—those who live in proximity to prisons or come into regular contact with infected prisoners or ex-prisoners.

Tuberculosis poses serious dangers to individuals within the prison system and to the communities that surround them. A review of tuberculosis rates in prisons evidences the ease with which the disease is transmitted. In 1997, for instance, there were thirty cases per one hundred thousand among New York State inmates, compared to thirteen per one hundred thousand in the total state population.[37] What is particularly problematic about this disease is that individuals can transmit it into surrounding communities unknowingly, as people with tuberculosis routinely do not exhibit symptoms.[38] The spread of tuberculosis occurs through airborne transmissions: the bacteria moves from one person to another simply through the air.[39] Given the environmental conditions that prevail in prisons—characterized by overcrowding in facilities with poor ventilation systems—the tuberculosis bacteria may spread quite easily within a prison facility. But the danger does not rest solely within the confines of the prison system. Joan Petersilia pointed out that, in the 1990s, New York City found itself dealing with a new multi-drug-resistant form of tuberculosis that was traced to Rikers Island Jail.[40] In addition, she documented a Los Angeles outbreak of meningitis in the county jail that moved into the surrounding neighborhoods.[41]

Like tuberculosis, hepatitis C is prevalent in the prison setting. The Centers for Disease Control and Prevention estimate that 1.3 million individuals with hepatitis C, or 39 percent of all Americans with this disease, are released from correctional facilities each year. Once back in the community, infected individuals may continue to transmit the infection, particularly if they remain undiagnosed and untreated. This situation presents a rare opportunity for targeted interventions aimed at reducing spread of the virus.[42] Hepatitis C, one of the leading known causes of liver disease in the United States, commonly causes inflammation of the liver. It is the most common reason for liver transplants; at least four million people in this country, it is believed, have been infected with hepatitis C.[43] Prisons estimate that 20-40 percent of prisoners are infected.[44] An estimated one out of three Americans with chronic hepatitis C infection rotates through correctional facilities annually.[45] Prevalence of hepatitis C infection in prisons is eight- to twenty-fold higher than in the community, with infection rates between 16 and 41 percent and evidence of chronic infection, 12–35 percent.[46]

D. HIV

But perhaps the most alarming health issue in the last few decades has been HIV/AIDS. By 1996, 2.3 percent of all state and federal prison inmates were known to be infected with the human immunodeficiency virus (HIV), a rate six times higher than in the general population.[47] Obviously, the long-term implications for the individual's health are quite serious. But when we add the stigma that attaches to the individual who is HIV positive, the burden on the formerly incarcerated individual who is trying to reintegrate into a community becomes more difficult. Given the homophobia that pervades communities of color, particularly the African American community, many individuals who may be at risk for HIV will be reluctant to seek testing or treatment for fear of community reaction. Thus, prison commitments that lead to infection run the risk of becoming death sentences.

By the mid-1990s, the epidemic proportions of HIV in prisons had become evident: the infection rate had begun to show that growing numbers of inmates had been infected with HIV.[48] In addition to relatively high HIV infection rates, the number of prison inmates with confirmed AIDS had also risen. From 1985 to 1996 the number of confirmed AIDS cases rose from 179 to 5,874.[49] The rate of confirmed AIDS among prison inmates (0.54 percent) is more than six times that of the general U.S. population (0.09 percent).[50] The transmission of HIV among correctional inmates has become a serious concern for prison and jail administrators in the United States.[51] In addition to affecting the health of inmate populations, it has also become a concern for safety, discipline, and the protection of correctional staff. Although it appears that most inmates are infected with HIV while outside the prison walls, the transmission of the virus in prison remains a very real problem.[52]

In addition to the environmental conditions contributing to the spread of HIV, rape is also difficult to detect and control in the prison setting. Prison rape has been assimilated into the cultural mainstream and is often the subject of late-night humor.[53] According to one poll, it is considered a socially acceptable price for offenders to pay for crimes they have committed.[54] There are no conclusive nationwide statistics on the prevalence of prison rape. Although the Prison Rape Elimination Act passed by Congress and signed by President Bush calls for research in this area, interviews and anonymous surveys of inmate populations have yet to determine accurate sexual assault rates. Victims and witnesses of sexual assault in prison often refuse to notify authorities out of shame or fear of reprisal.[55] In his important work on the issue of prison rape, James Robertson cites one study of midwestern prisons that concluded that 7 percent of male inmates experienced coerced anal or oral rape and about 21 percent had experienced some form of coerced sexual contact.[56] Prison rape is an area that has a dramatic impact on the inmate population both during and after a period of incarceration.[57] Failure to address the needs of the victims of prison sexual assault risks the spread of sexually transmitted disease both behind the walls and outside the prison in communities when offenders are released. In addition, profound psychological trauma can occur if the disease remains untreated, thus providing an additional obstacle to successful reentry.

While the numbers of men who are infected with HIV or who have AIDS have skyrocketed, they pale in comparison to the increase in rates of infection among female prisoners. The percentage of female prisoners who are HIV positive is actually higher than that of male prisoners.[58] For example, by the end of 1994, 2.4 percent of all males in state prisons were HIV positive, as compared to 3.9 percent of all females.[59] In the period beginning 1991 and ending in 1994, the percentage of male HIV-infected inmates in state prisons had grown since 1991 by 22.4 percent; the number of female inmates with HIV had exploded, increasing by 68.5 percent.[60]

E. Women

While medical care is generally substandard for all prisoners, women face additional barriers to care, reflecting the lower value society places on addressing the health of low-income women. Women enter prison with a high incidence of serious health concerns, including life-threatening diseases such as hepatitis C, as well as reproductive-related illnesses.[61] (A sizeable percentage of women enter prison while pregnant.) Incarcerated women are disproportionately affected by HIV as compared to incarcerated men.[62] In Massachusetts, one study found that though women account for only 7 percent of the inmates who are incarcerated, they represented 20 percent of the HIV-positive inmates.[63] This survey concluded that the number of female inmates with HIV is rising at a greater rate than that of men.[64] Today, the majority of U.S. women diagnosed with AIDS are women of color. African American women account for 53 percent of the cases, while Hispanic women account for 21 percent.[65]

F. Mental Health

Every year approximately seven hundred thousand adults with serious mental illnesses come into contact with the criminal justice system.[66] The inadequacy of general mental health care has made jails and prisons the de facto mental institutions of our age.[67] A study by the U.S. Department of Justice in 1999 reported that approximately a quarter of a million inmates in American jails and prisons, or about 16 percent of inmates in U.S. prisons, had a mental illness.[68] Studies have suggested that as many as 6 to 15 percent of persons in city and county jails and 10 to 15 percent of persons in state prisons have severe mental illnesses.[69] Part of the reason for the skyrocketing mental health problems includes the type of broken-windows policing that has become routine (i.e., quality-of-life crimes resulting in the arrest of large numbers of homeless individuals). In addition, many of the drug-related arrests include individuals who cannot afford, and have not had, access to adequate health care.

G. Legal Requirements to Treat the Mentally Ill Offender

The *Estelle* decision is less clear on the extent to which prison and jail inmates have a right to mental health treatment.[70] Cases decided by the United States Supreme Court and some appellate courts have helped begin outlining a standard of care required for incarcerated individuals. The United States Court of Appeals for the Ninth Circuit attempted to clarify *Estelle*'s "serious medical need" provision. In *McGuckin v. Smith*,[71] the court stated that a "serious medical need" exists if the failure to treat a prisoner's condition could result in further significant injury or the "unnecessary and wanton infliction of pain."[72] In the case of *Bowring v. Godwin*,[73] the United States Court of Appeals for the Fourth

Circuit attempted to address the extent and amount of mental health treatment that prisoners should receive pursuant to the Eighth Amendment of the United States Constitution. The court held that an inmate is

> entitled to psychological or psychiatric treatment if a physician or other health care provider, exercising ordinary skill and care at the time of observation, concludes with reasonable medical certainty (1) that the prisoner's symptoms evidence a serious disease or injury; (2) that such disease or injury is curable or may be substantially alleviated; and (3) that the potential for harm to the prisoner by reason of delay or the denial of care would be substantial. The right to treatment is, of course, limited to that which may be provided upon a reasonable cost and time basis and the essential test is one of medical necessity and not simply that which may be considered merely desirable.[74]

This standard articulated in *Bowring* established a constitutional right to mental health care based upon the Eighth Amendment. However, it is far from clear which inmates are legally entitled to treatment. The standard of those who have a "serious" medical need or for whom the treatment is a "medical necessity" is not as clear when one is referring to mental health treatment.

Still, the ruling in *Bowring* suggests that there is a constitutional right to mental health treatment in situations where the inmate has a serious medical need. This is perhaps the area where the legal mandates and the prescription for successful reentry diverge. Court, prison, and jail officials should be adequately funded to provide mental health services and referrals to those individuals who pass through their facilities. Given the prevalence of the problem and the extent to which the symptoms of mental illness contribute to the difficulties of reentry, we must address this problem in order to make any serious attempt to fix reentry.

Research has consistently demonstrated that a significant portion of the population entering the criminal justice system has moderate to serious mental health problems.[75] In New York City for example, approximately fifteen thousand people identified with mental health problems are confined and released each year, representing over 10 percent of the annual jail census.[76] A number of factors have contributed to the large number of incarcerated individuals with mental illness. Jails and prisons have always had many people with mental illness, but the numbers have increased in the last several decades due to massive deinstitutionalization from mental hospitals, cutbacks in social services, and the unavailability of community and inpatient psychiatric treatment. There is also an increasing criminalization of the mentally ill with municipal policies of "zero tolerance" based in large part on the "broken windows" theory that became a popular method of policing in the mid-1980s.[77] Another contributing factor is the rapid rise in the overall prison population and concomitant overcrowding, which increases tensions in prisons and causes more mental illnesses than previously existed.[78]

The prevalence of mental disorders[79] among persons with criminal justice system involvement is staggering.[80] The changing population in prisons and jails creates a dramatically different mission for these institutions, one that they have historically been ill-prepared to implement. It also raises unprecedented implications for offender reentry and the volume of services that will be needed in communities already stretched thin in their attempts to provide out-patient mental health services.

Corrections departments have typically not had the orientation, the physical facilities, staff, training, and clinical resources to meet the needs of the seriously mentally ill population they are currently called upon to serve. The courts have made it clear that these institutions are legally and constitutionally required to develop a capacity to provide adequate mental health services for the inmates in their custody.[81] In meeting these needs, institutions cannot rely solely on psychotropic medications, but instead need to develop a full range of mental health services to meet the foreseeable needs of the seriously mentally ill inmates in their custody. In addition, the courts have recognized that many mentally ill inmates face inordinate danger.[82]

Beyond legal problems, the mentally ill have many additional social service needs. This is particularly true for individuals with more than one disorder. Several reviews of the research literature found that the negative consequences of co-occurring disorders in the general population include greater stress and demands on family, increased risk of homelessness, increased vulnerability to infectious diseases such as HIV and hepatitis, increased risk for suicide, and higher rates of hospitalization and other service utilization.[83] To the extent that mental health problems have manifested prior to incarceration, they generally remain untreated in prison.[84]

Studies have shown that rates of mental illness and substance abuse are quite high in incarcerated populations; other studies have shown that the two problems are frequently co-occurring disorders. In a study on co-occurring abuse, Karen Abram and Linda Teplin determined that approximately three-quarters of inmates with mental health diagnoses have both alcohol and drug-abuse problems.[85] In a study on inmates with serious mental illnesses, Mark Munetz, Thomas Grande, and Margaret Chambers found that 70 percent of inmates with serious disorders were actively abusing substances at the time of incarceration.[86]

In addition to the human toll exacted by the unwillingness to treat mentally ill inmates, there is a financial burden on taxpayers as well. Nationally, over 283,800 individuals suffering from severe mental illness are in prison or jail.[87] American taxpayers pay approximately $8.5 billion a year to incarcerate the mentally ill (suggesting a rate of approximately $50,000 per person).[88] By refusing to address this massive public health issue while individuals are in custody and legally deserving of treatment, we instead tax our other community-based resources. Approximately half of the estimated two million homeless Americans—virtually invisible to much of society—are mentally ill.[89] In contrast, only 25 percent of the nation's mentally ill currently reside in public psychiatric hospitals.[90] Iowa, for example, incarcerates more than twice as many individuals with mental illness in prison than it treats in its four state mental health institutes.[91] An estimated 90 percent of the clients of the Des Moines' Churches United homeless shelter who have mental illnesses have been in jail or prison, some of them having been incarcerated repeatedly.[92]

Relatively few studies have specifically assessed rates of service needs of incarcerated populations. It is easy, however, to extrapolate the preponderance of medical, psychosocial, housing, treatment, employment, and other needs from the above-cited problems. Some studies have identified homelessness, sexually transmitted diseases, employment, and education as the most pressing needs for inmates preparing for release. Toward this end, one study estimated rates of homelessness among recently released mentally ill prisoners at 31 percent, with the most severely mentally ill inmates at the most risk.[93] Somewhere close to 20 percent will require some psychiatric intervention during their term of imprisonment.[94]

Some populations are disproportionately affected by the phenomenon of incarcerating the mentally ill. Research shows that as many as one in five incarcerated youth has a serious mental health disorder, such as schizophrenia, major depression, or bipolar disorder.[95] Mental illness is especially prevalent among women entering the correctional system.[96]

Female inmates display symptoms of serious mental illness in significantly higher proportion than males.[97]

One study of substance-abuse rates for women suggests that these rates may be higher for women than men.[98] According to the National Institute of Justice, 77 percent of women admitted to jails in the United States test positive for drugs (81 percent in New York City).[99] In addition to higher rates of substance abuse, incarcerated women are particularly likely to suffer from anxiety disorders.[100] Finally, incarcerated women have been found to have higher overall rates of mental illness than men (18 percent to 10 percent).[101] Women also have at least three times the risk for suicidal ideation and behavior when compared to the general community population.[102] Women are also medicated more often than men; approximately 17 percent of women in jails and 23 percent of women in prisons receive psychiatric medication.[103]

H. Disproportionate Effect on People of Color

Incarcerated women of color are particularly at risk for bouts of mental illness. In a chapter on the health status of Black women, Sandra Taylor describes the penal system as "yet another health hazard for African-American women."[104] Taylor goes on to point out the vulnerabilities of women in general and specifically women of color, who are being incarcerated at alarming rates. Despite the overpopulation of prisons with people of color, the possibilities of culturally competent mental health services in the prison context are discouraging.[105] Poverty seems to be one important factor in the lack of available treatment alternatives, and this poverty disproportionately affects African American families.[106] Links between poverty and mental illness have not been fully explained, though some experts believe that the correlations are due in part to the greater stress that living in poverty creates on individuals.[107] Only about half of all Blacks have private health insurance; one in five have Medicaid or Medicare and one in five have no health coverage.[108] Higher rates of poor health among African Americans are mirrored in higher rates of mental health problems.[109] Some researchers have also argued that African Americans may suffer from psychological stress associated with living in a pervasively racist society.[110]

The reasons for racial disparities in the receipt of mental health care are far from clear. However, a number of factors may affect the mental health care of Black males, including the fact that African Americans are less likely to receive their mental health care in private outpatient settings, where they could have a greater role in choosing care appropriate to their needs.[111] Also, bias on the part of clinicians is pervasive and affects the quality of care provided to African Americans.[112]

In addition to lacking adequate access to mental health treatment in prison and on the street, people of color also have to contend with chronic misdiagnoses of mental illness. Research suggests that African Americans are often misdiagnosed by mental health professionals. Diagnostic tests may be racially biased, elevating the observed rates of certain types of mental illness for African Americans.[113] White therapists may harbor negative views of African American patients, based on societal myths.[114] Studies found that Blacks were being disproportionately put into subcategories of schizophrenia that suggested dangerousness and a severity level that was greater than for Whites. They were also more likely to be committed to a psychiatric unit against their will.[115] Blacks are statistically overrepresented at state-run psychiatric institutions.[116] It is not coincidental that African American men were also more likely to be involuntary patients than any other race/gender group. Research suggests that Blacks and Latinos are more likely to be misdiagnosed with schizophrenia.[117]

The problem of subjectivity in the application of psychiatric diagnostic criteria is exacerbated when White, middle-class, and overwhelmingly male clinicians are called upon to interpret the signs and symptoms of patients who are different in race or ethnicity from the clinician. This situation often occurs in urban settings and public mental institutions and prisons.[118] This circumstance sometimes results in unnecessary commitment and harmful intrusive treatment not only for people of color but for immigrant populations as well.[119] Prisons and state hospitals often exacerbate this problem by not requiring full licensing.[120]

Because of racial bias in the mental health care profession, African Americans have generally relied on other forms of help for psychological difficulties. Research on the differences in help-seeking behaviors among Whites and African Americans has shown reluctance on the part of African Americans to seek mental health care treatment because of a fear of misdiagnosis or inappropriate treatment.[121] Arguably this can lead to African Americans suffering greater incidences of mental illness.[122] Community-based studies have found little variation in the types of mental illness that affect different populations.[123] However, there continue to be misdiagnoses and undertreatment for people of color with mental illness.[124] Contributing to the lack of adequate mental health services to communities of color is the range of cultural misunderstandings and communication problems between patient and provider, a distrust of mental health services, and racism.[125] To address this problem, cross-cultural training for psychiatrists and psychotherapists should be required.[126]

I. Focus on Prison/and Pre-Prison Release

Mentally ill offenders are often trapped in a cycle of petty crime, incarceration, release, homelessness, and reimprisonment. Half of the mentally ill inmates in state and federal facilities report having three or more prior sentences.[127] The United States Department of Justice reported that the nationwide cost for housing a prisoner in a state correctional facility is about $20,100 per year, or about $55 per day. Similarly, the cost of incarceration for federal inmates was estimated at $23,500 per year.[128] Some participants in the criminal justice system see this combination of high expenditures and low levels of treatment as inappropriate; one judge presiding over hearings involving mentally ill defendants suggested that these "inmates should be in treatment not in jail."[129] Mentally ill state prison inmates were more than twice as likely as other inmates to report living on the street or in a shelter within the previous twelve months.[130]

Mental health evaluations in prisons are generally conducted at the time of admission or following a crisis in which an inmate displays acute psychological problems. This type of screening may help to identify inmates who require services at the time of admission or after suffering an episode; however, it fails to address inmates who develop mental health problems after incarceration or whose problems become more acute after incarceration. Moreover, only about 60 percent of the mentally ill in state and federal prisons reported receiving mental health treatment after being incarcerated.[131] Treatment and preparation for release is conducted on a relatively small number of mentally ill inmates who need such services.

Counseling was the most common form of treatment, followed by medication.[132] An estimated 60 percent of the mentally ill in state and federal prisons received some form of mental health treatment during their period of incarceration. Fifty percent said they had taken prescription medication; 44 percent had received counseling or therapy; and 24 percent had been admitted to a mental hospital or treatment program.[133]

White mentally ill inmates reported higher rates of treatment than Black or Hispanic offenders. About 64 percent of White state prison inmates identified as mentally ill had received treatment, compared to 56 percent of Black offenders and 60 percent of Hispanic offenders[134] Reginald Wilkinson, the director for the Department of Rehabilitation and Correction for the state of Ohio gave a chilling description of the result of this lack of treatment in Ohio. Wilkinson testified before the legislature that "72% of inmates with mental illness leaving the Lucas County Jail, in northwest Ohio, were re-arrested within 36 months."[135] Wilkinson also noted that "[u]nless we provide these offenders with the services and treatment they need while they are incarcerated, we are virtually guaranteeing that they will commit new crimes when they return to the community. Nevertheless, few corrections systems are able to prepare inmates adequately for their release."[136] The need for mental health services, particularly for people of color, is not limited to those in custody. However, in order to provide better reentry services and to reduce recidivism, we need to also examine the obstacles to the availability of community-based treatment in communities of color.

When Surgeon General David Satcher released his report entitled "Mental Health: Culture, Race, and Ethnicity" in 2001, it came as no surprise to many that people of color were not receiving adequate mental health treatment outside the prison walls as well. Satcher's report suggests that the mental health of African Americans should be evaluated in light of the significant number of African Americans who are in "high need" populations. For example, proportionally 3.5 times as many African Americans as White Americans are homeless, thus compounding the problem of accurately assessing need.[137]

Financial barriers contribute at least in part to the disparities in access to mental health services. Many of the working poor, among whom African Americans are overrepresented, do not qualify for public coverage and work in jobs that do not provide private coverage. Better access to private insurance is an important step, but is not in itself sufficient.[138] The report also concludes that disparities other than financial are equally pressing. For example, few mental health specialists are available in communities where African Americans live.[139]

Latinos do not fare much better in access to mental health services. The report points out that the current system of mental health services in place fails to provide for the vast majority of Latinos in need of care and that this failure is especially pronounced for immigrant Latinos, who make the least use of mental health services. Latinos within known vulnerable groups are also of concern. Incarcerated Latinos, those who use excessive amounts of alcohol or drugs, and those exposed to violence—such as Central American refugees—are most likely to be in need of mental health care.[140]

The report also identified distrust and fear of the mental health system and mental health practitioners as barriers to accessing services. It also pointed out that the symptoms of illness may differ in different ethnic and racial groups: African Americans, Asian Americans, and Hispanics are more likely than non-Hispanic Whites to express mental distress through physical symptoms such as stomach aches, chest pain, dizziness, or other somatic complaints.[141] Spero Manson, director of the division of American Indian and Alaska Native programs at the University of Colorado's Health Sciences Center and a science editor for Satcher's report, said that in a review of the mental health literature, he found only two thousand studies over ten years, the bulk of them small and concerned primarily with alcohol and drug abuse treatment.[142] Yet the suicide rate among male Native Americans ages fifteen to twenty-four, the report noted, is two to three times higher than in the general population, and a 1997 study found that from 1979 to 1993, male Alaska Natives had "one of the highest documented suicide rates in the world."[143]

The likelihood of suitable treatment opportunities is quite low outside of the prison context. Even the surgeon general concluded that the existing mental health care system is ill suited to address the needs of people of color. The 2001 surgeon general's supplemental report on mental health emphasized the importance of considering race, culture, and ethnicity in addressing the mental health needs of a diverse population. The report confirmed that serious disparities exist regarding the mental health services delivered to racial and ethnic minorities. The supplemental report concluded that to achieve the benefits of effective mental health preventive and treatment services, cultural and historical context must be accounted for in designing, adapting, and implementing services and service delivery systems.[144]

J. Conclusions

The question then becomes, how do we prepare individuals with mental health needs for reentry back into society? Individuals in need of mental health services and those in need of non-mental-health-related reentry services bear some similarities. The issuance of necessary identification and qualification for health benefits (e.g. Medicaid, SSI, etc.) prior to release would help released individuals begin making the transition from prison to community. Also, especially in the case of those with mental health needs, better discharge planning must take place.

Individuals leaving prison often have multiple problems to address: housing, employment, previously strained familial relationships. The period just prior to release often has the added stress of the prisoner needing to identify and connect with services outside the prison walls; they frequently do not have sufficient knowledge about options or places where they can locate service, information, or help. Prison release can become a precursor to homelessness if comprehensive discharge planning is not implemented. Studies suggest that of the services provided to inmates with mental illness,[145] planning for discharge is the service least likely to be offered.

Addressing reentry through maintaining individuals in treatment upon release and identifying services in the community during the preparation for discharge will likely reduce the rates of mental illness and substance abuse (for those with co-occurring disorders) in the incarcerated populations nationwide.[146] One of the greatest obstacles to providing ex-offenders with mental health services is the difficulty in connecting the ex-offender with the appropriate community-based treatment provider.[147]

In preparing inmates for release, prison officials need to put plans in place that will assist inmates with health and mental health problems in maintaining some continuity of treatment upon reentry. Pre-release medical screening identifying treatment needs and preparing for release into the community will fundamentally improve the reintegration from prison. Connections to public health providers, coupled with adequate amounts of prescribed medications and links to other social service providers in the neighborhoods where the formerly incarcerated will return would also help facilitate reentry.

One tension in reentry and health care springs from privacy concerns over health care records. More research and proper consultations leading to informed consent are needed to determine how to get treatment records from custody facilities to community-based treatment providers.

In both jail and prison commitments, Medicaid is often suspended or terminated, depending on one's length of stay. Applying for reinstatement or initial consideration of Medicaid benefits prior to release can significantly improve a recently released individual's chances of success.

6

Reentry and Unemployment

Consider the case of Marc LaCloche. LaCloche served a term in the Clinton Correctional Facility in New York after being convicted of first degree robbery.[1] He spent twelve hundred hours in prison learning a barber's trade so that upon release, he would have a means of building a new life. Shortly before LaCloche was due to be paroled, he applied for a license as a barber's apprentice, but the state refused his application on the ground that the "applicant's criminal history indicates lack of good moral character." At least one judge in New York appreciated the irony of this situation, noting that "if the state offers this vocational training program to persons who are incarcerated, it must offer them a reasonable opportunity to use the skills learned thereby after they are released from prison."[2]

A. Obstacles to Employment

Employment is one of the key factors that prevent a former prisoner from committing new crimes. It often creates a sense of self-worth and of investment in the future that leads to full and legal participation in the community. Placement programs that specialize in rehabilitating ex-offenders frequently note the inverse correlation between recidivism rates and employment opportunities. However, despite the recognized importance of employment and the direct link to successful reentry, ex-offenders experience increasing difficulty locating jobs. Persons with a criminal record belong to one of the groups most discriminated against in hiring practices. A 2002 Urban Institute study found that employers were less willing to hire former felons than they were any other disadvantaged group. Applicants who had only earned a high school equivalency diploma (GED), were on welfare, had a spotty work history, or were unemployed tended to fare better than individuals with a criminal record.[3] In a 2002 survey, employers in five major cities said that they would not "knowingly hire an ex-offender," and approximately one-third "checked the criminal histories of their most recently hired employees."[4]

The law does provide some protection against discrimination. Where an employment policy that discriminates against the formerly incarcerated will have a disparate racial impact, employers must show a "business necessity" before automatically disqualifying them.[5] But the impact of a criminal record on job placement is strong even when there is no connection between the job and the crime committed because of the stigma created by a criminal conviction.[6] Discrimination that results from disclosure of criminal convictions often encourages applicants to lie on their applications. Because of the ease with which employers can check background records through the Internet, for example, there is little point in trying to hide a criminal record.[7]

Communities of color experience significantly more unemployment than other workers in the United States. The unemployment rate for African Americans remains steady at approximately twice the rate for White workers and has been so since 1958.[8] In 1988, the Black unemployment rate was 2.57 times the White rate and was the highest Black-to-White unemployment differential ever recorded.[9] Although the nation witnessed an economic boom in the decade of the 1990s, that increase was barely felt in the nation's African American communities.[10] In fact, the large discrepancies in unemployment rates between Blacks and Whites that existed in the 1970s and 1980s continued during the bullish times of the 1990s.[11] Black communities increasingly became associated with high and, more troubling still, "permanent" unemployment rates.[12]

When the characteristics of criminal history, race, and youth are combined, the unemployment rates for these population groups soar. "The unemployment rate for Black youths aged 16 to 24 years with less than a high school diploma was 36.7% in September 2001, while the unemployment rate for White college graduates was 2.0%."[13] If other factors indicative of disadvantage were added to the mix—such as family composition, child-care responsibilities, neighborhood of residence, and prior employment experience—the differences would be even greater. Unemployment and unemployability are closely identified with Black communities. In addition, residents of low-income Black communities are often deemed unworthy of employment relative to other demographic groups. One study found that employers bluntly described their biases in hiring, generalized about Whites and Blacks, and asserted that Whites had a better work ethic than Blacks.[14]

Black unemployment has been identified by sociologist William Julius Wilson as the primary reason for the hopelessness, despair, family breakdown, and isolation from mainstream society that define the underclass.[15] Wilson focuses on the loss of employment as the significant cause of the plight of the underclass in metropolitan areas in this country.[16] Wilson also describes the destruction wrought by long-term high unemployment in inner-city Black neighborhoods, arguing that market conditions coupled with government policies joined to make work disappear from inner-city neighborhoods. Residents confront a dismal labor market, characterized by a declining number of manufacturing jobs, falling wages, and racial discrimination. To compound the problem, many low-wage jobs have shifted from central cities into suburbs, leaving inner-city residents geographically isolated from employment.[17] For ex-offenders, the problems of transportation, hiring, and retention of employment are all compounded when the offender is a person of color.

Hurdles facing those released from prison seeking employment as a part of reentry include the reduction—and in some cases elimination—of vocational training and job preparatory courses in prison. In her very important writing on the subject of prisoner reentry, Joan Petersilia attributes the decline of job training programs since the 1990s to tight budgets, decreasing public willingness, and political rhetoric excoriating prisoners.[18] She points out that corrections now consume more than 4 percent of state budgets and that the increase in prison expenditures has focused more on staff, construction, and health care costs.[19] In addition to a massive reduction in employment preparation, occupational licensing requirements, lack of protection from state and/or federal civil rights legislation, the absence of jobs for potential employees with limited skills, and the failure of prisons to prepare inmates for jobs that actually exist have all contributed to the difficulties ex-offenders face in finding employment. Many low- or unskilled jobs continue to be relocated to countries with a cheaper pool of labor than the United States.

In addition to the problems that flow from a lack of unskilled-labor jobs, ex-offenders face a wide array of licensing barriers that have an equally devastating impact on their ability to gain employment. In California, for example, parolees are barred from working in real estate, nursing, or physical therapy. In Colorado, convicted felons cannot become dentists, engineers, nurses, pharmacists, physicians, or real estate agents.

In New York, depending on the nature of one's criminal history, an ex-offender may be prohibited from gaining employment in any place beer or liquor is sold for drinking in the place where it is purchased (for example, bars, restaurants), an insurance adjuster's office, a bank, a billiard parlor, any agency connected with horse racing, boxing or wrestling; they are also prevented from receiving licenses as an auctioneer, junk dealer, gunsmith, pharmacist, doctor, physiotherapist, osteopath, podiatrist, dentist, dental hygienist, veterinarian, certified public accountant, undertaker, embalmer, private detective, investigator, watch guard, attorney, billiard room operator, notary public, insurance adjuster, bingo operator, beer or liquor dispenser, real estate broker or salesman, check cashier, and union collector.[20]

Furthermore, "[i]n Virginia, felons may not work in the areas of optometry, nursing, dentistry, accounting, funeral homes, or pharmacology."[21]

"Occupational licenses are meant to protect the public interest by regulating certain activities."[22] A state's power to issue regulatory licenses flows from the state's police powers to account for the protection of the health, morals, and welfare of the public. Under these police powers, states have the right and the power to require a license as a prerequisite to engaging in a business, occupation, and a variety of vocations or trades. The state's power, however, does not extend to legitimate occupations or businesses that do not involve a public interest. The occupational license is the formal permission granted by a governmental body, generally for a fee, to a person, firm, or corporation to legally pursue some occupation or to legally carry on some business. Modern occupational licensing laws regulate a range of occupations, including professional, unskilled, and semiskilled occupations.

Because the occupational license is a regulatory license designed to protect the public, the terms and conditions for issuing the license must relate to the protection of the public good. Occupational licensing laws often are composed of a competency component and a character component. Through training and education, ex-offenders can acquire the necessary competency to be licensed in a particular occupation. The two most prevalent grounds for excluding ex-felons from obtaining occupational licenses on the basis of the character component relate to "moral character" and a felony conviction. According to Bruce E. May, under many licensing laws, the possession of a felony conviction is an automatic disqualification. In jurisdictions where no outright ban exists, the presence of the felony conviction on an applicant's record often creates an insurmountable obstacle to overcoming the "good moral character" component of the license.[23] Occupational licensing restrictions on ex-offenders are prevalent nationwide. Countless federal, state, and municipal laws single out the ex-offenders for possible exclusion from the majority of regulated occupations. "Occupational licensing laws have a significant impact on the ability of an individual to pursue an occupational or business goal. The failure to obtain a proper license may not only result in the imposition of civil or criminal penalties, but may also preclude the ability to enforce a contract."[24]

The greatest barriers to the ex-offender's job opportunities are those broad occupational licensing laws that exclude an applicant with any criminal conviction from obtaining a license. Statutes that involve automatic disqualification from license eligibility are particularly onerous on the formerly incarcerated. For example, Bruce May cites an Ohio criminal conviction that automatically barred an applicant from obtaining a dance hall license.[25] The applicant argued that despite two felony convictions, he possessed the good moral character necessary to operate a dance hall and obtain a license. Nonetheless, the court determined that evidence of his good moral character was not relevant because he possessed two felony convictions and the licensing authority was simply following a rule that all felons are denied licenses.[26]

Good-moral-character statutes present the second greatest barrier to the ex-felon obtaining an occupational license.[27] The "primary difficulties posed with good moral character statutes are twofold. First, the nature of character is often amorphous, thereby making statutory definitions of good character ambiguous and difficult to apply."[28] "Second, despite the legislative and judicial ambiguity of good moral character definitions, one definition has been generally accepted by the courts and licensing agencies: if a person has committed a crime, that person lacks the requisite good character for a license."[29] "Third, equating a criminal conviction with the lack of good moral character essentially converts the good moral character statute into the previously discussed criminal conviction statute which automatically bars an ex-felon from obtaining a license."[30]

In that matter "the revocation was overturned on the basis that a statute could constitutionally bar a person from practicing a lawful profession only for reasons related to fitness or competence to practice that profession."[31] Ex-felons who have brought constitutional challenges to occupational licensing laws have been generally unsuccessful.

Ex-offenders are excluded by statute from both licensed occupations and a number of public employment opportunities with federal and state agencies. One study reveals that state and federal restrictions bar the formerly incarcerated from upwards of 350 occupations, which employ ten million people, thus removing those with criminal histories from a significant number of jobs.[32] At least six states permanently bar ex-offenders from public employment.[33] In addition to the wide-ranging implications of occupational licensing bars, there is also the issue of access to criminal histories. In the representation and counseling of individuals with arrests and convictions, inevitably the question arises of how to answer questions in employment applications regarding criminal histories. There are some circumstances in which an individual has had a record sealed and may lawfully answer "no record." However, in the age of the Internet and online access to criminal records, employers can often check records on their own with fairly limited information from a potential employee. Acknowledging a criminal history leads to heightened scrutiny in the best cases and an immediate rejection in the worst cases. In some situations, failure to acknowledge a conviction can lead to termination if the conviction is discovered at a later time. In other circumstances, employers themselves can be found liable if an employee assaults a fellow employee or customer. This liability can be established under the principle of "negligent hiring."

B. Negligent Hiring

One of the most significant impediments for employers in the hiring of ex-offenders is the potential for civil lawsuits under the tort of negligent hiring. At least fourteen states, including California, Colorado, New York, New Mexico, Texas, and Florida, all recognize the tort of negligent hiring. Negligent hiring as a cause of action was born out of the increase in workplace violence in the last two decades. The theory of negligent hiring, supervision, and retention is similar to the legal doctrine of *respondeat superior* in that employers are held liable for the conduct of their employee. The difference is, however, that in negligent hiring, supervision, and retention cases, the law does not require a plaintiff to allege that the employee's misconduct was within the scope of his or her employment.[34] So, for example, if an employee caused harm wholly outside the scope of his or her employment, but while on duty, the employer could be subject to civil liability. Although the elements of negligent hiring vary from jurisdiction to jurisdiction, they generally include that (1) the employer owed the plaintiff a duty of reasonable care; (2) the employer breached the duty; and (3) that breach of duty proximately caused the third party's harm. Generally, the duty involves a reasonable investigation into the violent employee's background and it must be the case that such a reasonable investigation would have revealed the employee's violent tendencies. The elements suggest a broader interpretation of reasonable foreseeability and allow courts to look at an employer's hiring practices to determine whether that employer acted in a way that breached a duty of care to other employees or customers.

Negligent-hiring lawsuits continue to grow as an impediment to hiring ex-offenders. Courts have consistently articulated concerns about establishing a "chilling effect" on the employment of ex-offenders.[35] The perception is that potentially large jury awards will deter other employers from hiring ex-offenders.[36] To offset the cost of requiring employers to familiarize themselves with the criminal history of employees or potential employees, an employer-liability limit should be set.[37] Some states, as part of their tort reform movement (in an attempt to attract businesses to the state) have imposed limits on employer liability. The Florida legislature in its Tort Reform Act provided uniform limits on the liability of employers in negligent-hiring cases.[38] The legislation creates a presumption that an employer acts reasonably and, as a result, is not liable for negligent hiring when the employer conducts a background investigation that does not reveal any adverse information about the prospective employee.[39]

Although a majority of courts hold that as a general matter, no inquiry into a prior criminal record is required, gaps in employment, short residency periods, or an admission of a prior conviction all may trigger the need for further inquiry. Individuals exiting custody are subject to greater scrutiny and a greater likelihood that an employer will attempt to find some alleged legal business reason to forego the hiring of those with criminal records. Employers are often faced with the question, Why hire anyone with a criminal conviction, which raises the possibility of litigation if that employee ever engages in illegal acts against other employees or customers? First, employing former offenders, as it assists them in reintegrating into the community, seems to be good policy. Next, in some jurisdictions, a cause of action for wrongful denial of employment based upon improper use of conviction as a bar to employment is taking hold. Ex-offenders are routinely discriminated against when they truthfully answer questions; anecdotal information suggests that when individuals acknowledge a felony conviction, they are rarely granted interviews for jobs. Many employers fear those convicted of crimes or believe that ex-offenders will not be reliable employees.[40]

Federal law does not explicitly protect ex-offenders from employment discrimination. However, Title VII of the Civil Rights Act of 1964 makes it unlawful for private employers and state and local governments to discriminate in employment decisions on the basis of race, color, gender, national origin, or religion.[41] Title VII also makes it illegal for employers to "use[] . . . employment practice[s] that cause[] a disparate impact on the basis of race, color, religion, sex, or national origin. . . ."[42] In addition, the Equal Employment Opportunity Commission (EEOC) has ruled that policies that exclude individuals on the basis of arrests or convictions unrelated to the job for which they are applying may violate Title VII of the Civil Rights Act of 1964 because of the disparate impact on people of color, who are arrested more frequently than is proportionate to their percentage of the population.[43] The EEOC 1990 "Policy Guidance on the Consideration of Arrest Records in Employment Decisions under Title VII of the Civil Rights Act of 1964" establishes specific steps that an employer must take to avoid initiating a policy that might result in disparate-impact liability, as well as the legal requirements for an employer to establish a "business necessity" that passes constitutional muster.[44] Courts have scrutinized the "business necessity" defense very carefully.[45]

C. State Responses

A few states have included prior convictions in their antidiscrimination or civil rights laws. New York, Connecticut, Wisconsin, and Hawaii are among the states that have attempted to balance the need for public safety and the protection of the workplace with the need to assist ex-offenders with the difficult task of obtaining employment.[46] Wisconsin's Fair Employment Act (WFEA) goes beyond Title VII in an attempt to limit the impact of discrimination based on prior custody.[47] The WFEA designates fourteen different protected classifications.[48] Wisconsin acted specifically with ex-offender discrimination in mind.[49] Hawaii addressed the issue of employment discrimination of ex-offenders in the hiring process. State law makes it an unlawful employment practice to discriminate on the basis of an arrest and court record.[50] The law allows employers to inquire as to an applicant's criminal-conviction record from the past ten years, provided that the crime in the record bears a rational relationship to the duties and responsibilities of the position.[51]

Of all of the state statutes, New York provides perhaps the strongest protections for ex-offenders. New York Correction Law Article 23-A restricts employers' use of criminal conviction records to deny employment to applicants "unless: (1) there is a direct relationship between one or more of the previous criminal offenses and the [. . .] employment sought; or (2) [. . .] the granting of the employment would involve an unreasonable risk to property or to the safety or welfare of specific individuals or the general public."[52] Unlike similar laws in other states, this law sets forth the specific factors to be weighed in determining the relationship between the job and the criminal offense.[53] These factors include specific inquiries into how the job relates to the crime, the time that has elapsed since the criminal offense, the age of the person at the time of the criminal offense, the seriousness of the offense, legitimate interests in protecting property and the public, business safety, and evidence of rehabilitation provided by the applicant.[54] The list of considered factors begins with a statement that the public policy of New York is "to encourage the employment of persons previously convicted of criminal offenses."[55] New York balances the public policy of encouraging employers to hire ex-offenders with "[t]he legitimate interest [. . .] in protecting property, and the safety and welfare of [. . .] the general public."[56]

The New York courts have interpreted the statute to protect employers who, after engaging in the balancing put forth in 23-A, make the decision to hire ex-offenders. In *Ford v. Gildin*,[57] for example, an employer had hired a man convicted of manslaughter to fill the position of porter.[58] The New York Appellate Division refused to hold the employer liable for the negligent hiring of the employee when he molested a child twenty-seven years after his original manslaughter conviction.[59] Citing the "direct relationship" test, the court noted that even if the defendants had known of their employee's criminal history, the causal link between knowledge of the manslaughter conviction and the subsequent abuse was insufficient to find the employer liable.[60] The court held that "it was not foreseeable . . . that a person who had committed manslaughter [. . .] would molest a child [twenty-seven] years later."[61] Perhaps most important for ex-offenders, the court explicitly cited the potential harm to the policy of helping ex-offenders if they were to hold the employer liable: "an unacceptably chilling effect on society's efforts to reintegrate ex-offenders into mainstream society, contrary to precedent and the explicitly stated public policy of [New York] State."[62] Finally the court noted the potential consequences of holding an employer liable for negligent hiring where the employer has done a background check and made the decision to hire an ex-offender. The court stated that holding the employer liable would effectively "compel any employer to deny employment to anyone who was ever convicted of a violent crime [. . .] since the employer would [. . .] face potentially catastrophic liability for any crime committed by that employee which was even minimally connected to the place of his employment."[63]

Courts have been equally as protective of ex-offenders seeking work. In *Soto-Lopez v. New York City Civil Serv. Comm'n*,[64] the United States District Court for the Southern District of New York[65] held that the city could not deny the job of housing caretaker to an individual convicted of manslaughter and drug offenses because of the expressed public policy of the state to encourage employment of ex-offenders.[66] Examining the typical tasks involved in custodial jobs, the court found that Soto-Lopez's offense was not directly related to the employment, and that he did not present an unreasonable risk to persons or property. After analyzing the nature and duties, the court determined them to be unrelated to the facts and circumstances of the crime he had committed.[67] Moreover, the court found that these tasks were not "directly related" to a manslaughter conviction and did not present an unreasonable risk to persons or property.[68] The New York courts as well as the federal courts interpreting the statute have narrowly construed the notion of work being directly related to the offense committed by the prospective employee.

In a number of instances, the New York courts have been willing to deny the licensing and employment of ex-offenders where job responsibilities or access to vulnerable individuals might come into play. In *Arrocha v. Board of Educ. of New York*,[69] the licensing board denied an applicant's application to teach high school Spanish because he had been convicted of the criminal sale of cocaine. Similarly, in the case of *In re Application of Ronald Grafer v. New York City Civil Serv. Comm'n,*[70] a case involving a drunk-driving conviction and an application to become a firefighter, the court held that the drunk-driving conviction involved an "unreasonable risk" to public safety and property.

Employers in New York must consider the eight factors listed in the statute before denying an applicant employment on the basis of his or her conviction record.[71] However, even when that consideration is made, there is the appearance of a potential employer's "Hobson's choice," in which not hiring an employee due to a criminal record could violate Title VII, but not investigating a criminal background could lead to negligent-hiring liability. This situation has employers worried that their duty to the safety of the public and their other employees is compromised by the serious curtailment of their ability to do background checks under antidiscrimination statutes and Title VII regulations. The lack of uniformity among state and federal courts makes employers' tasks particularly challenging and has led to calls for a serious overhaul of negligent hiring litigation, and the development of further criminal-record discrimination regulations.

D. Conclusions

Research suggests that finding steady work after release is one of the few proven methods of reducing recidivism.[72] Researchers have consistently linked vocational training and post-release employment as prime factors associated with lower recidivism.[73] Notwithstanding those facts, the last decade has exhibited a massive reduction in the quality and quantity of prison-based vocational training programs. This reduction in programming has had a catastrophic impact on ex-offenders attempting to reintegrate into society. Inmates of color, in particular, have found employment opportunities increasingly difficult to find.

Joan Petersilia identifies a combination of cost, public sentiment, and political will as the reasons why vocational training and general work-preparedness programs have decreased in prison.[74]

In attempting to address issues of employment and reentry, the prospects for change can seem overwhelmingly dismal. Lack of preparation; licensing bars; bias in hiring, retention, and promotion; disincentives based on liability; and inconsistent policy in state and federal jurisdictions all conspire to cause inaction on the part of advocates for ex-offenders. States and the federal government should engage in a wide-ranging review of all the existing occupational licensing restrictions based on "ex-offender status." The goal here should be twofold: first, to identify those restrictions that serve a public safety function; second, to ensure that those restrictions are related in some way to the substantive crime that resulted in a conviction or is in some way related to the occupational license being sought. This type of revision in licensing restrictions and preclusions will require a new national movement to seriously address the administrative barriers to vocational opportunities for ex-offenders.

Next, states should draft legislation similar to Article 23-A in New York. New York's law is widely viewed as the preeminent piece of legislation protecting the rights of ex-felons.[75] One disparity in Article 23-A is the lack of attorneys' fees written into the statute to provide an incentive for lawyers to take on these troubling cases. New York should move to correct this flaw, and state and local jurisdictions should be aware of the need to encourage lawyers to represent individuals unjustly prevented from competing for employment.

New York's Human Rights Law uses a factor-specific approach in reviewing an employer's hiring decisions.[76] There are two exceptions. One exception allows the employer to deny an employment application if a "direct relationship" is present between the conviction and the job. The second exception gives the employer the right to eliminate a candidate from employment if that candidate would "pose an unreasonable risk to property or to the safety or welfare of specific individuals or the public."[77] These factors include, but are not limited to

(a) the public policy of ensuring employment to qualified individuals, (b) the specific duties and responsibilities of the job, (c) the bearing, if any, that a criminal offense (or offenses) has on the person's fitness to perform his or her job, (d) the amount of time elapsed since the criminal offense occurred, (e) the applicant's age when the criminal offense was committed, (f) the seriousness of the offense (or offenses), (g) mitigating factors produced by the applicant, including rehabilitation, and (h) an employer's legitimate interest to protect the public safety.[78]

Finally, New York courts emphasize the presumption of rehabilitation created by a certificate of good conduct or certificate of relief from disabilities.[79] This further assists those seeking to reenter the workplace after a conviction. The certificate has a number of steps consisting of documentation and, among other things, an interview with the parole officer. A "certificate of relief from disabilities" may be granted to relieve eligible offenders of any or all forfeitures or disabilities that were imposed automatically by reason of their convictions.[80] Without Article 23-A, many employers would probably refuse to hire most ex-offenders in order to avoid potential problems.[81] Employers should not face exorbitant damages awards if there has been good-faith compliance with the New York law that supports the hiring of ex-offenders.[82]

The key to legislation of this type is to limit it to cases where an employee commits an intentional tort, and to require that employers conduct a criminal background check, contact references and former employers, have a prospective employee complete a job application (including questions concerning previous criminal convictions and status as a defendant in intentional tort actions), check the employee's driver's license record (if relevant to the work to be assigned), and interview the prospective employee. Most importantly, this new limit on employer liability cannot and should not be a complete bar to litigation. It should establish a presumption but should acknowledge that different circumstances may require different conduct by employers. As a result, plaintiffs still have the opportunity to prove that an employer acted unreasonably, and juries still may conclude that an employer was negligent in hiring particular employees. The act simply determines that employer liability for acts committed outside the scope of an employee's job description must have limits. A liability limit will help alleviate this problem. With a statutorily prescribed liability limit, courts could more readily allow negligent-hiring cases to proceed to trial without fear of juries setting extremely high precedents for future awards.

There is some precedent for limiting liability and statutory coverage on the basis of the size of the prospective employer. For example, the Civil Rights Act of 1991 amended Title VII of the Civil Rights Act of 1964 to permit compensatory and punitive damages in cases of intentional employment discrimination.[83] Title VII does not apply to businesses with fewer than fifteen employees.[84] Forty-two U.S.C. § 1981a limits compensatory and punitive damages based on the size of the employer as well.[85]

Some commentators have recommended a federal legislative change in Title VII. Currently, Title VII does not list criminal history as a class or status entitled to protection from discrimination in employment.[86] As it stands, the only access to Title VII federal employment discrimination protection for criminal-record discrimination is achieved by using the disparate-impact test in order to show that the use of arrest or conviction records somehow operates to discriminate on the basis of a protected category (usually race). If the purpose is to protect ex-offenders who are struggling to obtain employment, this proposal misses the point.

If ex-offenders are to be self-sustaining, they need gainful employment. Employment problems are central to those seeking to ease reentry, especially as ex-prisoners return to low-income and of-color communities. Many ex-offenders return without skills, facing the stigma and legal limitations on employment related to their history of convictions.[87] State and federal governments have imposed a variety of legal barriers upon them, many of which apply both during and after incarceration.[88] Obtaining employment is likely to be a significant obstacle for prisoners attempting to reenter the community. Though half of state prisoners nationwide are employed before being incarcerated, only about 20 percent are able to find employment following imprisonment.[89] Involvement in job training and placement programs can lead to employment and lower recidivism. On average, participants in vocational programs were more likely to be employed following release and to have a recidivism rate 20 percent lower than nonparticipants.[90]

Encouraging private firms that receive government contracts to hire persons with criminal records would be a positive incentive for the hiring of the formerly incarcerated. Among the incentives that might be created for private employers are salary support and tax incentives, such as the Worker Opportunity Tax Credit.[91] It should be noted that one of the (potential) structural problems with tax credits is that employers, after making the initial hire and obtaining the tax credit, sometimes do not promote or even retain the ex-offender. So this type of structural protection needs to be built into any tax benefit. In addition to tax incentives, bonding programs such as the federal bonding program have shown some success in providing incentives for private employers.[92] It would seem a reasonable public safety measure for the government to take affirmative steps to help offenders obtain jobs, for there is a high correlation between steady employment and successful completion of a term of supervision.[93]

7

Reentry and the Political Process

"... *Iowa Governor Tom Vilsack, joined by a bipartisan group of legislators, issued an executive order that restores voter eligibility to thousands of disenfranchised Iowans. Previously, Iowa was among only a handful of states that permanently denies the right to vote to people with felony convictions. Felon disenfranchisement has been criticized across the country for unfairly excluding citizens from the electoral process and for its discriminatory impact on minority communities, who are disproportionately represented in the U.S. prison population. More than 80,000 Iowa residents are estimated to have lost the vote as a result of the policy. 'The right to vote is the foundation of our government and serves as a symbol of opportunity for our citizens,' Governor Vilsack said. 'Research shows that ex-offenders who vote are less-likely to re-offend and the restoration of voting rights is an important aspect of reintegrating offenders in society so that they become law-abiding and productive citizens.' 'Governor Vilsack has broken new ground in recognizing that voting is a civil right for everyone,' said Monifa Bandele, national field director for Right to Vote, a campaign to end felon disenfranchisement. 'This move will be particularly meaningful for African Americans who make up only 2% of Iowa's population but are nearly 25% of the state's disenfranchised citizens. This was the highest rate of disparity in the nation.' The Governor's executive order uses his power of clemency, which allows him to restore voting rights to individuals who have committed crimes. Although clemency was formerly granted on a case by case basis, the executive order creates a blanket restoration of voting rights as of July 4, 2005, that will include everyone who has completed incarceration and parole or probation. Nearly 50,000 people should have their eligibility restored under the order. The Department of Corrections will pass on information for the 29,000 individuals who are still under state supervision, once they have been discharged, in order to add them to the pool. Under the new sys-*

tem, the number of formerly disenfranchised people who will regain the right to vote will jump from approximately 500 people per year to 500 per month. 'The Governor's decisive action recognizes the right to vote as a central component of civic life, and moves Iowa out of the pantheon of states that cling to this antiquated law,' said Ludovic Blain III, Associate Director of the Democracy Program at Demos, a pro-democracy organization, and Right to Vote Campaign coalition member. 'Now there are four: Alabama, Florida, Kentucky and Virginia. They should immediately follow Iowa's lead.'"[1]

Voter registration card in hand, Jesse Miller stood in line for twenty minutes in November to cast her vote for governor. But fear turned her away before she got the chance.

Convicted on a drug charge more than a decade previously, Miller feared that the stigma of her felony would cause her problems, because even though she had served her time, and paid her court-ordered fines, she never received an official certificate of discharge restoring her rights.

"When I went to get in line I had so much fear in me because I knew I hadn't done the whole process," she said. "I was scared to vote."

Miller is one of an estimated 4.7 million people nationwide who are ineligible to vote because of a felony conviction, according to the Sentencing Project, an advocacy group in Washington, D.C. "Keeping people out of the loop, keeping people isolated from the larger community just creates more prisoners," said Monifa Bandele, national field director for Right to Vote, a New York–based advocacy group. The result of these laws is that it prevents people from voting. It doesn't prevent crime."[2]

A. The Vote and the Formerly Incarcerated

One subtle but devastating method of punishment exacted against our nation's formerly incarcerated is effected by stripping them of a basic right of citizenship: the right to vote. Felon disenfranchisement laws operate throughout the country to restrict the voting rights of individuals who have been convicted of felony offenses. In some instances, the laws dictate that individuals who have been convicted of felonies but who have served their debt to society will continue to pay for their crimes for the rest of their lives. These laws prevent individuals with felony convictions from ever voting in an election.

Until recently, this phenomenon has remained the well-kept secret of some states. On a daily basis ex-offenders are effectively silenced in the political process by virtue of their conviction and the triggering of these laws. And, because ex-offenders do not have an effective lobby or representative, these laws might have continued to operate largely under the radar screen had it not been for an exceptionally close presidential election in 2000. But the controversies surrounding George W. Bush's election as president helped to shine a light on the broad impact of felon disenfranchisement laws.

In Florida, more than 600,000 of those individuals excluded from voting have not only completed their sentences but have been discharged entirely from any supervision in the criminal justice system.[3] A study examining the impact on the outcome of the election had those individuals been permitted to exercise their right to vote found that Al Gore would have won the Florida election by more than thirty-one thousand ballots.[4] Not only did felon disenfranchisement laws deprive specific individuals of their opportunity to express their political views, but they effectively diluted the political power of voters who happened to share the political views of the disenfranchised.

B. The Politics of Exclusion: Tracing the Racist History of Disenfranchisement Laws

The disenfranchisement of felons in this country has its roots in the notion of "civil death," a permanent sanction under Greek and Roman law later adopted by the English. "Civil death" meant that those who violated the law forfeited the basic rights of citizenship, lost their ability to inherit or own property, and renounced all civil rights.[5] The approach to stripping the civil rights of an offender was passed on to the British colonies and became a part of the legal structure of the United States.[6] Some commentators have argued that disenfranchisement laws have a legitimate role to play in our society, because individuals who commit criminal offenses have violated the "social contract" and should be barred from participatory politics as a measure of the seriousness with which society views their conduct.[7]

An additional justification for denying suffrage to ex-offenders is the claim that they have proven a lack of moral virtue that is a prerequisite to participating in the election process. This has also been characterized as an attempt to maintain the "purity-of-the-ballot-box argument."[8] Here, both courts and commentators have opined that ex-offenders will corrupt the electoral process through election fraud or by voting for harmful policies. One of the most notorious cases supporting this argument is *Green v. Board of Elections of New York.*[9] There, the court concluded that it was not unreasonable for a state to bar ex-offenders from voting when they might participate in electing legislators or judges.[10]

The underlying premise of both prongs of the purity-of-the-ballot-box argument is that offenders weigh and calculate decisions before committing an act. In theory it is the same argument made in utilizing deterrence as a basis for a punishment scheme. In addition, it is the same argument that is used to deny felons the right to equal opportunity in other areas. Evidence and experience suggest that many crimes occur without the weighing and balancing requisite for deterrence to be effective. Using this deterrence justification in the disenfranchisement sense is problematic because there is little consistency in the way states handle felon disenfranchisement.[11] Offenders commit crimes for a variety of reasons—economic, sociological, and emotional—and all can contribute to lawlessness.[12]

Felon disenfranchisement also seems to offend a sense of proportionality when one examines individual rights, reintegration of the individual into society, and the goals of reentry.[13] Permanent loss of the franchise after the serving of a sentence continues punishment rather than beginning the process of civil and social reintegration. Even in a scheme that provides for the sacrifice of individual rights and interests for the greater social good or social utility, disenfranchisement seems to embody a penal philosophy that permanently separates the individual from society.[14]

The traditional goals of sentencing also leave little justification for disenfranchisement. Disenfranchisement essentially only serves the goals of retribution, and certainly does not address incapacitation or deterrence. Character tests for voting threaten to limit the scope of the franchise for the broadest sector of our population.[15] The foremost goal of offender reentry is the rehabilitation and reintegration of the former offender into society. During the periods in our history where rehabilitation was the predominant sentencing philosophy, many states abolished or revised their felon disenfranchisement statutes.[16] Finally, Alec Ewald offers one of the most eloquent attacks on disenfranchisement as "counterproductive" to the goal of rehabilitation when he points out that there is no data to suggest that "disenfranchising offenders—whether temporarily or permanently—[. . .] reduces crime."[17]

Notwithstanding the theoretical justifications for felon disenfranchisement laws, the history of this country indicates a radically different set of motivations for their imposition. During the post–Civil War period, disenfranchisement took on new significance after African Americans gained the right to vote. Not long after the Civil War, southern conservatives convened at a number of state constitutional conventions and consolidated the White backlash against Reconstruction and targeted the Black voters.[18] The conventions adopted various obstacles to voting. They included literacy and property tests,[19] poll taxes,[20] and grandfather clauses.[21] The express purpose of these voting restrictions was to disenfranchise as many Blacks as possible without violating the recently ratified Fifteenth Amendment, which prohibited denying the right to vote on account of race.

The efforts of these southern legislative conventions were extremely successful. While Blacks made up approximately 44 percent of Louisiana's potential voters just after the Civil War, they were less than 1 percent in 1920.[22] In 1867 in Mississippi, the eligible Black vote went from a high of almost 70 percent to less than 6 percent two years after the state's disenfranchising convention.[23]

Today, scholars "widely acknowledge the historically racist motives underlying criminal disenfranchisement in parts of the South."[24] The Supreme Court has also recognized this history. In 1985, the Court held in *Hunter v. Underwood* that an Alabama disenfranchising law aimed at certain felons was violative of the Equal Protection Clause of the Fourteenth Amendment because the law had a disproportionate impact on Blacks and was adopted with racially discriminatory intent.[25]

"*Underwood* marked the first time that a court struck down a criminal disenfranchisement law on account of racial discrimination."[26] Though many state constitutions were ratified with racially discriminatory provisions aimed at disenfranchising Blacks during the post-Reconstruction era, many have subsequently been amended and reratified, with an alleged attempt to exclude the animus of past discrimination.

Contemporary disenfranchisement laws are enacted on a state-by-state basis and have varied legislative histories and inconsistent implementation. Today's discrimination in criminal justice may be more difficult to distill if the primary method used involves crude statements or legislative histories. By adding a political prohibition to the other consequences of a felony conviction, disenfranchisement compounds and magnifies the effects of such systemic bias. In a time when even politically conservative White American politicians acknowledge that racial profiling is a serious problem, it requires turning a blind eye to argue that criminal disenfranchisement is not at least partly about race. Sensitivity to this history should spur Americans towards abolishing a policy that evokes memories of the connections between slavery and punishment.

C. Understanding Disenfranchisement Today

African American men account for an estimated 36 percent of all disenfranchised ex-felons.[27] As a result, these statutes restrict the voting rights of 13 percent of all adult African American males.[28] Despite the history of bias from which disenfranchisement statutes have emerged, states continue to keep disenfranchisement laws on books and to enforce them against the formerly incarcerated. The American Correctional Association has called on states to end felon disenfranchisement and, on the political front, Democrats in the House and Senate have introduced legislation to restore voting rights to ex-offenders.[29]

Recently, Florida joined seventeen other states that loosened voting restrictions on ex-felons since 1997, according to the Sentencing Project, an advocacy group.[30] In 2005, Governor Tom Vilsack (D-Iowa) signed an order to restore the voting rights of all felons in his state who have completed their sentences, overturning one of the strictest disenfranchisement laws in the nation.[31] In late 2005 and early 2006, the Advancement Project and other civil rights organizations mounted a vigorous but ultimately unsuccessful effort to push outgoing Governor Mark Warner (D-Va.) to sign an executive order restoring the voting rights of more than two hundred thousand former felons in his state.[32] New Mexico's political reentry movement won an important victory in 2001, by restoring ex-felons' voting rights immediately upon completion of their sentence.[33]

A number of states disenfranchise parolees while other states disenfranchise probationers. Remarkably, some states still deny felons the right to vote for the rest of their lives. "Approximately three-fourths of disqualified voters are no longer in prison, but are on probation or parole or have completed their sentences entirely."[34] Over six hundred thousand Floridians lost their voting rights through felon disenfranchisement.[35] Of those six hundred thousand, four hundred thousand had completed their sentences.[36] States that maintain indefinite periods of disenfranchisement have established some form of procedure providing ex-offenders with an opportunity to petition to regain the right to vote, but restoration procedures often make regaining the vote personally and procedurally cumbersome, in some instances purposefully so.[37] Maintaining inconsistent, confusing, and cumbersome procedures for returning the franchise to ex-offenders only increases the impression that we do not want to truly reintegrate individuals into society.

One of the primary goals of offender reentry is providing a means for ex-offenders to reintegrate themselves into the communities into which they are released. This may be somewhat misleading. As will become clear in other chapters of this book, many of these offenders were not previously "integrated" into the mainstream of the communities in question. Because of addictions to drugs and alcohol, lack of formal education, and lack of job skills, many offenders never participated in the traditional social structures in their communities. Many offenders have never voted, never paid taxes, and never attended a community forum. Reentry may provide a unique opportunity to prepare individuals to participate in the communities to which they will be returning and assist them in doing so.

Some continue to insist that disenfranchisement laws should be enforced today. They have attempted to return to the historical justifications, divorced from their overt racist justifications. Current voting laws have attempted to justify the disenfranchisement of felons as a protection against voter fraud and other election offenses—as a prevention of harmful changes to the law. This argument often goes unchallenged even in the absence of any data suggesting that ex-offenders vote consistent with some agenda that weakens law enforcement. These justifications address the continued disenfranchisement of the nonincarcerated felon. Two rationales have emerged from this language to support the state interest in denying the vote to ex-offenders in order to protect the ballot. First, proponents of ex-felon disenfranchisement have claimed that it is necessary to prevent voter fraud, which, if present, could have detrimental effects on the outcome of elections. Second is the claim that because of the individual's history of law breaking, the felon is more likely to violate election laws as well. These beliefs rest on a fundamental belief that the ballot box does not merely collect individual preferences but represents the body politic itself. If that body is to be healthy, it must be protected from corruption, immorality, and untrustworthy behavior.

In *Washington v. State*,[38] the Alabama Supreme Court upheld the conviction of a defendant who had been charged with voting illegally, given his prior conviction for larceny. The *Washington* court treated the disqualification "as withholding an honorable privilege, and not denying a personal right or attribute of personal liberty. . . ."[39] Since *Washington*, many courts and commentators have treated disenfranchisement as a regulatory, rather than a punitive practice, citing *Washington* and other nineteenth-century cases for this proposition.[40]

Such systematic voting restrictions stand in opposition to a democratic state. One of the hallmarks of democracy in this country is that the state is constantly improving and changing itself through voter input. Excluding ex-offenders from the franchise deprives a vast segment of the population, which has had an experience that sets them apart, of the right and the opportunity to influence the existing system, should they wish to do so, in the primary way democratic societies recognize— through the ballot box.

The other philosophical justification embraced in the contemporary defense of disenfranchisement has been the "social contract" theory. This approach informs a number of disenfranchisement opinions. Relying on contract theory to justify restricting the vote, courts have emphasized the deliberate nature of the offender's action. The *Wesley v. Collins*[41] court held that "[f]elons are not disenfranchised based on any immutable characteristic, such as race, but on their conscious decision to commit an act for which they assume the risks of detection and punishment."[42]

In *Wesley v. Collins*, the plaintiff argued that the Tennessee disenfranchisement laws resulted in "unlawful deterioration of the African American vote in violation of the U.S. Constitution and the Voting Rights Act."[43] The court dismissed the case for failure to state a claim.[44] On appeal, the court found that there was a showing of disproportionate racial impact based on statistical data; however, it held that this was not enough to establish vote dilution in violation of the Voting Rights Act.[45] The court focused on the text and the historical circumstances surrounding passage of the Fourteenth Amendment.

Despite the tenuousness of these arguments, the United States Supreme Court has implicitly adopted them as indicative of a rational exercise of state power.[46] Based on an analysis of the express language in Section 2 of the Fourteenth Amendment and the historical situation at the time of its passage, the Court held that state laws that permanently disenfranchise felons do not run afoul of the Equal Protection Clause.[47] The Court opined that the disenfranchisement of felons should be tested under a rational-basis standard because the language in Section 2 permits states to disenfranchise those convicted of rebellion or other crimes.[48]

D. Ignoring the Racial Impact of Disenfranchisement

Despite contemporary justifications that allude to states' rights to control the franchise and historical justifications for continuing the felon disenfranchisement, the status quo ignores the reality that we are denying the vote to a significant number of people of color. Even though many state disenfranchisement laws are race neutral on their face, they have a wildly disproportionate impact on racial minorities, particularly African Americans and Latinos.[49] Cloaking these current justifications in the garb of states' rights harkens back to the arguments that were made against the enforcement of civil rights in the 1950s and 1960s prior to the passage of a federal civil rights bill.

The impact of felon disenfranchisement is perhaps most acutely felt in the Black community. In Black communities nationwide a significant percentage of voter-age individuals cannot vote. This has a number of potentially significant outcomes. Lack of political clout in the Black community makes it increasingly difficult to bring needed legislative dollars and representation to communities where ex-offenders are being released. In addition, the failure to give the vote to those who have already paid their "debt to society" creates obstacles to reintegration into these communities. One study demonstrated that 13 percent of all adult Black men—1.4 million—are disenfranchised, thus represented one-third of the total disenfranchised population and reflecting a rate of disenfranchisement that is roughly seven times the national average.[50] The interaction of incarceration and disenfranchisement can skew the balance of political power within a state.

Raw numbers cannot fully capture the impact of felon disenfranchisement, but they give us an idea. There is a significant impact in the African American community; notwithstanding the fact that 4.6 million Black men voted in the 1996 election, 1.4 million were disenfranchised.[51] The dramatic impact of race was significantly concentrated in certain states: in Iowa, Mississippi, Virginia, and Wyoming, one in four Black men is permanently disenfranchised.[52] In Delaware, one in five Black men is subjected to permanent disenfranchisement. And the problem is even more striking in several of the states that use the most severe form of disenfranchisement—lifetime disqualification. In Alabama nearly one-third of all Black men are permanently disenfranchised, and in Iowa, Mississippi, Virginia, and Wyoming, roughly a quarter are permanently barred from voting.[53]

In African American communities, the right to vote not only brings with it the trappings of being a part of the citizen-state; it also carries with it a history of struggle that is inextricably bound with full civil rights. Notwithstanding the fact that it has been less than fifty years since African Americans were truly granted access to the franchise, there are still areas in this country where that right does not come easily. Felon disenfranchisement carries with it a history and legacy of racist politics.

In recent years, lower courts have applied a more exacting equal protection test to certain state provisions disenfranchising ex-offenders. In *McLaughlin v. City of Canton*,[54] a federal district court held that the state failed to provide a compelling interest justifying its decision to disenfranchise a group of potential electors solely because they were convicted of misdemeanors.[55] The court applied the compelling interest test because Section 2 only covers felonies, not misdemeanors.[56] Despite these small victories, the Supreme Court's decision to analyze ex-offender disenfranchisement generally using a lower level of scrutiny under the Equal Protection Clause means that voting rights are a fundamental right of citizens only as long as they are not convicted felons.

E. Felon Disenfranchisement and the Voting Rights Act

Article I, Section 10 of the Constitution provides that no state shall pass any bill of attainder, meaning that nonjudicial punishment applied by the legislature is prohibited. The Voting Rights Act was adopted to remedy racial discrimination in voting: it prohibits voting qualifications and practices that deny or abridge a citizen's right to vote on account of race or color.[57] In 1980, the U.S. Supreme Court interpreted the act as requiring the purpose to be a "discriminatory purpose" before state action would be prohibited.[58] However, the Voting Rights Act was amended in 1982 to prevent and prohibit voting qualifications and practices that result in loss of the right to vote and that are based on race, regardless of whether the enactment was adopted with discriminatory purpose or racist intent.[59]

Section 2 does not require discriminatory intent or purpose;[60] because voting is a fundamental right, ex-felon disenfranchisement should be judged according to equal protection strict-scrutiny standards. This would require states to demonstrate a compelling interest in order to justify such disenfranchisement. The challenge for plaintiffs using this strategy will be to connect past racial animus with current disenfranchising provisions. Though many state constitutions were ratified with provisions specifically targeted at disenfranchising Blacks during the post-Reconstruction era, they have since been amended and reratified, arguably to exclude the animus of the past though the franchise restrictions remain.[61]

The United States Court of Appeals for the Second Circuit, in *Baker v. Pataki,* addressed a claim similar to that raised in *Wesley v. Collins.*[62] In the *Baker* claim, Black and Hispanic incarcerated felons argued that New York's disenfranchising law disproportionately impacted minorities in violation of Section 2 of the act.[63] The court, sitting en banc, considered the applicability of this section to the disenfranchising statute.[64] The judges favoring a vote to affirm found that the Fourteenth Amendment's disenfranchising provision was not countered by a clear dictate from Congress indicating that Section 2 of the act was meant to address disenfranchisement.[65] The dissent concluded that the plaintiffs had a valid claim applying the results test of the act to the state disenfranchising provision.[66]

If racial minorities are considered a suspect group, this disenfranchisement then arguably places a disproportionately negative impact on the suspect group. Purposeful discrimination against minorities, especially Blacks, in order to dilute the voting pool establishes the fact that African Americans have "less opportunity to participate in the political process and to elect candidates of their choice."[67] This is further compounded by the voting disenfranchisement of the felons, which effectively decreases opportunities to participate in the election process and may shift the outcome of an election.[68]

There is no evidence that convicted felons are banding together to debase the election process or undermine the criminal law. If a felon attempted to effect significant, harmful changes in a particular jurisdiction or more generally in society, it is likely that this effort would fail because that vote would be overshadowed by the votes of law-abiding citizens. The arguments for incapacitation, or removal from the political process, simply do not adequately justify voter disenfranchisement for life. Most states seem to have recognized this argument, since only a limited number of states permanently disenfranchise voters for life. Yet states have chosen to enact and maintain voter disenfranchisement laws despite the weaknesses in the policy arguments.

Those critical of the felon disenfranchisement laws label the practice as penal in nature because of its effect and the coupling of disenfranchisement with conviction as a collateral consequence. They argue that the cruel and unusual nature of disenfranchisement is manifested by permanent ostracism from society and the denial of a right critical to the equality that U.S. society guarantees.

F. What Has Changed?

American criminal disenfranchisement law is marked by its association with this country's discriminatory legacy. The most direct link, of course, is the manipulation of this facially neutral voting restriction to prevent Blacks from voting in the post-Reconstruction South. States enacted felon disenfranchisement laws with a myriad of purposes. In a number of post-Reconstruction southern states, the intent was originally focused on disenfranchising Blacks. At that time the discrimination was de jure and the racist statements by primarily southern legislators clearly focused on Black political power. Today's discrimination is more difficult to detect in the legislative records, but the effect is still the same. The only type of legislative restriction of voting on a class of people that has continued to withstand an equal protection challenge has been the restriction of the voting rights of ex-offenders.[69]

Disenfranchisement furthers racial disparity and dilutes the minority vote when all felony convictions result in disenfranchisement and the authorities are engaging in race-targeted police enforcement. The scope of felon disenfranchisement and its disproportionate impact on of-color minority groups has received far greater national attention, and state-level political efforts have restored the voting rights of nearly a half-million people.[70]

One of the most dramatic effects of felon disenfranchisement laws is the stigma associated with losing the right to vote. If a felon were to internalize all of the theoretical and policy propositions held by the proponents of disenfranchisement, the felon might regard himself or herself as morally incompetent, unredeemable, and likely to recidivate. Reentry, by its very definition, is inconsistent with the notion of disenfranchisement. Black ex-offenders in particular are hindered in their rehabilitation efforts when their already severely weakened connection to the community is further strained by the creation of another barrier to reentry.

Where discrimination exists, community acceptance of the Black ex-offender will be reluctant if not nonexistent. He or she may feel even further removed from society if disenfranchisement accompanies such discrimination. Indeed, the negative effects of disenfranchisement are felt by Blacks who may already experience alienation and isolation from their community. For this reason, social policy and theory arguments, both general and race focused, condemning ex-offender disenfranchisement should play an important persuasive role in judicial review of the impact of felon disenfranchising statutes on the Black vote. Despite the real gains in antidiscrimination law made under constitutional amendments and the Voting Rights Act, felons—mostly African American and Latino males, many of them young—probably remain disenfranchised not only because they are non-White but also because they lack political support.

But outside the courtroom, the knowledge that a voting restriction that has racially discriminatory effects today is permissible only because of a passage in our Constitution that was written to allow states to bar Blacks from voting ought to give us pause. This is an area, a place that cries out for equal protection and equal justice. It speaks volumes against the notion of an outright ban. It seems that in making the decision to fully deny the ballot, states should be required to establish specific reasons as to what constitutes justifiable reasons for denying the ballot.

This might continue a presumption that those in custody as part of their punishment give up the right to vote. But it may also provide that in some cases someone who successfully completed his or her obligations in custody, as well as any parole commitment, may be immediately eligible to register to vote. If upon successful completion of their obligation to the state, individuals were also registered to vote, it might send a message that we now intend to have them participate fully in their community.

G. Eroding Community Connections and Collective Power

The philosophical underpinnings of offender reentry suggest the need to instill the desire and the will to function as a lawful contributing member of society. In addition to affordable housing, employment, and family connection, another way to give an individual a stake in his or her community is to engage him or her in the political process. This use of the franchise does two things. First, it empowers the individual; it allows the individual a modicum of input into the social, political, and economic direction of the community. Second, it forms an implicit and explicit collaboration between the individual and the community by encouraging coalitions of individual interests and community goals.

Although many of the areas that are home to returning ex-offenders are socially, politically, and economically depressed, when community residents rally around common issues of concern, the vote can empower these communities. In addition, elected officials from these jurisdictions can often create viable policy collaborations with other elected officials from different regions and different political parties. Disenfranchisement is one of the obstacles to empowering communities in this way. One author describes this effect of imprisonment as a "collective sanction."[71]

H. The Politics of Disenfranchisement

The politics of felon disenfranchisement has in many ways mirrored the politics of reentry. The massive prison building that coincided with the beginning of the mandatory minimums and current incarceration expansion have resulted in the empowering of correctional officers' unions, the economic revival of a number of rural communities where the new prisons were built, and the election and empowerment of rural state and federal elected officials due to the practice of census data placing inmates' residences in the location of their incarceration as opposed to the community from which they were sent to prison. In short, the politics of felon disenfranchisement is the politics of power. The interaction of incarceration and disenfranchisement can skew the balance of political power within a state between those who have power in the electoral process and those seeking access to the franchise.

In a very important article on felon disenfranchisement, Pamela Karlan points to the racial impact of the "usual residence rule" with which the Census Bureau counts incarcerated individuals as residents of the jurisdiction in which they are incarcerated.[72] Karlan points out that "[i]n many states, this results in largely White, rural communities having their population totals increased at the expense of the heavily urban, overwhelmingly minority communities from which most inmates come."[73] The fact that electoral districts are made up from these population numbers results in the overrepresentation of rural districts where prisons are located and prisoners are in custody. Prisoners generally do not benefit from the accumulation of social services and resources allocated to the districts where prisons are located, and they have fewer resources in the urban communities to which they return.

In addition to reducing the number of elected officials from these urban communities, the count also often results in a reduction of services and service dollars from these areas. What is particularly hypocritical about this practice is that most states require that ex-offenders be released back into these communities. Once they have returned, they find it difficult to receive services and cannot cast a vote.[74]

Because a disproportionate number of the disenfranchised are poor people and people of color, the current system skews electoral outcomes. A study conducted by Northwestern University and University of Minnesota students reveals that approximately 30 percent of those disenfranchised would have voted, and of that thirty, 70 percent would have voted Democratic if given the opportunity.[75] The study further suggests that since 1978, the outcomes in seven United States Senate races would have been reversed.[76] This may seem like a relatively insignificant shift, but it would probably have given Democrats control over the Senate throughout the decade of the 1990s.

I. Conclusions

Reentry, voter registration, and participation in elections provide us with a unique opportunity to reconnect the individual to the community to which he or she is returning. It is an opportunity to give that individual a stake in the community and in turn to give the community a stake in the individual. By involving returning ex-offenders in the political activity in a community, we are further weaving them into the social fabric of life in that community.

To address this problem with the depth of analysis and change necessary, a number of laws will need to be reviewed. Many resources, such as the Legal Action Center in New York City as well as the Sentencing Project in Washington, D.C., and other civil rights and human rights organizations around the country have identified the laws, compiled the statistics, and provided the information that we need to work on this important issue.

One of the primary problems in devising a national movement to address felon disenfranchisement is the lack of uniformity in the way the problem manifests itself. The fifty states use fifty approaches to implementing disenfranchisement and the procedures for returning the franchise in those that do allow for restoration of the vote. In states that allow ex-offenders to vote upon release from prison, part of the pre-release programming should be to register that individual to vote. Right now, all we can do is try to prepare formerly incarcerated individuals for the situation they are likely to encounter.

In jurisdictions that require extensive paperwork in advance of consideration for reenfranchising an ex-offender, outside-the-walls programming should include assistance in the process for obtaining the vote. In those jurisdictions, effort should be made to better streamline the process. In addition, there should be some move nationally to address the "usual residence rule" by the Census Bureau. In a number of jurisdictions an individual must be paroled to the county from which he or she was incarcerated. Particularly in those situations, it makes little sense to provide the added burden of decreasing the census numbers for a jurisdiction where by law the released inmate will be returned. Here, these urban communities need the resources that an accurate census count will provide. The most difficult obstacle to overcome in the matter of felon disenfranchisement is the political reality that many elected officials would have to participate in legislative activity for a constituency that currently does not have the ability to vote those officials into, or out of, office. The movement to address this issue will undoubtedly have to be a grassroots movement augmented by extensive press coverage, letters to editors, op-ed pieces, editorials, and support from a wide range of society.

Given the current philosophy of the United States Supreme Court, legislation rather than litigation is the proper strategy for change. Some states, including Tennessee[77] in 1996 and Texas[78] in 1997, have restored voting rights immediately upon completion of an individual's sentence. Delaware[79] and Nebraska[80] enacted legislation to replace their lifetime felon-voting ban with a five-year and two-year post-sentence prohibition on voting, respectively. Maryland[81] and Nevada[82] have also been successful in the legislative arena, increasing ballot access for some ex-felons. Connecticut provided voting rights to criminals on probation in 2001.[83] A grassroots movement in Rhode Island led to a ballot initiative that resulted in passage of a constitutional amendment in 2006 that extended the franchise to probationers and parolees.

8

Reentry and Parole

On August 6, 2004, six people were murdered in a Deltona, Florida, rental home. The community was shocked by the tragic murders that included an eleven-year-old girl. Investigators arrested and charged a number of individuals, including Troy Victorino, who was the alleged mastermind of the crime. At the time of the incident, Victorino was on parole and had recently reported to his parole officer.

Victorino had been charged with a new crime, and Florida law allowed the parole officer to exercise discretion in determining whether to arrest the parolee. The parole agent involved opted not to arrest Victorino, and this incident ensued. The press immediately jumped on the story, asserting that the parole department had failed to protect the public. One editorial went so far as to state that all felons caught violating the terms of their probation must be jailed promptly, asserting that the fact that this had not occurred in the Victorino case resulted in the deaths of six young people.[1]

Three days later, Florida prison officials fired four probation officers, including supervisors, essentially blaming them for the incident. Although officials stated that the parole agents did not follow proper procedure, the fact is that Florida law grants parole agents discretion in these instances, if they see other progress by the parolee. One of the parole supervisors whom the state terminated explained that "the parole officer made 'a judgment call' and 'he was a day late doing his paperwork.'"[2]

Predictably, one legislator has called for new laws eliminating discretion on the part of parole agents. The legislator states that "[v]iolent probation violators should not get a second bite at the apple"—and, further, that he "was surprised to learn that current law allows probation officers the 'discretion' of requesting an arrest if someone commits a violent crime while out on probation—but doesn't require it."[3] When parole agents in Florida and nationally read about the firings and recognized that officials and the public were blaming the murders on the fired agents and supervisors, there was a chilling effect on any exercise of discretion in favor of a second chance for parolees. Suddenly parole agents were being demonized along with parolees.

When the average citizen speaks about parole, he or she typically concentrates on its glaring failures. Willie Horton's crimes allegedly committed while on parole torpedoed a presidential campaign and helped launch a retributive phase of criminal justice policy. Polly Klaas's kidnapping and murder by parolee Richard Allen spawned "three strikes and you're out" legislation that sought to keep third-time offenders (violent and nonviolent) from ever seeing the light of day. But the story of parole, its limitations, and its potential to assist in the process of reentry is far more complex than the average citizen realizes and demands a closer look.

A. Role of Parole: A Historical Perspective

Parole has served a range of functions over the years since its inception. Initially, the parole function grew out of a tacit acknowledgment that individuals recently released from prison would require some assistance in their reentry back into the community. Parole offices recognized even at the beginning two principal needs that ex-offenders as a group experienced: securing housing and finding gainful employment. But parole offices further acknowledged that the process of successful reentry demanded more than just referral information. Parole agents were often expected to undertake a "counseling" role that, at least in theory, would help ease the variety of pressures that parolees faced in coping with family and community relationships as they worked their way back into the fabric of family and community life. Thus, the parole agent role was shaped, in part, by the ex-offender's needs around reentry.

Parole and parole supervision have traditionally been a critical part of the reentry process for ex-offenders. Planning for parole release served as motivation for inmates to participate in whatever programming was available. A grant of parole was often conditioned on the inmate's successful completion of prison programs, coupled with the development of a pre-release plan that identified ties to the community, job options, and a plan for housing. Upon release, parole supervision meant ensuring compliance with the plan or helping the ex-offender to adjust the plan to find work and housing. The supervision and regular case management that occurred on release on parole was thought to help minimize the risks of recidivism.[4] Also, advocates of parole supervision argued that the investment in this supervision ultimately saved tax dollars by helping the offender make a smooth transition back into the community and a law-abiding lifestyle, fostering public safety with a reasonable fiscal impact.[5]

Parole also served an important systemic function. It operated as a pressure valve for the indeterminate sentencing process that prevailed. The inmate knew that, by engaging in productive behavior in prison, he could ensure early release from his term of imprisonment. But the determination of when that release would occur was left in the hands of the parole board. The parole boards made a range of "assessments" about potential parolees. In most jurisdictions, the board assessed whether the inmate would be able to remain at liberty without violating either the law or other administrative conditions.[6] This meant that the parole board members had the perhaps unenviable task of predicting propensity for criminal behavior.[7] Parole boards also tried to determine future criminality, on the basis of various indicators. While such determinations were necessarily imprecise, the parole boards used a complex matrix of information that was contained in the inmate's file and then reconciled that information with statistics of successful parolee profiles, as well as the previous criminal record (if any) fitting a recidivist profile.[8] But once the parole board made its decision to release an individual back into the community, the parole agent became the interface between the state and the parolee.

The role of the parole agent changed dramatically from the pre-1980 to the post-1980 period. Prior to 1980, parole agents described their own work as "casework" with an emphasis on supervision and counseling. Once granted parole, the parole agent acted as the primary contact for an ex-offender in the quest to reenter society and to remain productively engaged in the community. The parole agent needed to know which employers tended to hire ex-offenders and helped to arrange for ex-offenders to find suitable employment. The agent knew where ex-offenders could obtain drug treatment and often brokered services for "clients."[9]

But the soaring numbers of parolees would shift the focus of parole and, in the end, would lead to a fundamentally reshaped role. In the

1970s and 1980s, parole agents focused principally on managing case-load numbers. The size of the caseload became the determining factor behind whether they could perform their jobs adequately. Parole case-loads began to inch up in the late 1970s, and by the beginning of the decade of the 1980s, there was a dramatic increase in both the number of parolees assigned to urban parole agents and the number of condi-tions placed on parolees to be monitored. After 1980, with the dramatic incarceration rates in the United States and the move to abolish parole as we know it, the primary role of the parole agent became that of a law enforcement officer. Surveillance, drug testing, and revocation be-came the fundamental tasks of the parole agent. The move to a more law-enforcement orientation coincided with more public attacks on the parole function that will be discussed more fully below.

B. How Parole Has Changed

Parole in the 1980s and 1990s came under vocal and persistent attack. The public, politicians, and the media perceived parole as ineffective. Of course, general lack of employment may have been a factor in the lack of success of parolees and parole agents. Parole agents began to experi-ence real difficulty locating jobs for the ex-offenders returning primarily to urban communities. These recently released individuals typically had little or no employment history; they often lacked skills. When we add the large number of collateral consequences that flowed from their con-victions—such as an inability to seek and obtain a wide range of gov-ernment, health care, and therapy-related licenses or the approvals nec-essary to get these jobs—ex-offenders had large amounts of free time on their hands.

Free time and parolees tended to be a dangerous combination. In-dividuals in urban settings typically did not want to remain in often crowded living conditions, with either extended-family living situations or in shelters or shared quarters. So, many of these individuals tended to congregate in public spaces, which only increased the chances of po-lice contact and/or opportunities to reengage in the activities that led to their incarceration in the first place. Previously, parole agents had been able to rely on their community expertise or knowledge of community-sponsored programming that might include job training, drug-abuse treatment, and mental health treatment. But many of these programs disappeared as a result of changes in budgetary priorities and budgetary politics over the last two decades. The net result was almost a complete elimination of community-based treatment and training. In *Poor Discipline,* author Jonathon Simon posits the notions that the parole function moved from a casework-focused role to one that simply attempts to manage risk among the varying levels of parolees, and that differentiating among individual parole agents only functions to carry out their surveillance function. The "new penology" that this represents focused on securing the most dangerous individuals away from the public and not on the ex-offender's reentry transition back to the community.

Not surprisingly, as the focus for parole supervision has changed from providing counseling and reentry services for ex-offenders, the rehabilitative functions associated with parole have atrophied. Some state laws still maintain on the books that parolees should have access to job training and other services,[10] but in reality, those services are rarely, if ever, provided. Much of the reduction in services can be traced to impossibly large caseloads of parole officers and the lack of public funding for rehabilitation programs.[11] The "limited contact between parole officers and parolees means that state officials making revocation decisions have little but the most rudimentary data about parolees and their prospects when making revocation decisions."[12] In addition, as will be discussed below, race and difference play a significant role in the revocation determination.

The "lack of individualized information about parolees as well as the lack of alternatives short of revocation once a parole violation is found" leads parole agents to respond conservatively.[13] Alternatives to reimprisonment, such as parole to a halfway house or tightened parole conditions under intensified supervision, often are unavailable due to budget limitations, the large number of parolees, and a punitive political climate.

One of the factors that undoubtedly contributed to the change in focus for parole agents was the media frenzy around crime and the ensuing social and political push toward crime control. Anyone and everyone connected with law enforcement was expected to be more "police-like" in the war on crime. And any behavior that seemed linked to rehabilitation was subject to attack as being "soft on crime." Discussion of the rights of parolees took a back seat to concerns about controlling their conduct.

Due process rights and protections for parolees would soon suffer in this war-on-crime environment. Parolees and probationers are in a netherworld between being free citizens and being prisoners. They live and circulate among the rest of us. They bear no obvious stigma. However, those on parole or probation remain in the legal custody of the state until the completion of their criminal sentences. Their liberty is conditioned upon compliance with state-imposed restrictions of varying degrees of severity. Many parolees and probationers are accused of violating a condition of their release, have their parole revoked, and are returned to prison.[14] Two decades ago the Supreme Court crafted due process protections that apply to the revocation process. In *Morrissey v. Brewer,*[15] the Court held that parolees accused of violating a condition of their parole are entitled to both preliminary and final hearings before their parole is revoked. In *Gagnon v. Scarpelli,*[16] the Court extended *Morrissey*'s due process protections to probationers accused of violating a condition of their probation.

The traditional judicial approach before *Morrissey* viewed parole as a gift bestowed upon the prisoner by the state and the parolee as but a privileged prisoner. Under this approach, parole revocation amounted to a mere transfer from one form of custody to another and did not entitle the parolee to due process protections. *Morrissey* marked a sharp shift from this approach. *Morrissey* classified parolees as being fundamentally different from prisoners for due process purposes. It regarded parolees a sharing "many of the core values" of unqualified liberty.[17] The *Morrissey* Court rejected the notion that state laws defining the parolee as being in the state's continued custody precluded due process protections, on the basis of its conclusion that revocation of parole inflicted a "grievous loss" on the parolee.[18]

While the law did not change, there was much less concern about any losses a parolee might suffer. Parole agents realized that to survive in this environment they needed to redefine their job role. The portion of the job that focused on public safety not only took precedence but also fit well with the prevailing simplistic and short-term definition of public safety. Rather than working to make sure that parolees on their caseloads had access to drug treatment and jobs, agents moved toward a decidedly law enforcement perspective. This meant looking for reasons to lock them up rather than reasons to keep them in the community.

The new focus was on technical violations. This nation witnessed large numbers of parolees committing violations and being sent back to prison—not for new crimes, but for technical violations of parole, including positive drug tests (which can be evidence of new criminality), curfew violations, and other prohibited activity. One study reported that with the transition from a casework orientation, in which parole officers work with ex-offenders to solve their reentry problems, to a more surveillance and monitoring and law enforcement mode, the number of parole revocations increased.[19] In 1993, for example, 42 percent of supervised releasees were revoked, but 29 percent were revoked for technical violations; however, figures for 1993 are consistent with the higher number that were revoked for technical violations.[20]

Toward the late 1990s the number of parole revocations accounted for a significant percentage of the new prison admissions. Over three-fourths of these parole violations were for technical violations only.[21] In Illinois, for example, the parole violation or revocation practice has been to imprison without possibility of bail every parolee accused of a parole violation no matter how minor the alleged violation.[22] It largely has done away with preliminary revocation hearings and typically delays final revocation hearings until after disposition of the new criminal charge that gave rise to the parole revocation action. In practice, this has meant that parolees often have been imprisoned for weeks or months before receiving a parole revocation hearing, even though they have been found eligible for release on bail in the new criminal case.[23] "Revocation hearings, if held before disposition of the new criminal charge, typically consist of the hearing officer reading a police report and asking the parolee to respond."[24] Parolees are rarely represented, and confrontation and cross-examination rights have been nonexistent.[25] The overwhelming result was that a number of individuals were being reincarcerated without the full panoply of trial rights, and parole officers had come to view their roles as more synonymous with those of police officers.

C. The Politics of Parole

Politically, the Left generally and the Democrats specifically had lost the high ground in the battle for the hearts and minds of Americans in the criminal justice debate. The media—a knowing or unknowing accomplice—had helped the Right with its sensational coverage of race, crime, and politics. From the crimes of parolees such as Willie Horton on the

East Coast to the kidnap and subsequent murder of Polly Klaas by a repeat violent criminal who had recently received early parole from prison on the West Coast, the media kept issues of crime on the front pages, the television screens, and the radios of America. Politicians were quick to attack the criminal justice system. Police and some prosecutors were characterized as out of touch with the communities in which they worked. Defense lawyers were painted as individuals without morals. Judges were termed "soft on crime" and characterized as attempting to "legislate from the bench." Parole agents were not exempt from criticism either; they were seen as ineffective, and parole generally was labeled a "failed liberal notion."

Finally, the chain of events that began with the Willie Horton incident and the Polly Klaas kidnapping and murder resulted in a flurry of political action. Although a previous attempt at passing "three-strikes-and-you're-out" legislation was unsuccessful, the legislation became state law in California. A similar three-strikes law passed overwhelmingly in Washington State. And a new retributive era began.

Parole and judges became the new targets of the conservative politician, political commentator, and man on the street. The kind of violence that occurred in the Polly Klaas case was perceived as the norm rather than as isolated or atypical, and the overwhelming media coverage of these events managed to silence those who believed that parole served a useful function. At the same time, the entire sentencing process came under scrutiny. Judges continued to sentence individuals, but, because of jail and prison overcrowding and in some places because of lawsuits, individuals could serve less time than had been mandated by the judge. Indeed, no one other than prison officials knew exactly how much time an individual would serve. As a result, the legislative and executive branches moved to place greater controls on the release of prisoners and urged states to abolish parole and pursue what was termed "truth in sentencing." Under the guise of "truth in sentencing," state officials successfully attacked the practice of granting "good time"—reductions in sentences for good behavior in prison.

The Federal Sentencing Guidelines were part of an effort that included the "abolition of parole." Whereas a number of jurisdictions allowed offenders to receive a subsequent sentence reduction of up to 33 percent for good conduct in prison, the Federal Sentencing Guidelines—and an increasing number of state sentencing guideline systems—defined "truth in sentencing" so that offenders receive a sentence reduction of no more than 15 percent for good conduct. Adoption of this definition (and of guidelines that include abolition of parole) was strongly encouraged by a 1994 federal statute that provided substantial funds for prison construction to states abolishing parole and requiring inmates convicted of serious crimes to serve at least 85 percent of their sentences.[26] The legislation also encouraged states to consider adopting guidelines, because prisoners in their states were previously serving a very low proportion of their sentences (sometimes less than 20 percent). With prisoners now required to serve at least 85 percent of their sentences, states are facing the prospect of massive increases in prison populations. The offer of prison-building funds was made to address those making fiscal arguments against states jumping on the "abolish-parole bandwagon."

D. Elections

In fact, in the 1994 campaign, we found that "three strikes and you're out" earn politicians more votes than anything they could say about any other issues, including health care, Medicare, Medicaid. "Three strikes and you're out" was the number one sound byte of that campaign, according to the pollsters. Although the initiative helped politicians' campaigns, it was extremely weak when subjected to any intellectually honest scrutiny. Still, "three strikes" quickly gained popularity across the country and was soon endorsed by Republicans and Democrats alike—including President Clinton. Finally, in a landslide, Virginians elected George Allen governor primarily because of his promise to obtain "truth in sentencing." If the election of Ronald Reagan was considered a mandate for conservatism and Republican rule, then the rhetoric of the 1994 elections represented a turn away from any semblance of compassion, prevention, or rehabilitation.

The force with which "three strikes," mandatory minimums, and general attacks on any type of rehabilitative policy took hold was amazing. In turn, the result was felt acutely in communities of color around the country. Arrests, convictions, and long sentences became the norm. In African American communities, where open-air drug markets thrived, wholesale roundups of young men continued. In Northern California, San Quentin prison looked more like an inner-city high school than a maximum security prison. Eventually, many of those young men have been, and will continue to be paroled to the communities in which they lived prior to incarceration. Parole then has become a way of life for many in the Black community.

E. Black Community and Parole

When one focuses on communities of color and specifically the Black community, parole takes on an entirely different dimension. Discrimination and discretionary criminal justice policies in arrests, charging, and sentencing have a disproportionate impact on the African American community. As a result, prison and parole are woven more directly into the fabric of these communities nationwide. Criminologist Joan Petersilia writes, "[S]erving a prison term is becoming almost a normal experience in some poor, minority communities."[27] Indeed Petersilia suggests that in some communities prison sentences are so routine that they are not viewed as a problem. In some cities, including our nation's capital, one in two young African American men is under the control of the criminal justice system.[28]

A closer examination of the relationship among parole, parole agents, and the African American community reveals that the concept of parole and the way it functions have always been somewhat different in Black communities. For the urban parole agent, the parolee ranks in the decades of the 1960s and 1970s were largely filled with African Americans.[29] However, the decades of the 1980s and 1990s would find dramatic increases in the numbers of African Americans who would face incarceration and parole. Finally, the War on Drugs has targeted massive numbers of drug users, addicts, serious abusers, and casual users alike and siphoned them out of society and into prison. As is often noted, there are fewer young Black men in college than are in the correctional system.[30] Indeed, researcher Marc Mauer, in his critique of crime-control policies, writes that for "African American males, the rates of incarceration can only be described as catastrophic."[31] No one who works in the criminal justice system could fail to notice that our jails and prisons have become repositories for young Black men. When probation and parole are included, one out of every three Black males in the 20–29 age group is under some form of criminal justice supervision.[32]

The picture of the future is equally harrowing: three out of ten African American baby boys will grow up and spend some time in prison.[33]

An African American young man who was born in 1991 stands a 29 percent chance of being incarcerated during his life, as opposed to a 16 percent chance for a Latino young man and a 4 percent chance for a young White man.[34] African American women in prison are significantly fewer in number than African American men, but the trend upward is startling. From 1985 to 1995, there was a 204 percent growth in the number of African American women in federal and state prisons as opposed to the 126 percent growth overall.[35] This supervision by criminal justice professionals was representative of government institutions for most inner-city Black men.[36]

F. Conclusions

Previously, in theory at least, the indeterminate sentencing regime called for collaboration between prison and parole officials to work with inmates to prepare them for release and, ostensibly, reentry. In reality, however, indeterminate sentencing was used as a means of controlling the behavior of prisoners rather than developing a comprehensive reentry plan. During that period, inmates had to devise a reentry plan, parole officers investigated the plan, and reports on the plan's feasibility were made to the parole board. If the inmate could not obtain substantial support from family or community, halfway houses were often used to assist in the transition. If someone was granted parole, he or she would be given conditions of parole, and the parole officer would see to guiding the offender to programs.

With the move to abolish parole and the discontinuation of indeterminate sentencing in the last decade, the process of prisoner release has altered dramatically. Many states and the federal government have severely limited or outright eliminated parole eligibility. In addition, a larger percentage of those released from prison, particularly with the most serious offenses and, in some instances, the highest risk to public safety, have no official supervision. They are released unfettered by conditions of parole and unassisted in the arduous reentry process. Many are given only a bus ticket and a few dollars. Often there is no direction and no sense of hope that they will have a real opportunity to improve their lives or circumstances.[37] Some have received high school equivalency diplomas or other job training education in prison, but find it difficult to employ those skills in today's workforce. With licensing bars in effect, they also cannot use other skills that they may have acquired while serving their sentences.

Rehabilitation through employment opportunities is one clear way to stem the tide of ex-offenders leaving and reentering society through the jailhouse doors. Incarceration has not served society well as a method to reduce recidivism.[38] "[W]ork and family are the keys to keeping an ex-convict from re-offending"[39] because they allow offenders to have legitimate employment and full, legal participation in their community. Placement programs that specialize in rehabilitating ex-offenders frequently note the inverse correlation between recidivism rates and employment opportunities. Lifetime stigma as a felon hinders ex-offenders from fully participating as active members of society.[40]

Whether parole agents take a casework or surveillance approach, caseloads will continue to be a factor in their ability to do their jobs. In the 1970s, parole officers maintained caseloads of approximately forty-five parolees, whereas today parole caseloads of seventy are not unusual.[41] With these types of numbers it is unrealistic to believe that parole officers can do much monitoring or provide much reentry assistance of parolees.

The role of parole and the parole agent must undergo a significant transformation if we are to slow the recidivism and reincarceration rate. Parole officials must work more closely with community service providers. High-risk offenders must be monitored and closely supervised to protect both themselves and those in the communities to which they return. To determine realistic goals, we must think about the nature of the government's responsibility to parolees and how that responsibility relates to concerns about public safety. If we have a genuine commitment to reentry and successful reintegration, we need to imagine the parole process as one that begins prior to release and reaches out to the communities where parolees will return.

Recently released offenders need a wide range of services. These individuals face significant hurdles to post-release services. Among the most significant concerns are the need to establish community-based treatment plans and the inability to finance needed services. Many inmates never received mental or physical health care services prior to incarceration and are thus unfamiliar with community-based care systems.[42] The range of needs include mental and physical health care, housing, and employment. Concerns about housing and employment may trump efforts to pursue mental health services. In addition, the cost of health care generally and the lack of availability of adequate referral services prior to release can make connecting to community-based services difficult.

"Community-based" means virtually any program operated outside a conventional correctional facility. One benefit of community-based care is the ability to manage services that include effective aftercare. Proximity to the community enables direct and regular family involvement with the treatment process as well as a phased reentry into the community. The use of community-based facilities, in which the community engages in the planning for and evaluation of programs, is also politically useful because it helps to build community consensus around priorities and services and also builds support for the kinds of comprehensive strategies, including job training and placement, that make the difference in the most successful programs.

For decades some sectors of the criminal justice community did not trust community-based organizations as viable partners in the reentry and rehabilitative process. Police, prosecutors, and judges often expressed skepticism about the viability of community-based treatment as an alternative to incarceration. The victim of a crime may initially be the most skeptical about community sentencing. Victims usually expect retribution for the crime. This attitude often emphasizes the need for the criminal to have been appropriately punished and does not coincide with restorative and rehabilitative measures. That skepticism often carried over to parole officers seeking reentry services. Focusing on restitution to and education of the public regarding the social and economic benefits of community sentencing may provide help in this movement.

The community justice movement that helped to establish community policing, community courts, and community prosecution and defense has significantly assisted in the legitimization of community-based nonprofits as viable reentry partners. The Department of Justice's Reentry Initiative specifically called for the development of "Reentry Partnerships" to assist ex-offenders with their reintegration back into communities.

Leena Kurki describes the foundation of community-justice programs as "community empowerment and participation."[43] The vision of community justice involves more of a focus on prevention than apprehension and on community and criminal justice agencies working in unison to prevent crime and empower communities.[44] The reality of community justice is that there are no set roles for the community in the administration of criminal justice.[45] Therefore, the implementation of any community-based criminal justice effort requires a redefinition of traditional roles.[46] Parole and probation officers themselves are beginning to rethink what it means to work in, and with, communities.

In a special issue of the *Federal Probation* journal entitled *"What Works" in Corrections,* Frances T. Cullen et al. offer parole officers a new three-pronged approach to working with offenders. First, they suggest being less focused on prohibited activities, as in the traditional stricture "no associating with known felons," and instead identifying specific problematic people, such as past co-offenders.[47] Second, they recommend working closely with the parolee not only to extinguish inappropriate conduct but also to replace it with pro-social activities.[48] Finally, and most importantly in the community-justice context, they recommend that the parole officer work closely with community members and help to develop personal relationships with both the parolee and the parolee's significant family and social contacts. This moves the parole officer from the constant threat of revocation to a positive role in reentry. The authors go on to recommend that a joint "problem-solving conference" involving the "intimate circle" of the parolee might serve an important preventive function.[49]

This new approach to actively involving community and family members in the reintegration of the individual parolee and probationer embraces the fundamental notions of community justice. Ed Rhine, one of the many innovative thinkers in corrections, defines the primary strategy involved with the new approach to community justice as "incorporating an ecological focus," which is seen as "essential to redirecting and guiding the daily work of probation and parole officers."[50]

Some may ask, Why the changes in approach and this new focus on community justice? The answer in some way points to the recent community-justice movement. Expectations inside and outside the criminal justice system have been raised. With all of the rhetoric of "community involvement," communities have responded. Many neighborhoods have conducted an unprecedented number of community meetings seeking input and involvement.

In addition to raising community expectations, the federal government has made funds available for agencies that partner with community groups. Beginning in fiscal year 2001 the Department of Justice instituted two programs to assist in the reintegration of offenders back into their communities.[51] The Reentry Partnerships Initiative, one of the initiatives, is an attempt to "create new accountability and support for released offenders by enhancing monitoring and follow-up" through individual and community support systems.[52] The hope is that by utilizing institutional corrections, community corrections, community policing, local businesses, and faith-based and grassroots community organizations, the initiative will create a collaboration that will work together to help prepare inmates for returning to their neighborhoods.[53]

The new effort works as a different incentive to probation and parole to develop reentry plans at both the community and individual level. The goals of these innovative community-justice partnerships are to keep communities safe, to reduce reincarceration for technical violations, and to help local economies.[54] Finally, in circumstances where the supervision is limited, the objective is to utilize these reentry partnerships to enhance supervision and increase accountability. This combination of collaboration with community justice and the Justice Department solicitation will lead to a more collaborative effort on the part of parole and community-based nonprofit and faith-based programs.

9

Reentry Courts

Being a judge in the reentry court radically transformed the role. In the traditional parole system, an administrative law judge would have contact with parolees, but only during revocation hearings. They would stand before him accused of failing to meet the conditions of their parole or facing allegations of new criminal violations. The judge could only talk to the parolee through his or her counsel, given the rules against ex parte communication with the accused. The hearing might last ten to fifteen minutes, and then the judge would make a decision and the hearing would end. He would only see the parolee once or twice at such hearings.

The judge preferred the practice of the reentry court. He had more direct interaction with parolees. He could now speak directly with the parolee about his or her progress and difficulties without the buffer of defense counsel. He could make parolees return to court frequently for drug tests and appearances before him. He could use the authority of the court to compel the behavior that he expected through the use of sanctions to punish behavior and rewards, such as relaxation of sanctions, to encourage compliance. He no longer believes that the independence of the judge should be the hallmark of this court hearing. For better or worse, he takes the job personally.[1]

According to traditional American jurisprudence, the role of the judge in a criminal case is to oversee courtroom proceedings relating to a defendant's guilt or innocence and appropriate disposition of the case. Over the last decade, however, drug courts and other problem-solving courts have been testing another model. Judges in these courts use the power of the courts to set and monitor explicit conditions for a defendant's behavior (e.g., "don't use drugs," "get regular drug testing," "go to treatment"). They use a mix of graduated sanctions and incentives as tools to change the defendant's behavior, and reinforce success if these changes are achieved. The concept of a "reentry court," first introduced in 1999 by Attorney General Janet Reno and Jeremy Travis, then-director of the National Institute of Justice, challenges criminal justice professionals and communities to apply the principles of the drug court to the back end of the system—to use the incentives and sanctions of judicial oversight to effectively address the complex challenges of offender reintegration. Reentry courts—there are now a small number springing up—generally include these core elements: a "reentry transition plan" acknowledged by the court and the ex-prisoner that is tailored to individual risks and needs and addresses an array of employment, treatment, housing, family, and supervision issues. The reentry court must have at its disposal a range of supportive and supervision resources to draw upon in order to implement the plan: regular oversight of the reentry plan by a court authority who has the discretion to swiftly impose a predetermined set of graduated, parsimonious sanctions and incentives to motivate good behavior, community service work, increased supervision levels, additional drug testing or treatment, or short periods of time in lockup, accountability to victims or community via strict attention to ongoing restitution orders, community service requirements, or even a citizen advisory board. Rewards for success, such as graduation ceremonies similar to those seen in drug courts. Aside from these central ingredients, reentry courts will vary tremendously depending on local needs, resources, and statutory frameworks. For example, the first generation of reentry courts includes a Delaware court that focuses on domestic violence cases, an Iowa reentry court for offenders diagnosed with mental health disorders, and a court in Florida that targets substance abusers. Importantly, because the authority for post-prison supervision is often not vested with the judicial branch, reentry courts operate on the basis of a variety of approaches, each consistent with local statutory frameworks. In Ohio, for instance, the Richland County Common Pleas Court judges use split sentences and a shock probation authority to supervise many of the returning inmates. In New York City, an administrative law judge—with authority from the parole board—manages reentry court participants within a community court setting. And in Fort Wayne, Indiana, the reentry court judge has actually been vested with authority by the Indiana Parole Commission to supervise returning prisoners on the commission's behalf.[2]

A. Background of the Reentry Courts

In an era when over 650,000 prisoners are being released annually, we, as a society, have only belatedly begun to ask critical questions about the far-reaching impact of these massive releases. This phenomenon has created hopelessly difficult scenarios for local officials and for those who are seeking to reintegrate into their communities. It has often caught local governments and social service providers completely by surprise as their already overtaxed systems attempt to address and absorb the concerns of so many individuals in need. It has left federal and state officials scrambling for an efficient way to provide a net that guarantees the safety of communities. On a daily basis, recently released individuals have not had the luxury of being able to wait for the government to figure out its next moves. Instead, they have faced the daunting task of navigating increasingly complex situations as they return to their communities. Unfortunately, those very communities have often been less than supportive and have seemed to believe that they no longer needed to think about these individuals once they had sent them to prison.

By now, most Americans are aware of the significant decrease in serious crime that has been documented recently. Communities continue to suffer from the residual effects of policies spanning the previous two decades that caught record numbers of individuals in the criminal justice net. Due to criminal justice initiatives in the 1980s and 1990s, the country increased the prison population to unprecedented numbers. Crime rates were on the upswing. Political leaders campaigned on tough-on-crime platforms. They often used the media to highlight the increasing violence of the era. Anxious to sell their products, the media relied heavily on sound bytes to keep a fearful public focused on the obvious: increased crime and rising crime statistics. Very little was done during this period to unravel and examine the factors that might have been contributing to rising crime rate. There was little or no discussion of the widening economic gap between the haves and the have-nots, as many personal incomes flourished and Americans reveled in newfound wealth, purchasing houses, cars, and disposable goods in record numbers. At the same time, the number of those falling deeper into poverty increased.

The news media bombarded Americans with stories of wealth and violence. Instead of analysis and discussion from policy makers, the nation got simple slogans such as "three strikes and you're out." Sensing the public's fear, officials embraced a new jargon laced with war-related imagery—particularly in the inner cities. We "waged wars on drugs" and "wars on crime," and we "targeted the enemy." The public seemed to crave quick-fix solutions in policy recommendations. Recognizing this, politicians did not waste time trying to explain to the public that meaningful solutions to complicated questions of crime and violence might take time. They did not caution the public about the long-term consequences of policy choices. They fed the public what they demanded—quick solutions and simple answers. These formed the foundational elements of the new retributive strategy.

As the nation began to move forward with this new strategy, harsh punishments became commonplace. Prosecutors used newly minted penalties to pursue long sentences. After all, this was the response the public seemed to want. On occasion, though, members of the public caught a glimpse of the consequences of short-term thinking. When they did, they expressed concern about the policy path that the nation had chosen. For example, when jurors were informed of the long-term consequences of mandatory-minimum sentencing, they were often less supportive. In California jurors began to rebel after finding that convictions for shoplifting food and merchandise worth less than ten dollars could result in sentences of twenty-five years to life if that shoplifting offense constituted a third strike against the offender. Post-conviction interviews with jurors began to surface their concern. Many indicated that had they known of the harsh penalties the accused would face, they would not have voted for guilt. The rules governing the evidence that jurors could consider often kept sentencing consequences away from jurors during deliberations. "Three strikes and you're out" statutes continued to flourish and to be used widely without much question.

One of the consequences of simplistic messages is limited information. Criminal justice practitioners knew that the people who faced long sentences would ultimately be released. They also knew that these individuals would need support. But policy makers chose to ignore that reality. Instead, they focused their attacks on parole. Parolees, exiting prison with some of the same problems and skill deficits that helped to incarcerate them in the first place, committed new offenses and gave politicians easy targets. Overburdened and understaffed, the parole system also became a ready political target. The media helped by focusing on parolees committing new crimes.

Fighting the tide of anticriminal sentiment, in January of 2002 the United States Department of Justice, in conjunction with Health and Human Services, Labor, Education, and Housing and Urban Development, launched a $100 million initiative to attempt to address the issue of reentry.[3] Given the sheer volume of formerly incarcerated individuals returning to communities, the federal government recognized that some coordination would be essential. But the federal initiative attempted to guide the form of coordination to be adopted. It encouraged the development of reentry courts throughout the nation.[4]

These reentry courts represent a new form of jurisprudence that presumably creates a partnership between courts and corrections. In this new collaboration, the ultimate goal is successful offender reintegration. The concept of the reentry court necessitates considerable cooperation between corrections and local judiciaries, requiring the coordination of prisons, community corrections, and various community resources in transitioning offenders back into the community through active judicial oversight.[5]

This chapter will suggest that too little attention was paid to the philosophy, structure, and implementation of these hybrid courts as a means of addressing the issue of reentry. Moreover, courts in many respects are a cumbersome and expensive vehicle for government to use to supervise ex-offenders' reintegration into society. Thrusting judges into the supervisory role—while at the same time retaining their adjudicatory powers—engages a number of ethical and procedural obstacles for parolees and for the court.

B. Helping Them Stay Out

"When I get out, I'm never coming back." So goes a promise that is as common to make as it is difficult to keep. The countless men and women who make plans in their heads about the ways in which they will change their behavior to ensure that they stay out of the criminal justice system are often ill prepared for the obstacles that they will encounter. This isn't meant to suggest that they are naïve about the attitudes awaiting them. To some extent, they will have already experienced and endured some biased attitudes based on race, gender, and class. But the intense power of hope tends to make them underestimate the difficulties they will encounter almost daily and to overestimate their innate abilities to overcome the obstacles that await them.

Indeed, their inner strength may be the only thing on which they may rely. Typically, countless numbers of ex-offenders are being released from jail or prison without any formal supervision. These individuals will not be on parole; they will not be subject to any release conditions; they will not have access to any real guide to employment, housing, or other necessary services. Instead, record numbers of ex-offenders will be left on their own to navigate their release and reintegration into the very communities in which they first found themselves enmeshed in the criminal justice system.

To compensate for this lack of supervision, the United States federal government proposed courts as one of the primary tools to supervise recently released individuals. When one unpacks the constituent parts of the reentry conundrum—guidance and supervision through the maze of employment, housing, health care, and child care—one might devise any number of strategies that would both assist the ex-offender and ensure the safety of the community. Strategies might range from formal entities charged with providing services with which ex-offenders might work to less formal networks of community partners and services. Interestingly, the federal government focused on the courts.

C. Why Did the Federal Government Choose to Create a Court?

The United States Department of Justice was fresh off the success of drug courts. There, the department utilized a team led by a judge to assist drug offenders in their efforts to kick their habits and avoid future criminal justice involvement. Using this model, the Justice Department reasoned that a court could fill the gap in supervision that had occurred as a result of two related phenomena: the choice to abolish some parole agencies and the overburdening of those offices that remained. What the Justice Department did not consider fully was the extent to which reentry supervision really belonged within the boundaries of a court. Practice has revealed significant drawbacks in design, particularly when we examine the expanded roles that judges play in these hybrid courts. Constitutional problems and ethical challenges abound as judges tend not to appoint defense lawyers to represent the interests of the ex-offender.

Still, using what it knew, the Justice Department committed itself to the course of developing specialized courts for reentry. This choice was to be expected. Not only did lawyers populate the Justice Department, but Attorney General Janet Reno had previous direct experience in creating hybrid courts to address seemingly intractable social and criminal justice problems. The attorney general had previously been the state's attorney (the local district attorney) in Dade County, Florida. During her tenure in 1989, she needed to find new ways to respond to a wave of criminal cases involving drugs. Reno, along with then–state court administrator Timothy Murray, created an experimental drug court.[6] The drug court evolved as a response to a critical criminal justice problem: the flood of cases due in large part to the War on Drugs, waged during the decade of the 1980s, threatened to cripple the state court systems. Criminal courts found themselves inundated with cases that were drug related, drug involved, or drug inspired. Cases tended to linger on court dockets because defendants often did not appear for their court dates, which resulted in warrants being issued for their arrest. Often these defendants were young, poor, of-color, and addicted to drugs.

The influx of drug cases affected every aspect of the court system. But cases involving drugs and particularly drug-addicted defendants presented new problems for the court. Conventional approaches to resolving those cases did not seem adequate to the task. So, the various court actors came together to devise a new strategy. Indeed, the criminal courts' main ally in attempting to deal with the flood of cases tended to be probation departments. Probation officers found themselves overwhelmed, understaffed, and underfunded. As a result, probation, drug treatment, social services, and the other community mechanisms began to crumble under the strain of these cases.

With this challenge, the Miami drug court experiment began. The objective of the court seemed quite different from that of its traditional counterpart: the drug court sought to address some of the root causes of crime.[7] This shift from punishment to treatment designed to help individuals deal with drug addiction represented a major reallocation of the court's resources. With the new objective came new methodologies. The courts were more informal and nonadversarial in their operation. They utilized a "teamwork" approach, putting the judge, defender, and prosecutor on the "same side."[8] The rationale behind the design was that by working together, all parties could help to create an individualized treatment plan and individualized justice for each defendant. If defendants successfully completed their programs of treatment, they graduated and the charges were dismissed. If they failed to meet the conditions set by the team, their criminal charges could be reinstated and they would face more conventional forms of punishment.

The experiment took hold. Urban courts that were on the verge of collapse due to the flood of drug cases were eager to try any program that might help them gain greater control over their dockets. The appeal of drug courts lay in their design: they siphoned off low-level nonviolent drug offenses from the courts' crowded calendars and placed them on a special docket devoted solely to drug cases. The availability of federal aid and technical assistance enabled courts nationwide to jump on the drug court bandwagon.

D. From Drug Courts to "Community Courts"

That success led to the widespread development of specialized courts. There was a growing recognition that with drug use and drug selling came a host of associated social and economic problems for communities. In the late 1980s, low-income communities and urban centers were experiencing various types of decline. Public urination, panhandling, graffiti, homelessness, littering, and loitering increasingly were all conspiring to reduce property values in residential areas, discourage tourism in certain commercial neighborhoods, and generally hamper the quality of life in a number of communities nationwide. Broken-windows theory led the way, and a wide range of policing brought unprecedented numbers of defendants on minor charges into criminal courts.[9] New York City mayor Rudy Giuliani used this theory to declare war on what he termed "quality of life" crimes. New York City launched a campaign of "zero tolerance" of these minor offenses, resulting in mass arrests. Criminal courts became inundated with low-level misdemeanors.

Courts, predictably, were unable to handle the volume. The regular participants of criminal courts (judges, prosecutors, and defense attorneys) viewed these cases as petty and unworthy of the time and emphasis wanted by politicians. The enforcement net was being cast wider, and the number of individuals being brought before the courts increased dramatically. At the same time, there was growing discontent among communities. Many residents contended that the courts were not solving the problems of quality of life in their neighborhoods. The criminal justice system was generally perceived as, at best, out of touch with the needs of the community or, at worst, hostile to their concerns. Mass arrests were disruptive of crime in the short run, but did little to make any lasting change.[10]

Conscious of the hostility toward the courts and aware of their ineffectiveness in addressing quality-of-life crimes, New York's chief judge for the court of appeals, Judith Kaye, working with the John Feinblatt, founder of the newly formed Center for Court Innovation in New York, made the choice to use the drug court model to create community courts. They designed the Midtown Community Court in Times Square. The focus of this court, which opened in 1993, was to "clean up" the midtown community, create a more hospitable environment for tourists, and, at the same time, try to provide more social services through the courts.

The methodology of the court is loosely based on the drug court model. It requires defendants to plead guilty and to remain in the court. After the defendant enters his or her guilty plea, the court orders him or her to undergo a pretrial assessment for such matters as drug abuse, work history, and homelessness. The information gathered is then used to devise an individualized sentence. The sentence for these defendants is usually some form of community service activity such as removing graffiti, cleaning subway stations, and stuffing envelopes for nonprofit community organizations. The court also attempts to set itself apart from traditional courts by providing community residents a means to participate in the criminal justice system. In devising its sentencing plans, the court takes care to acknowledge the harm done to neighborhoods and their residents by substance abuse and low-level offending.

Building on the drug court model, and utilizing federal and state funds and technical assistance from the Center for Court Innovation, community courts began to spring up in a number of cities. Because the success of these courts largely depended on using the symbols of the court and its coercive powers, the design required the participation of prosecutors, defenders, and other court personnel. But problems arose in the move to take the drug court model into this new context. The drug court model was based on considerable research into the most effective ways to treat addictive behavior. Their methods were in keeping with that research. But the newer hybrid courts lacked any foundational research to govern their methods. They seemed to be making it up as they went along.[11] In addition, some viewed the creation of a wide range of "boutique courts" as nothing more than net widening designed to punish conduct that previously had gone unpunished.[12]

These courts raised ethical concerns for the judges who were presiding. Because the courts attempt to maintain community ties through the use of community boards, questions arose about the extent to which the judges and other court personnel are affected by attendance at community meetings and other activities. Can they make independent choices or are they operating as an agent of the powerful voices in the community? Although such questions continue to be raised, the community court movement continues to spread. The culture of reentry courts continues to take root.

E. The Federal Government Responds to Reentry

Against this background, government officials were beginning to realize that the problem of prisoner reentry would be their next hurdle. Referring to prisoner reentry as "one of the most pressing problems we face as a nation,"[13] then–attorney general Janet Reno urged her staff to find a method to monitor and guide the more than 650,000 prisoners who would be released annually from prison. In looking at this problem, we see similarities with the drug court movement. Overwhelming numbers of individuals coming out of prison were in need of drug treatment, job training, and other social services. To the extent that parole existed in jurisdictions, parole officers were drowning in cases and lacking sufficient resources to do their jobs well. It appeared that a "court-oriented" approach might serve their needs because judges could fulfill the role of parole agent.

The Department of Justice made the decision to fund the establishment of reentry courts. The Office of Justice Programs (OJP) sent out invitations to state and local jurisdictions around the country to submit concept papers describing proposed reentry courts. In response, OJP received twenty-one proposals from jurisdictions throughout the country. Of these, OJP selected nine sites for the establishment of pilot reentry courts.

F. Faux Courts: The Faulty Design of Reentry Courts

The creation of a court does not occur against a blank canvas. Expectations about a court's mandate and the roles the participants will play precede the development of such an entity. Even the average member of the public is aware from popular culture that judges perform certain functions, as do the lawyers who appear before them. Although the public may tolerate a reduction in constitutional protections in an exceptional circumstance, we typically expect that the individual brought before any court will have the benefit of certain constitutional protections. But in developing these reentry courts, the designers have ignored convention and tried to reinvent themselves despite tradition. As a result, professional and ethical boundaries are blurred.

No single design is apparent when one looks at reentry courts, although the Office of Justice Programs has suggested that these courts do contain some core elements, including

- assessment and strategic planning assessment that involve the ex-offender, the judiciary, and other key partners and sometimes involve the development of a treatment plan;
- regular status and assessment meetings involving the ex-offender and various service providers and/or family members or members of the community;
- coordination of multiple support services, including substance abuse treatment, job training programs, faith institutions, and housing services;
- accountability to the community through the involvement of citizen advisory boards, crime victims' organizations, and neighborhood groups;
- graduated sanctions for violations of the conditions of release that can be swiftly, predictably, and universally applied;
- rewards for success (carrot-and-stick approach), especially through the negotiation of early release from parole after established goals are achieved or through graduation ceremonies similar to those used in drug courts.[14]

Although not all reentry courts look the same, they tend to have some common features. Structurally, they tend to consist of the reentry court judge, some service providers, and a parole agent. In addition to the plan, the court must have at its disposal some range of services. Some courts require the parolees to sign an agreement promising participation in the plan. Also an aspect of most of these courts is regular court appearances and oversight of the reentry plan by a court authority that has the discretion to impose sanctions swiftly and maintains accountability to victims or community through strict attention to ongoing restitution orders. In addition, there are sometimes community service requirements.

The courts borrow heavily from the drug court model. The court setting is informal to underscore its therapeutic aims. The philosophy behind this choice seems to be that the more formal setting carries punitive connotations and that the informality lends itself to the treatment-team approach. As in the drug court model, the reentry judge's role is to find ways to encourage the ex-offender to succeed. Despite the informal setting, the court does not abandon many of the formal trappings of a court. The judge will make clear that he or she will monitor the ex-offender's progress. The judge speaks for the team in handing down the reentry plan, and the judge serves as the final arbiter of any changes to the plan. Moreover, the judge retains power to sanction if the ex-offender fails to comply with the directives of the court. It is this power to sanction that raises questions about the lack of protections for the ex-offender.

G. Where Is My Lawyer?

When we examine reentry courts closely, we see the facade of a court, but some of the essential components are missing. More often than not, reentry courts operate without the presence of defense counsel or prosecutors. The parole agent in reentry court functions more as a representative of the state's interest. The parolee is ordered to the court usually within a few days of release. When the defendant appears before the court, he or she usually does not have representation. The parolee will be questioned about successes or failures in his or her reentry but will not have the benefit of counsel to assist him or her in complying with the court's plan or in navigating the procedures in court.

The justification for this choice seems to be that the court is assuming the traditional role performed by the parole agent. In parole meetings, the parole agent would speak with the ex-offender, explain parole terms and conditions, and make clear that the ex-offender would need to report his or her progress. The reentry court essentially mirrors this process, but adds a few more players. A team that consists of the judge, parole officers, and a clinical director meets with the ex-offender. Under such a scenario, there is no justification for defense counsel.

Or is there? A closer look at what occurs in the court makes clear that defense counsel should be present. Although the hearings in reentry courts are not initially intended for the purpose of revoking parole and imposing a prison term, that possibility exists. All of the courts utilize the process of graduated sanctions. If a parolee fails to comply with a condition, the court can force the defendant to engage in a range of activities as a sanction for failure to comply. Those sanctions are often predetermined and include community service, drug treatment, and incarceration.[15] The loss of liberty is possible as a component of these graduated sanctions. It is the existence of these sanctions that seems to implicate the Supreme Court decision in *Powell v. Alabama*,[16] which took the first step in identifying the centrality of the right to counsel. The *Powell* court recognized the link between the right to counsel and a fair trial.[17] However, there were still questions in noncapital cases as to appointment of counsel. In *Johnson v. Zerbst*,[18] the court moved the discussion forward by articulating the view that the Sixth Amendment requires counsel to be appointed where no intelligent waiver is made and a defendant's "life or liberty is at stake."[19] This ruling allowed for the appointment of counsel in federal courts. It did not, however, address the more thorny issue of the right to appointed counsel in state trials. Indeed, in the *Betts v. Brady*[20] decision, the court took the position that the Sixth Amendment did not require the appointment of counsel in state courts to guarantee a fair trial.[21] So this left open the question of the centrality of counsel to fair trials in state courts and set the stage for the *Gideon v. Wainwright* decision.[22]

Constitutional safeguards exist for an individual facing a potential sentence of incarceration. *Gideon* and cases that followed it[23] mandate the appointment of counsel in felonies and misdemeanors because of the potential loss of liberty. Following those cases, the United States Supreme Court recognized the critical role that defense counsel plays in pretrial and post-conviction settings such that the representation would be mandated.

The authority to appoint counsel in reentry courts is unclear. In most cases, as the parolee is essentially released to the court, there are no current criminal charges pending. Although the federal courts do not mandate the appointment of counsel in every parole revocation hearing, the states are inconsistent and some states do require the appointment of counsel in revocation hearings. The cases do suggest that failure to appoint counsel in situations where statements are being solicited by these reentry courts may violate the ex-offender's right to counsel. At the very least, failure to admonish the parolee that he or she has the right to counsel prior to the range of statements made to the court (that could ultimately revoke his or her parole) may run afoul of existing case law.

Reentry courts are attempting to build upon the legitimacy of the court. This would seem to require that the components of the court be in place. Some might suggest that appointment of counsel only at the time of revocation passes constitutional muster. However, in these informal courts the very statements elicited by the reentry judge can be used in the imposition of sanctions, including incarceration. For example, if a parolee has failed to comply with conditions and discusses those failures with the court, the court can then appoint counsel, and use the conversations as a basis to violate the parolee and return him or her to prison. This would make the right to counsel in these settings ring hollow.

Even where constitutional justifications call for the appointment of counsel, there may be practical obstacles. Defender offices may not have the resources to staff these courts. Many are already overburdened with skyrocketing caseloads. Most defenders typically view their relationship as terminating upon conviction or after appeal. Extensive planning with defender offices is necessary, much like what was done in the development of drug courts.[24]

Second, funding authorities might balk at the cost of providing counsel to these courts. Funding sources are already reluctant to adequately fund defender offices at rates that permit them to provide quality representation.[25] Because of the constitutional mandate, they grudgingly finance the delivery of indigent defense services. When the mandate is somewhat unclear, funding authorities may be unwilling to finance lawyers in these new courts. Government is already faced with a limited fiscal pie and many needy competitors. It is far from clear that governmental authorities would choose to recognize—and then fund adequately—defenders to serve in those courts representing parolees. Full funding may also detract from the political attraction of these courts.

Reentry courts that already exist have become accustomed to operating without defense counsel. It may prove difficult for defenders to enter existing courts and define a role where there has not been a role previously. It is very likely that defenders would find resistance from the other actors who had become accustomed to conducting business in certain ways. This would be particularly volatile in situations where defenders took positions that differed from the rest of the team. This could lead to disruption in the court's current operations.

Despite the practical obstacles, the role of defense lawyer is critical if these courts expect to operate in a way that is consistent with fairness and the appearance of fairness. Indeed, the driving force behind the effectiveness of courts—traditional or not—lies in the presence of separate parties serving separate functions. In drug courts, the courtroom trappings help to provide legitimacy to the judge's coercive power to move individuals into treatment. The newer problem-solving or community courts similarly benefit from the courtroom setting and actors. These courts have recognized that their power derives from the various actors performing their roles such that the judge can serve as the final arbiter. When both sides enjoy representation by counsel, the court has before it a more complete picture on the basis of which it can render decisions.

H. Stretching Judicial Boundaries beyond Recognition

The independent judicial role does not work in the reentry court. Everyone's roles intersect and require support from one another. The parole officers, clinical director, and judges have worked hard to juggle and refine their roles so they benefit the team context.[26] When one imagines the role of a judge, one typically perceives him or her, literally and figuratively, as stationed above the fray, the neutral arbiter of the events in contest before him or her. But with the advent of specialty courts, the judge's role has become less passive. Judges now seek to play a more active role in the life of a case. Still, this new role must operate, at a minimum, within ethical boundaries.

Reentry court judges appear to have lost sight of those boundaries. On a daily basis, these judges blend two quite distinct and potentially conflicting roles: an adjudicatory role and a probationary function. The judge presides over the ex-offender's progress and makes determinations about the most effective methods to assist, cajole, or force the ex-offender to adhere to a plan of action. This adjudicatory role is, in many ways, consistent with conventional boundaries. But when the judge also works with the parole agent to devise a plan and then sits in judgment over whether the ex-offender has complied, the judge has become less of a neutral decision maker and more of an interested party.

Even the adjudicatory role has devolved into a more interventionist one that raises ethical concerns. The ex parte conversations—conversations that take place with a party in the absence of counsel—would in any other setting be improper, but in reentry courts constitute the norm. Using the ABA Model Code of Judicial Conduct, the ABA Model Rules of Professional Conduct, and the ABA Standards for Criminal Justice, the United States Department of Justice, in conjunction with the national Drug Court Institute, has published guidelines for judges and lawyers functioning in drug courts. Canon One of these drug court guidelines states that "A Judge Should Uphold the Integrity and Independence of the Judiciary."[27] In particular, the *Ethical Considerations* make clear that "the informal nature of drug court proceedings should not be construed to relax the limitations on ex parte contacts."[28] This concern for communications held outside of open court and in the absence of the opposing party arises from the possibility, and indeed likelihood, that these types of contacts might improperly influence the decision making of the judge. Although the architects of the reentry court based the design on the drug court model, the implementation of its procedures seems to depend on ex parte communications about the cases before the reentry court judge.

The parole/probationary function often requires regular meetings and open discussions between the ex-offender and the parole officer. If they can develop a good working relationship of trust, the parolee is likely to share concerns and problems before they spiral out of control. But if the parole agent is the judge, who can impose sanctions, then the nature of the relationship changes. The judge is saying to the parolee "level with me about your problems," but if the parolee says the wrong thing or reveals too much, he or she may face sanctions, including jail time.

This causes yet another ethical dilemma when a judge is speaking directly with an unrepresented party and using that party's statements against him or her. The drug court *Ethical Considerations* require judges to act impartially and would seem to prohibit this use of statements of an unrepresented party against that party.[29]

The net result is that the neutral magistrate becomes more of a judicial inquisitor. Judges are developing plans, investigating violations, and deciding sanctions. They have taken on functions that stretch well beyond traditional boundaries. In the process they are not providing ex-offenders the due process protections that would exist in a formal proceeding. What occurs, in the end, is little more than a facade. The danger of such facades is that they may further erode the legitimacy of courts. Ironically, it is this very legitimacy that engaged the use of courts as a model in the first place.

The courts more frequently are being used as the filter through which services and supervision are provided because they represent an immediate means of implementing sanctions without the cumbersome constitutional protections. In addition, these problem-solving courts have begun to receive high degrees of political acceptability.

I. The Ever-Expanding Culture of Courts

The introduction of reentry courts is not surprising. It is the latest addition to the problem-solving-court landscape. But it is troubling that we are developing a culture of courts. The political instinct now is to develop a court to tackle any new social problem. The overwhelming tendency is to rely on legal structures when other models might serve us better.

What is wrong with a culture of courts? Using courts as the mechanism to deliver services is both costly and inefficient. Many problems occur as a result of poverty, homelessness, and mental illness.[30] Using courts is more expensive and less efficient in delivering services necessary to deal with social problems in part because of the added structural costs involved. The cost of the criminal justice apparatus—the salaries of judges, lawyers, court personnel—all add significant expenses to basic service delivery that could be provided to these communities without the additional costs of courts.

In addition to the added costs, there are also issues of training. Using the criminal justice system as the filter to make decisions in reentry belies the experience and training that probation and parole departments engage in to address these very difficult populations. The tendency in using the criminal justice system as the dumping ground for society's social problems is to turn social problems into legal problems.

Although they represent a more expensive way to deliver services, specialized courts retain a high degree of political acceptance. The notion of using courts in this way provides a level of psychic comfort to the public. There is a feeling that if individuals do not seek treatment, society must imprison them. As a result, government immediately turned to courts as a vehicle to deliver services to ex-offenders. The design of the reentry courts provides some clues to the answer to the question, Why a court? The reentry court prototypes have primarily been accepted.

J. Access to the Reentry Court: Who Gets In?

Community courts are often pitched as being able to respond to community concerns. However, this has routinely meant that nuisance or "victimless crimes," such as loud noise, graffiti, illegal vending, prostitution, and public urination—problems that typically do not command the attention of centralized courts—can be addressed. However, vocal community members are often able to utilize criminal justice resources to address administrative problems that they face. Studies have shown that communities are willing to pay more taxes[31] to have their own community court. In addition, judges themselves feel that the limits of the legal process in conventional courts do not allow them to be involved in some of the root causes of problems and desire more involvement.[32] It is against this backdrop of judges feeling powerless and citizens wanting more control over their communities that the popularity of these specialized courts has soared. Building on the sudden political successes has caused judges and elected officials to support the use of courts in the delivery of a wide range of services often unavailable to judges, lawyers, and defendants in traditional courts.[33]

Reentry courts then are a combination of lesser procedures and constitutional obstacles that create a different brand of coercive justice than the drug—or community—courts. They maintain the appearance of the same community-involved courts that have enjoyed widespread political popularity. The courts are a mix of types of cases and ex-offenders in various jurisdictions encompassing essentially what the market will bear. Reentry courts have started as a pilot and as a result, only a limited number of individuals are accepted into and supervised by these reentry court judges. The cases tend to be only what prosecutors, law enforcement officials, and politicians deem politically acceptable. This raises some fundamental questions about delivering these types of services through a court in the first place.

Examining the problem of offender reentry through the lens of Department of Justice employees brings with it certain limitations. These lawyers traditionally approach problem solving with an emphasis on using the law. Using the criminal justice system and courts to address reentry also speaks to issues of "place." The bulk of these new hybrid courts are going into communities that are low income and communities of color. Race plays a role in the decision to use a court. Groups that are negatively perceived (ex-offenders, the poor) often become targets for more interventionist strategies. If we look at the policies geared toward groups that are considered deserving, intelligent, and productive, we will often find policy tools that emphasize capacity-building techniques. Educational opportunities and resources in the form of incentives are the primary mechanism for delivering services. We use positive inducements to enable those groups to learn about options and opportunities, and we trust that they will take appropriate action on a voluntary basis. But for populations that are negatively construed, policies tend to focus on external controls to make those groups engage in activities that we expect.

In addition, the new iteration of courts as vehicles for service delivery has received some degree of popular support. This raises the obvious question of what other reentry efforts might look like and what components the current effort might contain if other agencies were involved.

K. Had Other Agencies Designed the Model, Would We Have a Court?

The issue of reentry, although raised most recently in the reentry court context by the Department of Justice, has actually been studied by a number of agencies and organizations that deliver services to ex-offenders. The National Institute of Corrections (NIC), as well as organizations consisting of federal probation officers, has also focused its attention on ex-offenders, courts, and corrections. Several states have been experimenting with different models of community corrections to assist parolees with their reintegration into communities. Minnesota, Tennessee, Kansas, and Wyoming are among the states that are encouraging collaborations between the Court Administrative System, court services, Departments of Corrections, and human services departments.[34] Working with the same population, and in many instances the most difficult clients in this population, experts in the field of ex-offender supervision are focusing on mechanisms other than courts to provide badly needed services.

Community corrections are created in their respective states by acts of legislation.[35] Under some of the states' plans they include the county departments responsible for traditional court services. So, rather than creating more courts, they instead act in lieu of court and directly link individuals to services. Community corrections represents a wide range of programs that include diversionary, alternative, and post-institutional programs. In thinking about service delivery and community corrections, some states have begun to recognize that beginning service delivery while individuals are still incarcerated—providing inmate education, drug treatment, and job-skill training— and then connecting these individuals with service providers and case managers at the point of release may be a more effective way to link individuals with services than simply ordering them to appear in reentry court on the date of release.

Unlike those charged in drug court or misdemeanor offenders charged with prostitution or spraying graffiti, who are channeled through a court with judge, prosecutor, and defender cheering them on, individuals who are leaving state prison often have had a very different experience in court and have been skeptical of the courts that were used to send them away. In large part the courts that these parolees were in before they were sent to prison were courts where the "providers" of criminal justice services were of a different race and/or ethnicity than the "consumers" of those services. As a result, the court-as-rehabilitative-mechanism is far from the ideal environment. The government's response to reentry should focus on assessing the wide range of collateral consequences that face formerly incarcerated individuals, including educational, vocational, and housing services that would greatly assist them in their reentry.

L. Conclusions

At least one evaluation of reentry courts has concluded that these courts tend to strengthen linkages among the courts, probation, and other institutional criminal justice players.[36] These types of connections driven by the courts and court administration are not unexpected, nor are they that profound. Where there is greater access to services, the programs tend to be more successful.[37] In the more intractable areas like familial relations and reintegration into the community, however, reentry courts are less than successful.[38] Other findings help to identify the strengths of reentry courts; for example, some of those interviewed suggested that reentry court supervision officers work their cases harder because the judge sees them often and [. . .] these case workers view their clients more holistically."[39] These conclusions are not unexpected.

My own conclusions about reentry courts focus more on their design and articulated purpose. Reentry courts have been described as a mandating a "sentence management" role for judges.[40] This notion of the judge as "reentry manager" was first articulated by Jeremy Travis in his important writing on reentry, *But They All Come Back: Rethinking Prisoner Reentry.*[41] Travis makes a compelling argument about the need for reentry management. He quite correctly observes that we cannot expect the formerly incarcerated to navigate the treacherous waters of reentry without some significant assistance. Judges with the bully pulpit of the bench, coupled with virtually unlimited services, would seem like a good fit. The success of drug courts only underscores what services and courts can accomplish in the pretrial situation. However, in the reentry context Travis arguably puts the management responsibility in the wrong hands. One of the main problems in suggesting that judges serve as some form of sentence manager is their lack of influence in corrections. The system of corrections is the primary body responsible for providing education and vocational training for inmates. Unless we guarantee that those individuals who are incarcerated receive services while in the charge of corrections, judges will be acting as little more than parole agents with a robe in the reentry court.

The concept of the reentry court requires considerable cooperation between corrections and local judiciaries since it requires the coordination of the work of prisons in preparing offenders for release.[42] This type of coordination by and large does not exist. If we attempted to involve courts and corrections agencies actively with various community resources in transitioning offenders back into the community through judicial oversight, new departments and lines of communications would have to be created.

Some scholars have articulated the view that reentry courts are merely another term for parole supervision or simply reflect the age-old paradigms of carrot-and-stick practices of parole supervision.[43] Given the public's loss of confidence in the parole function, a judge may in fact help bolster the appearance of authority and credibility in the supervision of the formerly incarcerated. Reentry courts allow for the public perception that the criminal justice system is simultaneously tough and safe. Absurd press releases such as the one from Senator Joseph Biden's office in Delaware proclaiming that "Biden Introduces Tough New Court Program for Released Inmates" suggest that an inmate is safe enough to release (and has presumably paid his or her debt to society) but needs a court to supervise him or her.[44] Biden, like many politicians, has used the "political cover" that reentry courts provide to look tough on crime while doing little to substantively assist large numbers of the formerly incarcerated. When we look at the limits of the judiciary, the lack of capacity of the courts to assist large numbers of parolees, as well as the lack of influence over the types of vocational and educational programming in prisons, the bench inherently seems to be an inappropriate center of gravity for providing reentry services.

Conclusion

Close examination of this country's retributive criminal justice policy decisions over the last three decades reveals the devastation left in their wake. Each decision taken separately created a host of consequences. But when one steps back and examines the impact of those policies as a whole on individuals and communities, one can see the massive toll on both lives and potential that short-sighted decisions can take.

Americans patted ourselves on the back and declared ourselves victorious in the War on Drugs because we believed we regained control of our streets by sending low-level drug dealers into prisons for extended periods of time. But we failed to prepare for the postwar devastation by ignoring the impact of releasing poor, unskilled, and chemically dependent individuals back into communities. In our zeal to remove "comforts" from prisoners, we withdrew education, drug treatment, and vocational training and never implemented real health care as a central part of the prison system. And when a few notorious failures in the parole system came to the public's attention, we responded by withdrawing political support for the parole function, even though the parole agent offered a way to monitor and facilitate the transition of prisoners back into their communities. The claim of victory was as premature as it was inaccurate.

But there is still time to change that story. Notwithstanding the bleak picture that I have painted thus far, there are a number of new and innovative efforts that should provide hope. The collaboration of government and nonprofit agencies has provided some promising results. The faith community has refocused some of its efforts into street-level activism, moving outside the church walls and into the surrounding communities. Faith-based organizations work with young people and the formerly incarcerated to better reintegrate them into their communities. Resources in these communities are already stretched thin, and the influx of individuals with a variety of needs only serves to further destabilize neighborhoods on the brink of collapse. So as we begin to contemplate solutions, we should be mindful that there may be greater needs in reentry planning for people of color.

Invariably, people of color released from prison return primarily to communities of color. In many African American and Latino communities there are such a large number of people returning from jail and prison that the cycle of incarceration and reentry actually transforms the neighborhoods. Without the requisite social and economic resources, these communities hover at the edge or, as one group of authors puts it, the "tipping point," beyond which incredibly high levels of personal and neighborhood disorganization and chaos occur.[1] These neighborhoods can be affected by what researchers John Hagan and Bill McCarthy term "criminal embeddedness."[2]

Once released from prison, a large number of people of color return to inner-city environments filled with criminogenic risks and threats.[3] Increasingly we see that not only cities and states are affected by the recent incarceration boom, but neighborhoods and communities are directly affected as well. Jeffery Fagan, Valerie West, and Jan Holland, in their important work on the effects of crime and incarceration in New York City, reveal that incarceration is no longer simply a consequence of neighborhood crime but rather may be integral to the ecological dynamics that actually elevate crime in given neighborhoods.[4] Fagan et al. analyze the incarceration rates in New York City and attribute the skyrocketing rates of the last two decades to increased street-level drug enforcement.[5] Overwhelmingly the target of this enforcement has been "mainly minority neighborhoods."[6] Analyzing patterns of incarceration and return, the Fagan et al. research contributes significantly to the conversation about reentry and its implications for communities of color. Their research suggests that "it is not uncommon for certain residents to cycle between the prison system and their communities several times."[7]

The media and popular culture have intentionally or inadvertently conspired to demonize prisons and offenders. As troubling as the television news, dramas, and movies have been in portraying inmates and recently released ex-offenders, some of the worst depictions have been saved for offenders of color. The lens of race and ethnicity in the media only serves to contextualize how difficult the prospect of reentry can be in many real communities. This constant focus on race and crime, along with the dearth of people of color in nonstereotypical roles in prime-time television, only contributes to the continuation of stigma.

Many of us who teach, think, and write about reentry continue to raise the question, What is a successful reentry program?[8] Programs that are successful in some communities find little or no success in others. Reentry initiatives that reap success for a few falter when they are "brought to scale." In addition to these problems, there also exists the issue of who should "own" reentry and where programs should be housed. In the past, many of us have scanned the field for best practices in the hope of replicating these programs. Perhaps one of the key lessons about reentry and our inability to create a "movement" around reentry is that many programs are not conducive to duplication.

A. Coordinating from Pre-Release to Reentry

The reentry process has devolved into a series of events that the prisoner encounters rather than a coordinated release strategy. As a first step toward coordination, one might examine the various points of contact for the offender on the trip from prison to home. Such an examination would be likely to suggest a role for corrections officials.[9] For example, corrections officials might ensure that upon release an offender will receive adequate state-issued identifications. Health care services, drug treatment placements, and employment services should all be connected from facilities to communities. This ensures that the ex-offender has a map of sorts to follow that might prevent interruption of services and might provide transitional support as she begins her reintegration.

Still, the most pressing problems facing the formerly incarcerated are the obstacles that interfere with their ability to make a smooth transition to being productive members of their community. Collaborative efforts should consider that the communities receiving the largest number of ex-offenders are also the communities most often at risk. Overwhelmingly, commentators and statistics have made clear that the primary recipients of prison sentences during the height of the War on Drugs and the war on crime have been African Americans. This high rate of incarceration has placed added stresses on low-income communities of color. The loss of young men who are potential wage earners and supports for families has a detrimental effect on the social organization of poor communities while the young men are in prison. After the individual is released, lack of employment and lack of meaningful connection with the community perpetuate the cycle of poverty and disaffection.[10]

B. Faith-Based Initiatives

Another area of concern in reentry is that of the faith-based initiatives. These initiatives, launched and supported by President George W. Bush, have found some success. At the same time critics have been quick to point out that there are both substantive and philosophical problems with these religious programs. Let's look at the Prison Fellowship Ministries (PFM), founded by former Watergate conspirator Charles Colson. In 1997, then-Texas governor George W. Bush gave PFM control over a wing at the state prison in Richmond, Texas.[11] PFM implemented its InnerChange Freedom Initiative (IFI) curriculum in this unit.[12] The curriculum is nonsecular and focuses on day and night prayer meetings for rehabilitation.[13] Moreover, although the IFI is obligated by law to take inmates of all religions, the teachings are clear that "Jesus is God."[14] One of the supervisors of the IFI program, Tommie Dorsett, confirmed that "about a dozen Muslims have completed the program in Texas, and most but not all converted to Christianity." Charles Colson, the PFM founder, stated that Muslims in IFI prisons "can see that [Christianity] is something far superior" to Islam, which he called "a religion which breeds hatred."[15]

The president's defense of faith-based programs as the answer to reentry has caused many to take a closer look at these programs. The Richmond, Texas, program has a mentorship component where individuals from Houston and Dallas are recruited to come into the prison to mentor soon-to-be-released offenders.[16] Inmates are allowed to work as volunteers five days a week in the community.[17] The IFI program is located only three and a half hours from the inmates' Dallas and Houston homes (closer than most facilities to prisoners' families).[18] The vocational-training offerings are greater in number and availability than at other Texas prisons, and participants are given employment contacts through the network.[19] Finally, there is aftercare for parolees through PFM. ("Aftercare" is the term for the delivery of services after release from custody.)

Faith-based or not, the basic program components are ones that tend to be present in successful reentry. There is the availability of educational classes and vocational training. The ratio of participants to computers in the training program is better than in other prisons and prison programs.[20] Efforts are made to bring families to the prison and to have inmates stay in contact with family members prior to release. There is a focus on employment and intensive support and contacts for jobs. Aftercare and support is provided through the program. This type of programming and support tends to be successful in a secular setting as well. One of the long-term problems with reentry has been the unwillingness of politicians and corrections officials to provide this type of programming on a large scale. Encouraging churches to get involved with prison and after-prison care should be applauded, but it cannot and should not replace the primary governmental responsibility. The IFI program has been attacked as coercive.[21] According to the Texas corrections department there are over six hundred inmate-on-inmate assaults each year. The less violent atmosphere of the IFI wing is desirable for safety's sake.[22] Some participants have suggested that their motivation for participation is to avoid the ongoing racial violence that exists at other Texas Department of Corrections facilities.[23]

Despite the constitutional, political, and programming questions surrounding the current version of the faith-based corrections effort, one of the institutions that has endured over generations in communities of color, particularly the African American community, has been the church. Recognizing the important role that the church can play should not relieve the government of its responsibility to play a role in the reentry process. The church must maintain accountability to the community as a whole and cannot serve the few. Collaboration between government and the faith community raises concerns about the separation between church and state. This tension should be discussed openly and not avoided. In making the decision to embrace the faith community, certain difficult realities must be addressed. Some critics have pointed out that many in the faith community have been biased against gays and lesbians.[24] In addition, the Nation of Islam—which has realized tremendous success in working inside prisons and in a reentry role in the Black community—often cites Whites as the reason for the socioeconomic and moral decay in the African American community.[25] This tenet has made many uncomfortable with allowing the Nation of Islam to participate in these types of reentry collaborations.

Engaging the faith community, policy makers should first obtain solid empirical evidence of the success of faith-based initiatives. One article on government funding of faith community efforts cites two impressive anecdotes on the success of faith-based interventions, involving the 1992 collaboration between the Boston Police Department and the African American clergy in that city.[26] Between 1990 and 1999 Boston saw an 80 percent decline in the homicide rate after an intensive street ministry where the Black clergy walked the most troubled neighborhoods and connected young people with services.[27] Some argue that faith-based organizations are uniquely situated to provide those services to prisoners and the recently released and to remind us all of the importance of rehabilitation and reintegration to a vibrant and caring community.[28] Aside from the constitutional debates, there are some statistics and solid arguments for the effectiveness of faith work.[29] Those arguing the effectiveness of faith outreach say that there are some statistical indications that "faith works."[30] The national Center on Addiction and Substance Abuse (CASA) at Columbia University released a two-year study suggesting that faith has "enormous potential for lowering the risk of substance abuse among teens and adults."[31] The study does point out that faith is effective "when combined with professional treatment."[32]

Other studies show evidence of the success of faith-based services. One such study of New York prisons showed that prisoners who participated in the Prison Fellowship Bible studies program and took part in at least ten classes had a much lower rate of recidivism.[33] A 2001 study found that religious involvement reduced the number of youth-committed serious crimes in high-crime areas.[34] However, even some of those who tout the faith community as an important component in dealing with issues of criminal justice suggest that there is little empirical data to bolster that claim.[35]

Despite the obvious need for more studies on the effectiveness of the faith community in reentry efforts generally, one cannot ignore that in communities of color the church is a long-standing institution that can and should be a part of reentry policy planning and implementation. At its core, reentry is the healing and reestablishment of social relationships. Princeton sociologist Robert Wuthnow emphasizes the importance of paying greater attention to the healing nature of relationships, and writes that churches foster a sense of volunteerism and civic involvement.[36] According to a survey conducted by Wuthnow, 73 percent of the public said that helping people in need was absolutely essential or very important.[37] Black churches have traditionally served multiple functions within their communities, including being places of spiritual sustenance, community service, and political activity.[38]

C. Probation, Parole, and Other Government Responses

Transformation of the parole function back into one that provides some level of counseling and service in addition to law enforcement and surveillance is also necessary. Parole and probation officers, under the watchful eye of the National Institute of Corrections (NIC), the American Correctional Association (ACA), and other state and local organizations, have begun to reevaluate their function in light of the high number of prison returnees and the increasing caseloads that they face. These organizations are coming to recognize that case management systems must differentiate between high-risk and low-risk offenders and that the resulting counseling and coordinating of services and referrals must be appropriate to each population.

Some parole agencies are advocating closer collaboration and cooperation with community-based nonprofits and working with local law enforcement. Others, such as social service providers and a variety of other state, local, and federal agencies, as well as the families of offenders, can help monitor and deliver services that ultimately better utilize correctional costs and more directly address the root causes of criminal activity. This coordination will significantly decrease recidivism and returns to prison for technical violations.

As parole redefines itself, we are also seeing that judges, prosecutors, and defense attorneys are thinking about offenders, and the extent to which their functions are implicated by the large number of returns. In recent years, as part of the community justice movement, the criminal justice system has tried to reinvent itself. Community courts, community prosecutors, and community defenders have all burst onto the scene with new mandates and largely preventive ideologies. While this is good in a number of contexts, we must be careful not to embrace the notion that "the lawyers can solve all of the social ills." This may sound strange coming from a lawyer and law professor, but I have learned in my experiences in the law that we need to be very careful where we engage the machinery of the courts to solve a problem. We often create more problems than we solve with a vast array of "new" courts.

In our haste to use the criminal justice system to solve all the problems of poor communities, we have put into play another dynamic: people feel comforted by the idea that police, judges, and law enforcement will use courts and the not-so-subtle threat of imprisonment to address many of society's problems. With the decrease in the range of social services generally available, we are beginning to create a system that uses courts in poor communities and communities of color to deliver services where they don't exist in other places. One of the factors contributing to the success of drug courts is that they have the conventional trappings of "real courts" with prosecutors, judges, defenders, and procedures. The new hybrid reentry courts do not always come with the components of conventional courts. These "knock-offs" can be dangerous if they do not provide all of the substantive protections of other courts, because they can be perceived as unfair by those who appear before judges and negotiate parole without the protections of counsel.

This should not be interpreted as diminishing the role of traditional courts in reentry. Judges should craft dispositions that take into account the needs of the particular offenders before them. Perhaps with the assistance of the legislature, new, innovative approaches to sentencing can better prepare offenders for the burdens of reintegration.

Prosecutors, as "ministers of justice," must better prepare themselves to think carefully about charges, plea offers, and sentence recommendations as they relate to eventual reentry. Indeed, community prosecutors deeply involved in the communities in which they work can assist in the reentry process. Bringing an awareness of the phases of relapse and recovery and being in contact with treatment and service providers can help community prosecutors fashion more appropriate responses to the reentry needs that individuals present.

Poverty lawyers, civil and criminal, who go to work every day in poor communities and communities of color in this country, may be in the most critical position to address offender reentry. Because we, as educators, lawyers, and researchers, have been slow to devise a specialized curriculum and discipline for reentry, information has been scattered and difficult to obtain. There are few classes for law professionals that focus on reentry[39] or that examine and identify multidisciplinary approaches to reentry. Nonetheless, civil legal services, lawyers, and public defenders should be required to obtain the expertise necessary to serve ex-offenders, who are often a significant part of their client base.

In the same way that lawyers had to grapple with profound changes in the immigration laws in the late 1980s and the 1990s, collateral sanctions and reentry represent critically important areas of the law that must be learned now. The first place that many recently released individuals turn is to civil legal services and to the public defender. For years, the response has been, "We can't help you." Some of that automatic response emerged from the difficult and incoherent policies that had been thrust on civil legal services from the Legal Services Corporation and Congress. Some of it was a result of the compartmentalization of our practice and our approach to providing indigent defense services. Under the strong leadership of the National Legal Aid and Defender Association (NLADA), reentry has become a unifying issue.[40] Civil and criminal indigent legal service providers are beginning to collaborate in training, as well as to share data and referrals. We are also witnessing the establishment of substantive conversations between both lines of service. This has led to recognition of the need to focus on reentry by other service providers and policy makers.

D. Policy Review and Political Change

In addition to changes in community recognition of the reentry problem and changes on the part of probation and parole agencies, perhaps the most important of the changes necessary to address ex-offender reentry is the need for a thorough examination of the panoply of collateral consequences often unrelated to the offenses and the circumstances of incarceration for criminal conduct. Ex-offenders have little or no political clout. Politicians have continued to engage in rhetoric that mandates increasing penalties, else they be cast as "soft of crime." This continued ratcheting up of obstacles to reentry is having the unintended cost and consequence of inhibiting law-abiding conduct by individuals trying to integrate back into the social and political fabric of the community.

The politics of reentry are complicated. Brent Staples, in a September 17, 2004, editorial, makes the case that felon disenfranchisement is a vestige of slavery days.[41] He accurately traces the origins of the concept of felon disenfranchisement back to the Reconstruction period, where the intent was to bar African Americans from voting.[42] Today, those with felony convictions number in excess of fourteen million.[43]

We know from a number of studies that this population is overwhelmingly people of color largely based in urban centers. This demographic has implications for the consideration of the restoration of voting rights. It also should inform how and where we count prisoners and soon-to-be ex-offenders in the census.

The Census Bureau has determined that counting offenders in the prison communities where they are present at the discretion of the relevant state department of corrections and from which they can be moved virtually without any administrative or judicial review has created an unexpected result. Rural, upstate, nonurban jurisdictions that have fewer prisons and generally smaller populations derive real benefits from this count. In addition to high corrections budgets, which pay for the offenders in the "community" in which they are counted, electoral power, political resources, and services are taken from the urban and highly populated and diverse communities and moved to less densely populated communities that tend to be more conservative politically and less diverse.

In economically difficult times, prison becomes an industry. In many rural communities prisons become economic lifelines. Young people aspire to be corrections officers. Surrounding property is developed for correctional employee housing at reasonable rates. Economies thrive from the existence of the prison. In turn, correctional officer unions endorse candidates that push policies resulting in more work and higher pay for these officers. Ironically, young people from the inner cities who have never enjoyed such employment opportunities get caught up in criminal activity and populate these facilities, thereby creating these opportunities for others.

The economics and politics of crime often become the politics of prison and, by default, the politics of race. Studies and some experts suggest that voting and political activity only increase ex-offender participation in community and society, and there is very little reason to bar ex-offenders from the franchise. While acknowledging that reentry is an important issue, courts and elected officials have thus far refused to provide relief. Counting individuals in their custodial place of residence removes them as citizens of their home towns and so depletes the neighborhoods and communities where they will return and from which they will need services. This perpetuates an illogical and unfair political structure.

E. Looking Back at Legislation

Apart from the issue of fundamental fairness in the political arena, there are questions about how we can maximize chances for success in reentry. One observation I have made in the last few years in working in reentry is the difficulty of success without implementation of certain changes based on the lessons we have learned. For example, there is a great deal of work necessary on the local, state, and federal level in reviewing, repealing, and implementing new laws.

At the federal level we must concentrate on addressing the fundamental lack of affordable housing stock in the cities of this country. The effects of *HUD v. Rucker* have been catastrophic. The ensuing housing authority decisions to exclude virtually all of those coming back from prison should be addressed. Although we immediately need transitional housing, it is just that, transitional. We need to create permanent housing for the large numbers of those returning home.

Federal officials should review the employment training, preparation, and incentives used to assist inmates and former inmates to get jobs. More specifically, we should no longer implement antiquated vocational training. Job preparation should be in fields where inmates might actually get work—few are using printing presses and there are no jobs printing license plates. In addition, the federal government should work with states to remove unnecessary licensing restrictions that exist in jobs that inmates are training for in prison. If there is a licensing bar to auto body work in a state where prison vocational training in auto body repair takes place, the ex-offender is doomed from the start and taxpayers are wasting their money. There should be a logical relationship between occupational bars and the committed crimes.

Another area for the federal government to review is that of employer incentives. Tax credits to employers for hiring ex-offenders should not continue if the employer does not retain and promote these employees. Negligent-hiring protections for employers that complete due diligence and make reasoned hiring decisions of ex-offenders should be legislated. Finally, some sort of federal employer's insurance should be implemented to protect employers who hire from the ranks of those reentering communities from prison.

On the state level some of the solutions mirror what should take place on the federal level. A comprehensive review of state restrictions and the administrative interpretations of those restrictions should be completed. Housing and employment are two areas that can make a fundamental difference in the success or failure of reentry. A fair retort is that "affordable housing is a problem for many." While this is true, it is a sound public safety investment to ensure that communities can house those ex-offenders being released to prevent immediate homelessness on their part.

Prison programming, health care, and aftercare should be a part of the pre-release and parole process. A system that is more cohesive and actually thinks in advance about the release process would go a long way toward minimizing some of the problems associated with reentry.

Legislative action on the state and local level that sends a clear message of support for those who hire, house, and help ex-offenders would be welcome. Congress's "Second Chance" legislation, New York State's Article 23-A, and new human rights legislation recently passed in Boston are prime examples of the type of legislation and legislative history that give ex-offenders a chance. Adding attorneys' fees to this type of legislation will enhance its enforceability as well.

I have suggested at various points in this book that while reentry is bad for all who have been incarcerated, it is particularly problematic for people of color. Given that reality, we should create programming and service that is culturally competent.[44] Organizationally, this means that the staff, as part of its recruitment training and promotion, is prepared to work with a diverse population. We must provide staff with literature concerning effective service delivery to racial and ethnic minorities and train staff to recognize how various structural and culture-specific experiences are essential to achieving culturally competent delivery of client services.[45] This education should be included in the broad preparation to provide treatment and service reentry. It is vitally important that culture-specific training, partnering with outside-the-walls nonprofits, and creating content in the policy, protocol, training, and practices underlying traditional correctional interventions be treated as essential.[46]

F. Research

Finally, perhaps the most important observation I can offer about reentry is the need for more research. A number of people have helped to move this conversation forward, but we need to continue to generate more research focused on evidence-based practices. We should think across disciplines and fields. Corrections data, particularly under the leadership of Allen Beck at the Bureau of Justice Statistics, has made a considerable contribution to this effort. Prisoner reentry and a focus on public health and other implications of individuals returning from custody have also opened the door to other important issues. Jail reentry and the unique problems of short stays—or "frequent flyers," as they are called—are fodder for important future research. The implications of this research are monumental, particularly in communities of color. If we are a nation that truly believes that people should get a fresh start when they have paid their debt to society, then we must address the myriad issues in reentry.

Notes

NOTES TO THE INTRODUCTION

1. Jeremy Travis et al., Urban Institute Justice Policy Center, From Prison to Home: The Dimensions and Consequences of Prisoner Reentry (2001), *available at* http://www.urban.org.

2. James P. Lynch & William J. Sabol, *Prisoner Reentry in Perspective*, 3 Crime Pol'y Rep. 15 (Sept. 2001).

3. Jeremy Travis et al., *supra* note 1 ("More than 95 percent of the nation's state prisoners will eventually return to the community.").

4. George W. Bush, State of the Union Address (Jan. 20, 2004), *available at* http://www.whitehouse.gov.

5. E.g., Remarks of the Honorable Janet Reno, Attorney General of the United States, on the Reentry Court Initiative, John Jay College of Criminal Justice (Feb. 10, 2000), *available at* http://www.usdoj.gov.

6. Second Chance Act of 2007 (HR 1593), along with Representatives Cannon, Conyers, Coble, Scott of Virginia, Smith of Texas, Jones of Ohio, Forbes, Schiff, Sensenbrenner, Chabot, Jackson-Lee of Texas, Cummings, Johnson of Georgia, Clarke, and seventy-five other members of Congress. A companion bill (S1060) has been introduced into the Senate, sponsored by Senators Biden, Specter, Brownback, Leahy, Obama, and ten other senators.

7. Gerald Frug, *City Services*, 73 N.Y.U. L. Rev. 23, 73 (citing Jeff Jacoby, *Crime Is Down, So Why Don't We Feel Safer?*, Boston Globe, Aug. 17, 1995, at 19).

NOTES TO CHAPTER 1

1. Laura Ofobike, *An Unforgiving Society Ties Itself in Moral Knots: How Are Ex-Offenders to Carry Their Own Weight?*, Akron Beacon J., Dec. 20, 2005, at B2.

2. Bureau of Justice Statistics, Office of Justice Programs, U.S. Dep't of Justice, Sourcebook of Criminal Justice Statistics 2000 (2001) [hereinafter U.S. Dep't of Justice, Sourcebook 2000]; Bureau of Justice Stat., Office of Justice Programs, U.S. Dep't of Justice, Prisoners in 2001 (2002) [hereinafter U.S. Dep't of Justice, Prisoners in 2001].

3. U.S. DEP'T OF JUSTICE, SOURCEBOOK 2000, *supra* note 2, at 488 tbl.6.2; U.S. DEP'T OF JUSTICE, PRISONERS IN 2001, *supra* note 2, at 11.

4. KATHERINE BECKETT, MAKING CRIME PAY: LAW AND ORDER IN CONTEMPORARY AMERICAN POLITICS 4–5; 14–27 (Oxford Univ. Press 1997) (suggesting that public concern about crime was a product of media attention and political anticrime initiatives, rather than crime rates, and that the resulting crackdown on crime was a socially and politically engineered response); KATHLYN TAYLOR GAUBATZ, CRIME IN THE PUBLIC MIND 5–8 (Univ. of Mich. Press 1995).

5. Anthony C. Thompson, *Stopping the Usual Suspects: Race and the Fourth Amendment,* 74 N.Y.U. L. REV. 956 (1999).

6. JEROME G. MILLER, SEARCH AND DESTROY: AFRICAN AMERICAN MALES IN THE CRIMINAL JUSTICE SYSTEM (Cambridge Univ. Press 1996).

7. Alfred Blumstein, *Incarceration Trends,* 7 U. CHI. L. SCH. ROUNDTABLE 95 (2000); NICHOLAS LEMANN & MICHAEL TONRY, MALIGN NEGLECT: RACE, CRIME, AND PUNISHMENT IN AMERICA (New York: Oxford Univ. Press, 1995); Jeffrey Fagan et al., *Reciprocal Effects of Crime and Incarceration in New York City Neighborhoods,* 30 FORDHAM URB. L.J. 1551 (2003).

8. U.S. SENTENCING COMM'N, REPORT TO CONGRESS: COCAINE AND FEDERAL SENTENCING iv–v (2002); *see also* Laurence A. Benner, *Racial Disparity in Narcotics Search Warrants,* 6 J. GENDER RACE & JUST. 183, 197–98 (2002). A study of drug warrants issued in San Diego County found that in the district that included the city of San Diego, 39 percent of the warrants were for crack cocaine and only 2 percent of the warrant subjects for crack cocaine were White. *Id.* African Americans were 50 percent of the targets for crack cocaine warrants and Hispanics were 48 percent. *Id.*

9. Ann Bailey, *Legal Services, Poor Clients, and the "War on Drugs,"* 24 CLEARINGHOUSE REV. 504 (1990).

10. KATHERYN K. RUSSELL & HERNAN VERA, THE COLOR OF CRIME: RACIAL HOAXES, WHITE FEAR, BLACK PROTECTIONISM, POLICE HARASSMENT, AND OTHER MACROAGGRESSIONS 26–46, 110–29 (Univ. of Chicago Press 1998); David A. Harris, *Profiles in Injustice: Why Racial Profiling Cannot Work,* 21 CRIM. JUST. ETHICS 66 (2002); Samuel R. Gross & Katherine Y. Barnes, *Road Work: Racial Profiling and Drug Interdiction on the Highway,* 101 MICH. L. REV. 651, 655 (2002).

11. DAVID COLE, NO EQUAL JUSTICE: RACE AND CLASS IN THE AMERICAN CRIMINAL JUSTICE SYSTEM 4–5 (New Press 1999).

12. *Id.* at 9.

13. *Id.* at 9–11.

14. MARC MAUER, RACE TO INCARCERATE 124 (New Press 1999).

15. Sharon L. Davies, *Study Habits: Probing Modern Attempts to Assess Minority Offender Disproportionality,* 66 LAW & CONTEMP. PROBS. 17, 19 (2003).

16. Andrew E. Taslitz, *Foreword: The Political Geography of Race Data in the Criminal Justice System,* 66 LAW & CONTEMP. PROBS. 1, 1–3 (2003).

17. Dinesh D'Souza, THE END OF RACISM: PRINCIPLES FOR A MULTICULTURAL SOCIETY 260–61 (Free Press 1995).

18. The 2001 National Household Survey on Drug Abuse found rates of illicit drug use to be 7.4 percent among African Americans, 7.2 percent among Whites, and 6.4 percent among Hispanics. Yet African Americans represent more than 57 percent of those incarcerated for drug offenses in state prisons. *See, e.g.,* SUBSTANCE ABUSE & MENTAL HEALTH SERV. ADMIN., OFFICE OF APPLIED STUDIES, U.S. DEPT OF HEALTH & HUM. SERV., 2001 NATIONAL HOUSEHOLD SURVEY ON DRUG ABUSE: HIGHLIGHTS, *available at* http://www.oas .samhsa.gov. The survey reports that 7.1 percent of the U.S. population twelve years of age or older used an illicit drug during the month immediately prior to the survey interview.

19. *Id.*

20. James A. Inciardi, *Beyond Cocaine: Basuco, Crack, and Other Coca Products,* 14 CONTEMP. DRUG PROBS. 461, 461–92 (1987).

21. John J. Lieb & Claire Sterk-Elifson, *Crack in the Cradle: Social Policy and Reproductive Rights among Crack-Using Females,* 22 CONTEMP. DRUG PROBS. 687, 687–88 (1995).

22. JAMES A. INCIARDI, THE WAR ON DRUGS II: THE CONTINUING EPIC OF HEROIN, COCAINE, CRACK, CRIME, AIDS, AND PUBLIC POLICY (Mayfield Pub. Co. 1992).

23. JIMMIE L. REEVES & RICHARD C. CAMPBELL, CRACKED COVERAGE: TELEVISION NEWS, THE ANTI-COCAINE CRUSADE, AND THE REAGAN LEGACY (Duke Univ. Press 1994).

24. WILLIAM N. ELWOOD, RHETORIC IN IHE WAR ON DRUGS: TRIUMPHS AND TRAGEDIES OF PUBLIC RELATIONS 46–56 (Praeger 1994).

25. David Jernigan & Lori Dorfman, *Visualizing America's Drug Problems: An Ethnographic Content Analysis of Illegal Drug Stories on the Nightly News,* 23 CONTEMP. DRUG PROBS. 169, 192–93 (1996); *see also* STEVEN R. BELENKO, CRACK AND THE EVOLUTION OF ANTI-DRUG POLICY 30 (Greenwood Press 1993).

26. BELENKO, *supra* note 25.

27. RUSSELL & VERA, *supra* note 10, at 3; Erika L. Johnson, *"A Menace to Society": The Use of Criminal Profiles and Its Effects on Black Males,* 38 How. L.J. 629 (1995).

28. Tom Morganthau et al., *Crack and Crime,* NEWSWEEK 16 (1986) *reprinted in* 132 Cong. Rec. 4418 (1986).

29. *Id.*

30. *Newsweek,* in June 1986, stated that "crack should be a leading target for the nation's policymakers." *The Drug Crisis: Crack and Crime,* NEWSWEEK, June 16, 1986, at 3.

31. Leonard M. Baynes, *White Out: The Absence and Stereotyping of People of Color by the Broadcast Networks in Prime Time Entertainment Programming*, 45 ARIZ. L. REV. 293, 304 (2003).

32. Dorothy Roberts, *Crime, Race, and Reproduction,* 67 TUL. L. REV. 1945, 1947 (1993).

33. Bias's death was widely attributed to a crack overdose, spurring Congress to enact a sentencing statute that imposed far higher mandatory penalties for trafficking in crack cocaine than for trafficking in powder cocaine. Post-autopsy reports suggest Bias actually died of powder cocaine poisoning. Judge Louis F. Oberdorfer, *Mandatory Sentencing: One Judge's Perspective—2002,* 40 AM. CRIM. L. REV. 11, 16 (2003).

34. Graham Boyd, *New Voices on the War on Drugs: Collateral Damage in the War on Drugs,* 47 VILL. L. REV. 839, 846–47 (2002); JUST. POLICY INST., CELLBLOCKS OR CLASSROOMS? THE FUNDING OF HIGHER EDUCATION AND CORRECTIONS AND ITS IMPACT ON AFRICAN AMERICAN MEN (2002).

35. Gaubatz, *supra* note 4, at 5–8; ELLIOT CURRIE, CRIME AND PUNISHMENT IN AMERICA (Metropolitan Books 1998) [hereinafter CURRIE, CRIME AND PUNISHMENT]; ELLIOT CURRIE, RECKONING: DRUGS, THE CITIES, AND THE AMERICAN FUTURE 148–212 (Hill and Wang 1993); JEFFREY H. REIMAN, THE RICH GET RICHER AND THE POOR GET PRISON: IDEOLOGY, CLASS, AND CRIMINAL JUSTICE 12–50 (Wiley 1979).

36. STUART A. SCHEINGOLD, THE POLITICS OF LAW AND ORDER: STREET CRIME AND PUBLIC POLICY (Longman 1984); Ted Chiricos, *The Media, Moral Panics, and the Politics of Crime Control, in* THE CRIMINAL JUSTICE SYSTEM: POLITICS AND POLICIES (George F. Cole & Marc G. Gertz eds., 1998).

37. DAVID GARLAND, PUNISHMENT AND MODERN SOCIETY: A STUDY IN SOCIAL THEORY (Univ. of Chicago Press 1990); Ray Surette, *News from Nowhere, Policy to Follow, in* THREE STRIKES AND YOU'RE OUT: VENGEANCE AS PUBLIC POLICY (David Shichor & Dale Sechrist eds., 1996).

38. Beckett, *supra* note 4 (suggesting that public concern about crime was a product of media attention and political anticrime initiatives, rather than crime rates, and that the resulting crackdown on crime was a socially and politically engineered response).

39. David Garland, *The Culture of Control: Crime and Social Order in Contemporary Society* 61-63 (Oxford Univ. Press 2001).

40. MAUER, *supra* note 14 (focusing on overwhelming focus on African Americans in 1990s incarceration boom.

41. Anthony C. Thompson, *It Takes a Community to Prosecute,* 77 NOTRE DAME L. REV. 321, 340 (2002); NAT'L CTR. ON INSTS. AND ALTERNATIVES, THE REAL WAR ON CRIME: THE REPORT OF THE NATIONAL CRIMINAL JUSTICE COMMISSION 115 (Stephen R. Donziger ed., HarperPerennial 1996).

42. Describing the overall trend of the Senate's biannual crime debates, Sen-

ator Howard M. Metzenbaum (D-Ohio) said that "[t]he truth is, we're engaged in a crass political contest about which of us—Democrats or Republicans—hate crime more." Gwen Ifill, *Bush Drops Plan for a Court for Aliens*, N.Y. TIMES, June 21, 1991, at A14; *see also* Gwen Ifill, *Senate's Rule for Its Anti-Crime Bill: The Tougher the Provision, the Better*, N.Y. TIMES, July 8, 1991, at A6.

43. Robert Martinson, *What Works? Questions and Answers about Prison Reform*, 35 PUB. INT. 22, 25 (1974).

44. GWEN A. HOLDEN ET. AL., U.S. DEP'T OF JUST., TREATMENT OPTIONS FOR DRUG-DEPENDENT OFFENDERS: A REVIEW OF THE LITERATURE FOR STATE AND LOCAL DECISION MAKERS 32–33 (1990); D. A. Andrews et al., *Does Correctional Treatment Work? A Clinically Relevant and Psychologically Informed Meta-Analysis*, 28 CRIMINOLOGY 369, 369 (1990).

45. Lawrence M. Friedman & George Fisher, *Governing through Crime, in* THE CRIME CONUNDRUM: ESSAYS IN JUSTICE 171 (Lawrence M. Friedman & George Fisher, eds., Westview Press 1997).

46. Maralee Schwartz & Lloyd Grove, *TV Ads to Depict Gov. Dukakis as Coddling Criminals*, WASHINGTON POST, Sept. 4, 1988, at A14.

47. Sidney Blumenthal, *Willie Horton and the Making of an Election Issue: How the Furlough Factor Became a Stratagem of the Bush Forces*, WASH. POST, Oct. 28, 1988, at D1. "Then the announcer [asks]: '[w]hich candidate for president gave weekend passes to first-degree murderers who are not even eligible for parole?' On one side was a picture of a smiling Bush, bathed in a golden sunny glow. On the other was a picture of a disheveled, double-chinned swarthy Dukakis. His picture came forward in answer to the question. Finally, [the announcer asks]: 'Which candidate can you really trust to be tough on crime?' Bush's picture came forward." *Id.*

48. Thomas B. Rosensteil, *Regional Advertising Proves Tough on Dukakis*, L.A. TIMES, Oct. 28, 1988, at 16; *see* Susan Estrich, *The Politics of Race*, WASH. POST, Apr. 23, 1989, at W20.

49. Craig Reinarman & Harry G. Levine, *Crack in Context: Politics and Media in the Making of a Drug Scare*, 16 CONTEMP. DRUG PROBS. 535, 556 (1989).

50. Oberdorfer, *supra* note 33, at 16 ("There is no material pharmacological difference between crack cocaine or powder cocaine; the primary difference is that crack can be broken into bits and sold relatively cheaply on the street, while powder is usually bought and sold more discreetly indoors.").

51. RANDALL KENNEDY, RACE, CRIME, AND THE LAW 370–72 (Pantheon Books 1997). Kennedy notes that President Clinton and Congress rejected reducing the sentencing disparity between crack and powder cocaine largely because of the message that doing so would send. *Id.* at 381. It should be noted that African American members of Congress did eventually shift their position

on crack. *See* Joe Davidson, *The Drug War's Color Line: Black Leaders Shift Stance on Sentencing,* NATION, Sept. 20, 1999, at 42.

52. MAUER, *supra* note 14, at 152.

53. *Id.* at 61.

54. *Id.* Until this opinion judges had not taken on the federal guidelines so directly as racially bias; however, since *Clary* a number of judges have attacked the guidelines on both race and fairness grounds.

55. United States v. Clary, 846 F. Supp. 768, 776 (E.D. Mo.), *rev'd,* 34 F.3d 709 (8th Cir. 1994).

56. 34 F.3d 709 (8th Cir. 1994).

57. David A. Sklansky, *Cocaine, Race, and Equal Protection,* 47 STAN. L. REV. 183 (1995).

58. *Id.* at 1308. *See* Paul Butler, *By Any Means Necessary: Using Violence and Subversion to Change Unjust Law,* 50 U.C.L.A. L. REV. 721, 735.

59. *Inside Politics* (CNN television broadcast Jan. 18, 2001), *available at* http://www.cnn.com.

60. Neil A. Lewis, *Justice Department Opposes Lower Jail Terms for Crack,* N.Y. TIMES, Mar. 20, 2002, at A24 (quoting U.S. Deputy Attorney General Larry D. Thompson).

61. *Federal Sentencing Issues Discussed at ABA Hearings,* CRIM. L. REP., Nov. 19, 2003, at 127.

62. Martin Finucane, *Supreme Court Justice Says Judges Need More Flexibility,* WASH. POST, Sept. 22, 2003. Justice Breyer, as a member of the first Sentencing Commission, is considered the justice with the deepest expertise in sentencing issues.

63. Mark Sauer, *Drug Law Reform Campaign Flexes Its Muscles,* SAN DIEGO UNION TRIB., Nov. 14, 2000, at E1; *Shadow Conventions: Rep. Maxine Waters Calls for Resignation of Drug Czar General Barry McCaffrey,* U.S. NEWSWIRE, Aug. 15, 2000; *U.S. Drug Laws Called Racist,* ORLANDO SENTINEL, Aug. 23, 2001, at A13.

64. Drug arrests in the United States rose from approximately one million in 1991 to nearly 1.6 million in 2000. FEDERAL BUREAU OF INVESTIGATIONS, U.S. DEP'T. OF JUSTICE, UNIFORM CRIME REPORTS: CRIME IN THE UNITED STATES, 2001 216 (2001).

65. Ironically, the gap in vocal representation led to political commentary from what had once been seen as part of the problem—hip hop culture. Hip hop artists increasingly began to dabble in political commentary about a range of criminal justice matters, from drug sweeps to overincarceration to the September 11th attack on the World Trade Center.

66. EDWARD C. BANFIELD, THE UNHEAVENLY CITY: THE NATURE AND FUTURE OF OUR URBAN CRISIS 53–54 (Little, Brown 1970); GERALD D. SUTTLES,

SOCIAL ORDER OF THE SLUM: ETHNICITY AND TERRITORY IN THE INNER CITY 3–12 (Univ. of Chicago Press 1968).

67. THOMAS BYRNE EDSALL & MARY D. EDSALL, CHAIN REACTION: THE IMPACT OF RACE, RIGHTS, AND TAXES ON AMERICAN POLITICS 231 (Norton 1991).

68. ANDREW HACKER, TWO NATIONS, BLACK AND WHITE: SEPARATE, HOSTILE, AND UNEQUAL 225 (Scribners 1992).

69. *Id.*

70. *Id.*

71. Thomas Byrne Edsall & Mary D. Edsall, *Race,* ATLANTIC MONTHLY, May 1991, at 53.

72. BECKETT, *supra* note 4, at 107.

73. WILLIAM JULIUS WILSON, THE TRULY DISADVANTAGED: THE INNER CITY, THE UNDERCLASS, AND PUBLIC POLICY 100–102 (Univ. of Chicago Press 1987).

74. CHRISTOPHER JENCKS & PAUL E. PETERSON, THE URBAN UNDERCLASS (Brookings Institution 1991); Michael B. Katz, *The Urban "Underclass" as a Metaphor of Social Transformation, in* THE "UNDERCLASS" DEBATE: VIEWS FROM HISTORY 3 (Michael B. Katz ed., Princeton Univ. Press 1993).

75. Robert J. Sampson & Janet L. Lauritsen, *Racial and Ethnic Disparities in Crime and Criminal Justice in the United States,* 21 CRIME & JUST. 311, 338 (1997).

76. ELLIS COSE, THE RAGE OF A PRIVILEGED CLASS 107 (HarperCollins 1993).

77. KENT GREENAWALT, DISCRIMINATION AND REVERSE DISCRIMINATION 10–11 (Knopf 1983).

78. Bruce Western, *The Impact of Incarceration on Wage Mobility and Inequality,* 67 AM. SOC. REV. 526 (2002).

79. *Id.*

80. Eric Rasmussen, *Stigma and Self-Fulfilling Expectations of Criminality,* 39 J. L. & ECON. 519, 540 (1996).

81. John Hagan & Ronit Dinovitzer, *Collateral Consequences of Imprisonment for Children, Communities, and Prisoners in Prisons,* 26 CRIME & JUST. 121, 136–37 (1999).

82. John H. Laub & Robert J. Sampson, *Long-Term Effect of Punitive Discipline, in* COERCION AND PUNISHMENT IN LONG-TERM PERSPECTIVE 20 (Joan McCord ed., Cambridge Univ. Press 1995).

83. For a discussion of the consequences of stigma on families of prisoners, see Donald Braman, *Families and Incarceration, in* INVISIBLE PUNISHMENT: THE COLLATERAL CONSEQUENCES OF MASS IMPRISONMENT 129–34 (Marc Mauer & Meda Chesney-Lind eds., New Press 2002).

84. ROBERT J SAMPSON & JOHN H. LAUB, CRIME IN THE MAKING: PATHWAYS AND TURNING POINTS THROUGH LIFE 143 (Harvard Univ. Press 1993); *see also*

Hagan & Dinovitzer, *supra* note 81, at 126–28 (noting that "the stigma of imprisonment risks not only making parents into outlaws, but their children as well").

85. Todd Clear & Dina Rose, *Incarceration, Reentry, and Social Capital: Social Networks in the Balance, in* PRISONERS ONCE REMOVED: THE IMPACT OF INCARCERATION AND REENTRY ON CHILDREN, FAMILIES, AND COMMUNITIES 35(Jeremy Travis & Michelle Waul eds., Urban Institute Press 2003).

86. CURRIE, CRIME AND PUNISHMENT, *supra* note 35, at 33. Combining the 762,000 Black men counted in the official 1995 unemployment figures with 511,000 in state or federal prison raises the unemployment rate for Black men from under 11 percent to almost 18 percent—an increase of two-thirds. *See also* Bruce Western et al., THE LABOR MARKET CONSEQUENCES OF INCARCERATION 47 (Princeton Univ., Indus. Relations Section 2001).

87. Devah Pager, *The Mark of a Criminal Record,* 108 AM. J. SOC. 937 (2003).

88. Anthony C. Thompson, *Stopping the Usual Suspects: Race and the Fourth Amendment,* 74 N.Y.U. L. REV. 956, 983 (1999).

89. Jerome S. Bruner, Jacqueline J. Goodnow, and George A. Austin discuss the process by which human beings group the world of particulars into ordered classes and categories. *See generally* JEROME S. BRUNER ET AL., A STUDY OF THINKING (Transaction Publishers 1986) (1956).

90. Renato Tagiuri, *Person Perception, in* THE HANDBOOK OF SOCIAL PSYCHOLOGY 395, 422 (Gardner Linzey & Elliot Aronson eds., 2d ed. 1969).

91. JOHN R. ANDERSON, COGNITIVE PSYCHOLOGY AND ITS IMPLICATIONS 132–33 (W.H. Freeman 1980).

92. *Id.* at 133.

93. MARY ELLEN GOODMAN, RACE AWARENESS IN YOUNG CHILDREN 19–21 (Addison-Wesley Press 1952); *see also* William A. Barnard & Mark S. Benn, *Belief Congruence and Prejudice Reduction in an Interracial Contact Setting,* 128 J. SOC. PSYCH. 125, 126 (1988).

94. Shelley E. Taylor, *A Categorization Approach to Stereotyping, in* COGNITIVE PROCESSES IN STEREOTYPING AND INTERGROUP BEHAVIOR 83, 84–86 (David Hamilton ed., L. Erlbaum Associates 1981).

95. GORDON W. ALLPORT, THE NATURE OF PREJUDICE 23 (Addison-Wesley 1954).

96. Anthony G. Amsterdam & Jerome S. Bruner, MINDING THE LAW 13 (Harvard Univ. Press 2000).

97. *Id.* at 7–8; *see also* ALLPORT, *supra* note 95, at 23.

98. SUSAN T. FISKE & SHELLEY E. TAYLOR, SOCIAL COGNITION 98 (McGraw-Hill 2d ed. 1991); Hazel Markus, *Self-Schemata and Processing Information about the Self,* 35 J. PERSONALITY AND SOC. PSYCH 63 (1977).

99. FISKE & TAYLOR, *supra* note 98, at 98.

100. RUSSELL & VERA, *supra* note 10, at xiii–xiv (noting that images of the criminality of other racial and ethnic groups have tended to be crime specific rather than, as for African Americans, general presumptions of innate criminality in all circumstances). *But see* Kevin R. Johnson, *The Case for African-American and Latina/o Cooperation in Challenging Racial Profiling in Law Enforcement*, 55 FLA. L. REV. 341, 346–47 (2003) (noting that both African Americans and Latinos are "demonized as criminals, drug dealers, and gang members, are the most likely victims of police brutality, and are disproportionately represented in the prison population").

101. Social comparison and social identity describe the process of comparing one's own group. MICHAEL A. HOGG, THE SOCIAL PSYCHOLOGY OF GROUP COHESIVENESS: FROM ATTRACTION TO SOCIAL IDENTITY 90 (N.Y.U. Press 1992).

102. Barnard & Benn, *supra* note 93, at 126.

103. Self-esteem maintenance, also known as ego maintenance, occurs when an actor's discrimination itself enhances the actor's own ego. *See* James Sidanius et al., *A Comparison of Symbolic Racism Theory and Social Dominance Theory: Explanations for Racial Policy Attitudes*, 132 J. SOC. PSYCH. 377, 380 (1992).

104. Jody D. Armour, *Race Ipsa Loquitur: Of Reasonable Racists, Intelligent Bayesians, and Involuntary Negrophobes*, 46 STAN. L. REV. 781, 787 (1994).

105. Desiree A. Kennedy, *Consumer Discrimination: The Limitations of Federal Civil Rights Protection*, 66 MO. L. REV. 275 (2001).

106. Edwin H. Sutherland, *White-Collar Criminality*, 5 AM. SOC. REV. 1, 1 (1940) (discussing crimes committed by those in upper- or white-collar class versus crimes committed by those in lower classes).

107. Edwin H. Sutherland, *Is "White-Collar Crime" Crime?*, 10 AM. SOC. REV. 132, 137–39 (1945).

108. Elizabeth Szockyj, *Imprisoning White-Collar Criminals?*, 23 S. ILL. U. L.J. 485, 486–87 (1999) (noting that not only do definitions of "white-collar crime" vary, but harm inflicted by white-collar crime varies as well in that it may be financial, physical, or social).

109. STANTON WHEELER ET AL., SITTING IN JUDGMENT: THE SENTENCING OF WHITE-COLLAR CRIMINALS (Yale Univ. Press 1988).

110. *Id.* at 102.

111. Michelle S. Jacobs, *Loyalty's Reward: A Felony Conviction: Recent Prosecutions of High-Status Female Offenders*, 33 FORDHAM URB. L.J. 843, 857 (2006).

112. *Id.* at 859 ("During the renegotiation of the second plea, it was widely reported that Ms. Fastow was interested in a plea that would allow her children to stay at home with one parent while the other was incarcerated, rather than running the risk that both parents would be incarcerated at the same time.").

113. *Wife of Former Enron CFO Likely to Face Trial*, Houston Chron., Apr. 8, 2004, at A1, *available at* 2004 WLNR 12368141.

114. Greg Farrell, *Fastow's Wife Gets Reduced Charge; Will Plead Guilty to Misdemeanor*, USA Today, Apr. 30, 2004, at B1 (comments by Columbia University securities expert Jack Coffee), *available at* 2004 WLNR 6243138.

NOTES TO CHAPTER 2

1. Tania Ralli, *Who's a Looter? In Storm's Aftermath, Pictures Kick Up a Different Kind of Tempest*, N.Y. Times, September 5, 2005, at C6.

2. George Gerbner & Larry Gross, *The Scary World of TV's Heavy Viewer*, Psychol. Today, April 1976, at 89.

3. George Gerbner, The Killing Screens: Media and the Culture of Violence (Media Education Foundation 1994); J. M. Hough & Julian Roberts, Attitudes to Punishment: Findings from the British Crime Survey 179 (Home Office Research, Development and Statistics Directorate 1998).

4. P. T. Bryant & E. Morris, *What Does the Public Really Think?*, 60 Corrections Today 26, 26–79 (1998).

5. *Id.*

6. Sarah Eschholz, Brenda Sims Blackwell, Marc Gertz, & Ted Chiricos, *Race and Attitudes toward the Police: Assessing the Effects of Watching "Reality" Police Programs*, 30 J. Crim. Just. 327, 328 (2002).

7. Gray Cavender & Lisa Bond-Maupin, *Fear and Loathing on Reality Television: An Analysis of* America's Most Wanted *and* Unsolved Mysteries, 63 Soc. Inquiry, 305–17 (1993).

8. P. Kooistra, J. Mahoney, & S. Westervelt, *The World of Crime according to* Cops, *in* Entertaining Crime 141-58 (M. Fishman & G. Cavender eds. Aldine De Gruyter 1988).

9. Eschholz et al., *supra* note 6, at 329.

10. Hough & Roberts, *supra* note 3, at 289.

11. *Id.*

12. *Id.*

13. Kathleen Daly, *Celebrated Crime Cases and the Public's Imagination: From Bad Press to Bad Policy?*, 28 Austl. & N.Z. J. Criminology 6 (1995).

14. Michael Welch, Lisa Weber, & Walter Edwards, *"All the News That's Fit to Print": A Content Analysis of the Correctional Debate in the New York Times*, 80 Prison J. 245, 245–64 (2000).

15. *Id.*

16. *Id.*

17. *Id.*

18. *Id.*

19. *Id.* at 253.

20. RICHARD V. ERICSON ET AL., REPRESENTING ORDER: CRIME, LAW, AND JUSTICE IN THE NEWS MEDIA 244–47 (Univ. of Toronto Press 1991) (discussing a study showing that stories about violence against the person constitute at least one-third of popular newspaper, television, and radio stories); PHILIP SCHLESINGER & HOWARD TUMBER, REPORTING CRIME: THE MEDIA POLITICS OF CRIMINAL JUSTICE 140 (1994).

21. Franklin Gilliam Jr., S. Iyengar, A. Simon, & O. Wright, *Crime in Black and White: The Violent, Scary World of Local News* 1 3 HARV. INT'L J. OF PRESS/POLITICS 6, 6-23 (1996).

22. Robert Entman, *Blacks in the News: Television, Modern Racism, and Cultural Change,* 69 JOURNALISM Q. 341 (1992).

23. JULIAN V. ROBERTS & LORETTA J. STALANS, PUBLIC OPINION, CRIME, AND CRIMINAL JUSTICE (Westview Press 1997).

24. BUREAU OF JUSTICE STATISTICS, U.S. DEP'T OF JUSTICE, SERIOUS VIOLENT CRIME VICTIMIZATION 128–29 tbl.2.47 1988, *available at* http://www.ojp.usdoj.gov.

25. *Id.* at 134–35 tbl.2.50 (indicating attitudes people have concerning the severity of the courts in their area). While only 5 percent of those surveyed in 1996 believed that courts in their area dealt "too harshly" with criminals, and 11 percent said that criminals were treated "just right," 78 percent believed that courts in their area treated criminals "not harshly enough."

26. Sean O'Sullivan, *Representations of Prison in Nineties Hollywood Cinema: From* Con Air *to* The Shawshank Redemption, 40 HOWARD J. 317 (2001).

27. Internet Movie Database, http://www.imdb.com.

28. Stephen King, *Rita Hayworth and the Shawshank Redemption, in* DIFFERENT SEASONS 1 (Viking Press 1982).

29. Roger Ebert, *Review of* The Shawshank Redemption, CHICAGO SUN-TIMES, Oct. 17, 1999, at 5 ("Behind bars, Red is king. He's the prison fixer, able to get you a pack of cigarettes, a little rock pick or a Rita Hayworth poster. On the outside, he has no status or identity. We've already seen what happened to the old librarian (James Whitmore), lonely and adrift in freedom.").

30. Ebert, *supra* note 29, at 5 ("Mostly the film is an allegory about holding onto a sense of personal worth, despite everything.").

31. *Id.*

32. Janet Maslin, Film Review: *Prison Tale by Stephen King Told Gently, Believe It or Not,* N.Y. TIMES, Sept. 23, 1994, at C3.

33. Gary Levin, *The Inside Story on HBO's* Oz. *True to Form, Its Final Season Won't Be Pretty, Either,* USA TODAY, Jan. 2, 2003,at 8D.

34. *Id.*

35. *Id.*

36. Rate it All, The Opinion Network, *available at* http://www.rateitall.com. Examples of perceptions of *Oz:* "Well written, superbly acted. Raw, gritty, and

brutally honest. One of the best dramas on TV." "I've only had the pleasure of seeing two episodes of *Oz* but those two episodes made me look at prisons and prisoners in an entirely different light. *Oz* is an extremely powerful show, set in a prison where every day is a struggle to survive." "Excellent content. I assume that it's true to life, which makes it even more interesting." "Makes you wonder if it's really like that in jail."

37. Not all viewers were so impressed: "For a show that packages itself as a kind of hyper-real, socially relevant statement of sorts, it is almost laughably unbelievable. The inmates simply have too much access to drugs, weapons, and unsupervised areas in this supposedly high security prison. Similarly, is there a penal colony anywhere in the world where so many people are murdered so often?" Rate It All, The Opinion Network, *available at* http://www.rateitall.com.

38. Julian V. Roberts & Mike Hough, *The State of Prisons: Exploring Public Knowledge and Opinion*, 44 HOWARD J. 286 (2005). In a poll of knowledge of prisons in Britain, 74 percent of respondents said they knew "a great deal/fair amount" about the police, compared to 30 percent of respondents claiming the same level of knowledge of prisons. Seven percent claimed to know "hardly anything/nothing at all" about the police, while 31 percent claimed to know nothing at all of prisons. The numbers are even lower for probation service. I did not see a similar survey for the United States.

39. *Id.*

40. D. Gibbons, *Who Knows What about Corrections?*, 9 CRIME AND DELINQUENCY 137, 137–44 (1963).

41. Alexis Miller, Richard Tewksbury, & Christopher Hensley, *College Students' Perceptions of Crime, Prison, and Prisoners*, 17 CRIM. JUST. STUD. J. 311, 314 (2004).

42. *Id.*

43. *Id.*

44. B. Applegate, *Penal Austerity: Perceived Utility, Desert, and Public Attitudes toward Prison Amenities*, 25 AM. J. OF CRIM. JUST. 253-68 (2001).

45. *Id.*, citing FLA. DEP'T OF CORRECTIONS, CORRECTIONS IN FLORIDA: WHAT THE PUBLIC THINKS: RESULTS OF A SURVEY OF FLORIDIANS (Fla. Dep't of Corrections 1997).

46. DOBLE RESEARCH ASSOCIATES, CRIME AND CORRECTIONS: THE VIEWS OF THE PEOPLE OF OKLAHOMA (Doble Research Assocs. 1995).

47. Steve Farkas, *Pennsylvanians Prefer Alternatives to Prison*, *in* SENTENCING REFORM IN OVERCROWDED TIMES: A COMPARATIVE PERSPECTIVE (Michael H. Tonry & Kathleen Hatlestad eds., Oxford Univ. Press 1997).

48. Belden, Russonello, and Stewart, RESEARCH AND COMMUNICATIONS REPORT OF EXISTING PUBLIC OPINION DATA ON JUVENILE JUSTICE ISSUES (1997).

49. Later on, in looking at how politicians have used code words for race,

this is a group that is often described as "lazy or shiftless" and is also often suggestive of race.

50. Francis T. Cullen, Bonnie S. Fisher, & Brandon K. Applegate, *Public Opinion about Punishment and Corrections*, 27 CRIME & JUST. 1, 31 (2000); DOBLE RESEARCH ASSOCS., CRIME AND CORRECTIONS: THE VIEWS OF THE PEOPLE OF NEW HAMPSHIRE (Doble Research Assocs. 1998).

51. DOBLE RESEARCH ASSOCIATES, CRIME AND CORRECTIONS: THE VIEWS OF THE PEOPLE OF NORTH CAROLINA (Doble Research Assocs. 1995).

52. DEP'T OF CORRECTIONS, CORRECTIONS IN FLORIDA: WHAT THE PUBLIC THINKS: RESULTS OF A SURVEY OF FLORIDIANS (Fla. Dep't of Corrections 1997).

53. *Id.*

54. Benjamin D. Steiner, William J. Bowers, & Austin Sarat, *Folk Knowledge as Legal Action: Death Penalty Judgments and the Tenet of Early Release in a Culture of Mistrust and Punitiveness*, 33 LAW & SOC'Y REV. 461 (1999); see also Stephen P. Garvey, Sheri Lynn Johnson, & Paul Marcus, *Correcting Deadly Confusion: Responding to Jury Inquiries in Capital Cases*, 85 CORNELL L. REV. 627 (2000).

55. Julian V. Roberts & Anthony N. Doob, *News Media Influences on Public Views of Sentencing*, 14 LAW & HUM. BEHAV. 451, 454 (1990) (giving examples of several studies demonstrating the public's misconceptions regarding prison sentencing and parole); Tom R. Tyler, *Public Mistrust of the Law: A Political Perspective*, 66 U. CIN. L. REV. 847, 849 (1998) (analyzing dissatisfaction with the criminal justice system based on a widespread belief that sentences are too lenient).

56. Kathleen Hall Jamieson's commentary on the Bush campaign's use of the Willie Horton advertisements during the presidential campaign of 1988 is especially illustrative of this point. KATHLEEN HALL JAMIESON, DIRTY POLITICS: DECEPTION, DISTRACTION, AND DEMOCRACY (Oxford Univ. Press 1992).

57. JAMIESON, *supra* note 56, at 31–33.

58. DAVID C. ANDERSON, CRIME AND THE POLITICS OF HYSTERIA: HOW THE WILLIE HORTON STORY CHANGED AMERICAN JUSTICE 217 (Times Books 1995).

59. TALI MENDELBERG, THE RACE CARD: CAMPAIGN STRATEGY, IMPLICIT MESSAGES, AND THE NORM OF EQUALITY 178 (Princeton Univ. Press 2001).

60. CHARLES E. LINDBLOM & DAVID K. COHEN, USABLE KNOWLEDGE: SOCIAL SCIENCE AND SOCIAL PROBLEM SOLVING (Yale Univ. Press 1979).

61. *Id.* at 45.

62. Howard Kurtz, *A Guilty Verdict on Crime, Race Bias: TV Viewers Often Assume Suspects Are Black*, WASH. POST, Apr. 28, 1997, at C1 (defining the assumption whereby Whites "automatically associate a crime story with a non-White guy").

63. ANDREW HACKER, TWO NATIONS: BLACK AND WHITE, SEPARATE, HOSTILE, AND UNEQUAL 181 (Scribners 1992).

64. Martin Gilens, *Race and Poverty in America: Public Misperceptions and the American News Media,* 60 PUB. OPINION Q. 515, 516, 520, 527, 531 (1996); Marlene Cimons, *Myths Color Views on Who Receives Aid,* CHICAGO SUN-TIMES, Jan. 29, 1995, at 24 (opining that most Americans believe that the average AFDC recipient is a Black female when in reality it is a rural White person).

65. The priming effect of this standard crime script is so powerful that in video experiments that made no reference to a perpetrator, 60 percent of respondents erroneously recalled seeing a perpetrator, and in 70 percent of those cases, they identified the perpetrator as Black. *See* Franklin D. Gilliam Jr. & Shanto Iyengar, *Prime Suspects: The Influence of Local Television News on the Viewing Public,* 44 AM. J. POL. SCI. 560, 564 (2000).

66. Franklin D. Gilliam Jr. et al., *Crime in Black and White: The Violent, Scary World of Local News,* 1 HARV. INT'L J. PRESS/POL. 6, 8 (1996); Lori Dorfman & Vincent Schiraldi, *Off Balance: Youth, Race, and Crime in the News,* Apr. 10, 2004, *available at* http://www.buildingblocksforyouth.org. The most sophisticated analysis of juvenile law media coverage disclosed that (1) the press reports juvenile crime out of proportion to its actual occurrence; (2) violent crime, although representing only 22-24 percent of juvenile crime from 1988 to 1997, dominates media coverage; (3) the media present crimes without an adequate contextual base for understanding why the crime occurred; (4) press coverage unduly connects race and crime; and (5) juveniles are rarely covered by the news other than to report on their violent criminal acts.

67. ROBERTS & STALANS, *supra* note 23, at 4.

68. REID HASTIE & ROBYN M. DAWES, RATIONAL CHOICE IN AN UNCERTAIN WORLD: THE PSYCHOLOGY OF JUDGMENT AND DECISION MAKING 80-81 (Sage 2001).

69. Meda Chesney-Lind, *Girls in Gangs: Violent Equality or Media Hype,* EXTRA!, Mar.—Apr. 1994, at 12.

70. Lori Dorfman & Vincent Schiraldi, *Off Balance: Youth, Race, & Crime in the News,* J. POLICY INST., *available at* http://www.buildingblocksforyouth .org.

71. *Id.*

72. *Id.*

73. Barry C. Feld, *The Transformation of the Juvenile Court, Part II: Race and the "Crack Down" on Youth Crime,* 84 MINN. L. REV. 327, 345, 361 (1999). Feld ties the origin of the "get tough" policies of the new punitive juvenile justice system (including its expanded transfer or waiver mechanisms, its use of juvenile adjudications for adult sentencing enhancements, and its eroded confidentiality protections) to the unrest of the 1960s, including civil rights un-

rest, when fear of crime became a popular concern and crime became an explicit political issue.

74. MENDELBERG, *supra* note 59, at 135–65; JAMIESON, *supra* note 57.

NOTES TO CHAPTER 3

1. T. J. Banes, "Female Offenders Get Touch of Home," INDIANAPOLIS STAR, June 21, 2004, at 1B.

2. Tina Greigo, *Women Seize Hope from Miracles*, ROCKY MOUNTAIN NEWS, July 3, 2004, at 6A, *available at* 2004 WLNR 1259171.

3. Monica Pa, *Towards a Feminist Theory of Violence*, 9 U. CHI. L. SCH. ROUNDTABLE 45, 45–48 (2002).[o]

4. Myrna S. Raeder, *Gender and Sentencing: Single Moms, Battered Women, and Other Sex-Based Anomalies in the Gender-Free World of the Federal Sentencing Guidelines*, 20 PEPP. L. REV. 905, 922–24 (1993) (citing Meda Chesney-Lind, *Patriarchy, Prisons, and Jails: A Critical Look at Trends in Women's Incarceration*, 71 PRISON J. 51, 57–58 (1991).

5. Leslie Acoca & Myrna S. Raeder, *Severing Family Ties: The Plight of Nonviolent Female Offenders and Their Children*, 11 STAN. L. & POLICY REV. 133, 134 (1999).

6. U.S. CENSUS BUREAU, HISTORY OF POVERTY TABLES: POVERTY OF PEOPLE BY SEX, 1966 TO 2003, tbl.7, *available at* http://www.census.gov.

7. U.S. CENSUS BUREAU, HISTORY OF POVERTY TABLES: POVERTY STATUS OF PEOPLE, BY AGES, RACE, AND HISPANIC ORIGIN, 1959 TO 2003, tbl.3, *available at* http://www.census.gov.

8. JOAN PETERSILIA, WHEN PRISONERS COME HOME: PAROLE AND PRISONER REENTRY 26 (Oxford Univ. Press 2003).

9. MEDA CHESNEY-LIND, CRITICAL CRIMINOLOGY: TOWARD A FEMINIST PRAXIS, *available at* http://critcrim.org.

10. *Id.*

11. CLARICE D. FEINMAN, WOMEN IN THE CRIMINAL JUSTICE SYSTEM 28 (2d ed. 1986).

12. Matthew Zingraff & Randall Thomson, *Differential Sentencing of Women and Men in the U.S.A.*, 12 INT'L J. SOC. L. 401, 410 (1984).

13. Boni Brewer, *Incarceration of Pregnant Women Doubles at Jail*, VALLEY TIMES, June 17, 1990, at A1.

14. Nicole S. Mauskopf, Note: *Reaching beyond the Bars: An Analysis of Prison Nurseries*, 5 CARDOZO WOMEN'S L.J. 102 (1998).

15. ADRIAN NICOLE LEBLANC, RANDOM FAMILY: LOVE, DRUGS, TROUBLE, AND COMING OF AGE IN THE BRONX 118–19 (Scribners 2003).

16. Eda Katherine Tinto, *The Role of Gender and Relationship in Reforming the Rockefeller Drug Laws*, 76 N.Y.U. L. REV. 906 (2001).

17. Shimica Gaskins, *"Women of Circumstance": The Effects of Mandatory Minimum Sentencing on Women Minimally Involved in Drug Crimes*, 41 Am. Crim. L. Rev. 1533, 1534 (2004).

18. *Id.*

19. Stephanie R. Bush Baskette, *The War on Drugs as a War against Black Women, in* Crime Control and Women: Feminist Implications of Criminal Justice Policy 113 (Susan Miller ed., Sage Publications 1998).

20. Joan Petersilia, When Prisoners Come Home: Parole and Prisoner Reentry 49 (Oxford Univ. Press 2003).

21. The Henry J. Kaiser Family Found., Racial and Ethnic Disparities in Women's Health Coverage and Access to Care: Findings from the 2001 Kaiser Women's Health Survey (2004) [hereinafter Kaiser Family Found., Racial and Ethnic Disparities].

22. *Id.*

23. Jacobs Inst. of Women's Health & the Henry J. Kaiser Family Found., Women's Health Data Book: A Profile of Women's Health in the United States (D. Mirsa ed., 3d ed. 2001).

24. *Id.*; Kaiser Family Found., Racial and Ethnic Disparities, *supra* note 21.

25. Paula M. Ditton, Office of Just. Programs, U.S. Dep't of Just., NCJ 174463, Mental Health and Treatment of Inmates and Probationers (1999), *available at* http://www.ojp.usdoj.gov/bjs/pub/pdf/mhtip.pdf (last visited July 29, 2007).

26. Bureau of Just. Stat., Office of Just. Programs, U.S. Dep't. of Just., Criminal Offenders Statistics: Women Offenders, *available at* http://www.ojp.usdoj.gov/bjs/crimoff.htm#women (last visited July 29, 2007).

27. Christopher J. Mumola, Incarcerated Parents and their Children 1 (U.S. Dep't of Just., Office of Just. Programs, Bureau of Just. Stats. 2000), *reprinted in* Amy E. Hirsch, Every Door Closed: Barriers Facing Parents with Criminal Records (Community Legal Services 2002).

28. One study found that 67.5 percent of women in state prisons in the late 1980s had at least one minor child, while only 54.4 percent of men did. Peter M. Genty, *Procedural Due Process Rights of Incarcerated Parents in Termination of Parental Rights Proceedings: A Fifty-State Analysis*, 30 J. Fam. L. 757, 758 (1991).

29. Barbara Bloom & David Steinhart, Why Punish the Children? A Reappraisal of Incarcerated Mothers in America 15 (Nat'l Council on Crime and Delinquency 1993). A 1981 survey found slightly more than fourteen hundred women in federal facilities. By 1991, this number had risen to over five thousand. American Correctional Ass'n, Female Offenders: Meeting Needs of a Neglected Population 1 (American Correctional Ass'n 1993).

30. Marilyn C. Moses, Nat'l Inst. of Justice, U.S. Dep't. of justice,

Keeping Incarcerated Mothers and Their Daughters Together 4 (1995), *available at* http://www.ncjrs.org.

31. Federal Bureau of Prisons, Institutions Housing Female Offenders, *available at* http://www.bop.gov.

32. Dorothy Roberts, Shattered Bonds: The Color of Child Welfare 206 (Basic Books 2002).

33. *Id.*

34. Nicole S. Mauskopf, Note: *Reaching beyond the Bars: An Analysis of Prison Nurseries,* 5 Cardozo Women's L.J. 101, 112 (1998).

35. Santosky v. Kramer, 455 U.S. 745, 745–53 (1982).

36. Susan C. Boyd, *Mothers and Illicit Drugs: Transcending the Myths* (Univ. of Toronto Press 1999) (arguing that female drug users are being unfairly demonized).

37. Susan Vivian Mangold, *Challenging the Parent-Child-State Triangle in Public Family Law: The Importance of Private Providers in the Dependency System,* 47 Buff. L. Rev. 1397, 1436 (1999).

38. Personal Responsibility and Work Opportunity Reconciliation Act, Pub. L. No. 104-193, § 115, 110 Stat. 2105 (1996). *Welfare Reform: Punishment of Drug Offenders: Congress Denies Cash Assistance and Food Stamps to Drug Felons,* 110 Harv. L. Rev. 983, 986 (1997).

39. Adoption and Safe Families Act, Pub. L. No. 105-89, 111 Stat. 2115 (1997).

40. TANF is the block grant that replaced the 60-year-old Aid to Families with Dependent Children program. It ends any federally based individual entitlement to benefits, sets a five-year lifetime limit on federally funded assistance, and limits recipients' access to education and job training. It is governed by Title I of PRWORA. *See* 42 U.S.C. § 601–619 (1996). The federal law also denies assistance for ten years to a person convicted in federal or state court of having fraudulently misrepresented her residence in order to obtain TANF, food stamps, SSI, or Medicaid benefits. The most severe welfare reform provision based on criminal records is a lifetime bar on benefits for individuals with felony drug convictions.

41. As of April 2006, thirteen states have completely repealed the Welfare Reform Act and twenty-three others have modified it. The Sentencing Project, Life Sentences: Denying Welfare Benefits to Women Convicted of Drug Offenses (1996), *available at* http://www.sentencingproject.org.

42. Regina Austin, *"The Black Community," Its Lawbreakers, and a Politics of Identification,* 65 S. Cal. L. Rev. 1769, 1791 (1992).

43. Canterino v. Wilson, 546 F. Supp. 174, 179 (W.D. Ky. 1982).

44. *Id.* at 188.

45. *Id.* at 207.

46. *Id.*

47. Kim A. Hull et al., *Analysis of Recidivism Rates for Participants of the Academic/Vocational/Transition Education Programs Offered by the Virginia Department of Correctional Education*, 51 J. CORRECTIONAL EDUC. 256, 256–61 (2000).

48. LAWRENCE A. GREENFIELD & STEPHANIE MINOR-HARPER, WOMEN IN PRISON 6 (U.S. Dep't. of Just., Office of Just. Programs, Bureau of Just. Stats. 1991).

49. Heidi Rosenberg, *California's Incarcerated Mothers: Legal Roadblocks to Reunification*, 30 GOLDEN GATE L. REV. 285, 314 (2000).

50. *Id.*

51. UNITED STATES GENERAL ACCOUNTING OFFICE, WOMEN IN PRISONS: ISSUES AND CHALLENGES CONFRONTING U.S. CORRECTIONAL SYSTEMS 19 (December 1999).

52. This begs the question of why women are being incarcerated at such a high rate today.

53. Kara Stinson, *Letting Time Serve You: Boot Camps and Alternative Sentencing for Female Offenders*, 39 BRANDEIS L.J. 847, 855 (2001).

NOTES TO CHAPTER 4

1. Amanda Ripley, *Outside the Gates*, TIME, Jan. 21, 2002, at 56.

2. ELIJAH ANDERSON, STREETWISE: RACE, CLASS, AND CHANGE IN AN URBAN COMMUNITY 86–87 (Univ. of Chicago Press 1990).

3. Sometimes families respond to loved ones living with them on parole by becoming "agents" for parole. By taking on this "early warning system" role, they often convey to the parolee that they are "watching" him or her and this also can become a point of contention where the parolee feels that he or she should not be under this type of scrutiny at home.

4. Including essential documents such as one's prison release certificate, birth certificate, addresses, etc[o]. Jeanne Flavin & David Rosenthal, *La Bodega de la Familia: Supporting Parolees' Reintegration within a Family Context*, 30 FORDHAM URB. L.J. 1603, 1608 n.33 (2003). Privacy rights are "more important than ever" when people are in crisis because they "need a confidential place where they feel safe communicating with helping professionals, so they can start to assemble the sources needed to get back on solid ground." Kate Taylor, *Shelter Remodeling Will Give Families More Privacy*, THE OREGONIAN, Nov. 30, 2006, at 4.

5. NATIONAL COALITION FOR THE HOMELESS, HOW MANY PEOPLE EXPERIENCE HOMELESSNESS? (2002) (discussing problems of estimating homelessness generally, as well as distortions inherent in both point-in-time surveys and yearly estimates of homelessness), *available at* http://www.nationalhomeless. org.

6. Paula A. Franzese, *Housing and Hope: The Crisis in Homelessness, Dis-*

crimination in Housing, and an Agenda for Landlord/Tenant Reform, 29 SETON HALL REV. 1461, 1461 (1999) (discussing two million figure); National Law Center for Homelessness & Poverty, *Homelessness and Poverty in America,* available at http://www.nlchp.org.

7. JONATHON KOZOL, RACHEL AND HER CHILDREN: HOMELESS FAMILIES IN AMERICA 11 (Ballantine Books 1988) ("Any poor family paying rent or mortgage that exceeds one half of monthly income is in serious danger [of eviction].").

8. Even though 1998 produced the highest incomes ever recorded, the poverty rate was higher than almost every year throughout the 1970s. *See* Brian Maney & Sheila Crowley, *Scarcity and Success: Perspectives on Assisted Housing,* 9 J. OF AFFORDABLE HOUSING & COMMUNITY DEV. L. 319, 322 (2000). About 34.5 million people lived in poverty in 1998. *Id.* The higher rate of poverty may be related to the decrease in families receiving financial assistance and food stamp benefits.

9. Michael H. Schill & Susan M. Wachter, *The Spatial Bias of Federal Housing Law and Policy: Concentrated Poverty in Urban America,* 143 U. PA. L. REV. 1285 (1995).

10. John Atlas & Peter Dreier, *From "Projects" to Communities: Redeeming Public Housing,* J. HOUSING, Jan.–Feb. 1993, at 21.

11. According to a study published in the *Journal of Urban Affairs* in 1999, 29 percent of African Americans live below the poverty level, while only 8 percent of Whites do. *See* Robert M. Adelman & Charles Jaret, *Poverty, Race, and the U.S. Metropolitan Social and Economic Structure,* 21 J. URB. AFF. 35, 44 (1999).

12. The only metropolitan area where they are close is in Portsmouth, New Hampshire, where the poverty rate is 6.6 percent for Whites and 9.4 percent for Blacks. *Id.* at 44.

13. Florence Wagman Roisman, *Intentional Racial Discrimination and Segregation by the Federal Government as a Principal Cause of Concentrated Poverty: A Response to Schill and Wachter,* 143 U. PA. L. REV. 1351, 1358 (1995).

14. *Id.*

15. *Id.*

16. Michael H. Schill, *Distressed Public Housing: Where Do We Go from Here?,* 60 U. CHI. L. REV. 497, 504–17 (1993) (describing historical patterns of discrimination in setting of public housing).

17. An important factor in the current racial segregation of public housing is the different residential makeup of family and elderly housing. A majority of tenants in elderly public housing are White, and elderly public housing is less likely to be located among concentrations of poverty. A HUD report confirms that "most African-Americans living in public housing live in a largely African American and poor community, whereas Whites, living in elderly housing,

typically live in areas with large numbers of Whites who are not poor." JOHN GOERING ET AL., THE LOCATION AND RACIAL COMPOSITION OF PUBLIC HOUSING IN THE UNITED STATES: AN ANALYSIS OF THE RACIAL OCCUPANCY AND LOCATION OF PUBLIC HOUSING DEVELOPMENTS 1 (U.S. Dep't of Housing & Urban Dev., Office of Pol'y Dev. & Research 1994). Indeed, regression analysis points to the differences in housing conditions between White elderly households and African American families as a substantial cause of segregation in public housing. *Id.* at 741.

18. DOUGLAS S. MASSEY & NANCY A. DENTON, AMERICAN APARTHEID: SEGREGATION AND THE MAKING OF THE UNDERCLASS 77 (Harvard Univ. Press 1993).

19. *Id.*

20. *Id.*; Nancy A. Denton, *Are African Americans Still Hypersegregated?*, in RESIDENTIAL APARTHEID: THE AMERICAN LEGACY 74 (Robert D. Bullard et al. eds., CAAS Publications 1994).

21. John O. Calmore, *Race/ism Lost and Found: The Fair Housing Act at Thirty*, 52 U. MIAMI L. REV. 1067, 1113 (1998).

22. *Id.* (citing Louie Albert Woolbright & David J. Hartmann, *The New Segregation: Asians and Hispanics*, in DIVIDED NEIGHBORHOODS: CHANGING PATTERNS OF RACIAL SEGREGATION 138 [Gary A. Tobin ed., 1987]); Rachel F. Moran, *What If Latinos Really Mattered in the Public Policy Debate?*, 85 CAL. L. REV. 1315, 1338 (1998). With the exception of Puerto Ricans, Moran concedes that Latinos are advantaged over Blacks in the context of open housing access. *Id.*

23. ARNOLD R. HIRSCH, MAKING THE SECOND GHETTO: RACE AND HOUSING IN CHICAGO, 1940–1960 (Cambridge Univ. Press 1983); DAVID L. KIRP ET. AL., OUR TOWN: RACE HOUSING AND THE SOUL OF SUBURBIA (Rutgers Univ. Press 1995); SUDHIR ALLADI VENKATESH, AMERICAN PROJECT: THE RISE AND FALL OF A MODERN GHETTO (Harvard Univ. Press 2000) (examining Chicago's Robert Taylor Homes).

24. United States Housing Act of 1937, Ch. 896, § 3, 50 Stat. 888, 888–99 (codified as amended at 42 U.S.C. §§ 1437–1437z 7 [2000]).

25. TIMOTHY L. MCDONNELL, THE WAGNER HOUSING ACT: A CASE STUDY OF THE LEGISLATIVE PROCESS 1–28 (Loyola Univ. Press 1957).

26. *Id.*

27. Housing Act, § 1, 42 U.S.C. § 1437 (1937).

28. Peter Kivisto, *Changes in Public Housing Policies and Their Impacts on Minorities*, in RACE, ETHNICITY, AND MINORITY HOUSING IN THE UNITED STATES 3 (Jamshid A. Momeni ed., Greenwood Press 1986).

29. United States v. Certain Lands, 9 F. Supp. 137, 142 (W.D. Ky.), *aff'd*, 78 F.2d 684 (6th Cir. 1935); United States v. Certain Lands, 12 F. Supp. 345, 348

(E.D. Mich. 1935). The federal government did not appeal the Kentucky decision and terminated the program.

30. Housing Act, Pub. L. No. 81 171, 63 Stat. 413 (1949) (codified as amended as 42 U.S.C. § 1441 [1994]).

31. Rachel G. Bratt, *Public Housing: The Controversy and the Contribution, in* Critical Perspectives on Housing 335 (Rachel G. Bratt et al. eds., Temple Univ. Press 1986).

32. R. Allen Hays, The Federal Government and Urban Housing: Ideology and Change in Public Policy 96–97 (State Univ. of N.Y. Press, 2d ed. 1995).

33. Daniel Roland Fusfeld & Timothy Mason Bates, The Political Economy of the Urban Ghetto 45–66 (Southern Ill. Univ. Press 1984).

34. Kenneth T. Jackson, Crabgrass Frontier: The Suburbanization of the United States 190–245 (Oxford Univ. Press 1985).

35. Irving H. Welfeld, Where We Live: The American Home and the Social, Political, and Economic Landscape from Slums to Suburbs 191 (Simon & Schuster 1988).

36. Bratt, *supra* note 31, at 336–42.

37. Lawrence J. Vale, *Destigmatizing Public Housing, in* Geography and Identity: Living and Exploring the Geopolitics of Identity 439 (Dennis Crow ed., Maisonneuve Press 1996).

38. Mark L. Matulef, *This Is Public Housing,* J. Housing, Sept.–Oct. 1987, at 175, 176.

39. Examples of negative popular sentiment are also recounted in Schill, *supra* note 16, at 497–98. For political conservatives, high rises that do have severe social and structural problems have become symbols of the failure of government intervention in affordable housing. For political liberals, decaying public housing developments are the inevitable product of HUD and local governments' conscious efforts to build public housing in areas of high racial and economic segregation.

40. Brian Maney & Sheila Crowley, *Scarcity and Success: Perspectives on Assisted Housing,* 9 J. of Affordable Housing & Community Dev. L. 319, 322 (2000). About 34.5 million people lived in poverty in 1998. *Id.* The higher rate of poverty may be related to the decrease in families receiving financial assistance and food stamp benefits. *Id.*

41. Schill & Wachter, *supra* note 9.

42. Atlas & Dreier, *supra* note 10, at 21.

43. Maney & Crowley, *supra* note 40, at 321.

44. *Id.* at 322.

45. Donald MacDonald, Democratic Architecture: Practical Solutions to Today's Housing Crisis 17–18 (Whitney Library of Design 1996).

46. The term came into popular use in Ronald Reagan's presidential campaign speeches, in which he told the story of a Cadillac-driving Chicago welfare queen who was collecting dozens of welfare checks under different names. Robert Friedman, *Sorry, We Have No Time for Apologies,* St. Petersburg Times, June 26, 1988, at 5D.

47. It is the image of the "lazy welfare mother who breeds children at the expense of the taxpayers in order to increase the amount of her welfare check" that is used to sell programs to the public that will adversely affect women. David T. Ellwood & Mary Jo Bane, *Understanding Welfare Dynamics, in* Welfare Realities: From Rhetoric to Reform 28, 45 (David T. Ellwood & Mary Jo Bane eds., Harvard Univ. Press 1994).

48. Donald MacDonald, *supra* note 45, at 7.

49. Atlas & Dreier, *supra* note 10, at 351.

50. Paige M. Harrison & Allen J. Beck, Bulletin: Prisoners in 2001 (U.S. Dep't of Just., Bureau of Just. Stats. 2002) (reporting that 10 percent of African American men, ages 25–29, are incarcerated).

51. President William J. Clinton, State of the Union Address (Jan. 23, 1996).

52. 42 U.S.C. § 1437d(l)(6).

53. Rucker v. Davis, Not Reported in F. Supp., 1998 WL 345403 (N.D. Cal. June 19, 1998) (NO. C 98-00781 CRB).

54. *Id.*

55. *Id.*

56. *Id.*

57. *Id.* at 6; Emelyn Cruz Lat, *One-Strike Evictions,* S.F. Examiner, Aug. 23, 1998, at A1.

58. *Id.* at 1.

59. *Id.*

60. *Id.* at 43a (affidavit of Pearlie Rucker).

61. *Id.*

62. *Id.*

63. *Id.* at 1.

64. *Id.* at 13a, 42a.

65. *Id.* at 36a.

66. *Id.*

67. *Id.* at 37a.

68. *Id.* at 39a.

69. *Id.* at 39a.

70. Rucker v. Davis, 237 F.3d 1113, 1124 (citing Scales v. United States, 367 U.S. 203, 224 25 [1961]).

71. *Id.* at 1125.

72. Dep't of Hous. and Urban Dev. v. Rucker, 535 U.S. 125, 135 (2002).

73. *Id.* at 134.

74. LEGAL ACTION CTR., HOUSING LAWS AFFECTING INDIVIDUALS WITH CRIMINAL CONVICTIONS (2000) [hereinafter LEGAL ACTION CTR., HOUSING LAWS], *available at* http://www.lac.org/pubs/gratis/housing_laws.pdf (last visited July 29, 2007).

75. *Id.* Other convictions include any household with a member subject to a lifetime registration requirement under a state sex-offender registry.

76. Carl Horowitz, *Housing Rights versus Property Rights,* Heritage Foundation Reports: The Heritage Lectures No. 312 at 8 (Apr. 3, 1991).

77. PETER HENRY ROSSI, DOWN AND OUT IN AMERICA: THE ORIGINS OF HOMELESSNESS 8–10 (Univ. of Chicago Press 1989); Kenneth M. Chackes, *Sheltering the Homeless: Judicial Enforcement of Governmental Duties to the Poor,* 31 J. URB. & CONTEMP. L. 155, 155–56 (1987).

78. Robert Hayes, *Litigating on Behalf of Shelter for the Poor,* 22 HARV. C.R.-C.L. L. REV. 79, 83–85 (1987).

79. Jeremy Travis, Amy L. Solomon, & Michelle Waul, *From Prison to Home: The Dimensions and Consequences of Prisoner Reentry* 35–36 (The Urban Institute 2001) [o](discussing difficulties ex-offenders face finding suitable housing when they are released from prison).

80. Daniel Glaser, *Supervising Offenders outside of Prison, in* CRIME AND PUBLIC POLICY 207, 220 (James Q. Wilson ed., 1985). "Most offenders have little successful employment experience, limited job qualifications, and few economic resources." *Id.* at 220. Since parolees and probationers are usually not eligible for unemployment insurance because they did not work in the year prior to their release, the idea of forcing a person who is an extremely high unemployment candidate into a strange community (presumably without housing) is irresponsible and short sighted. *See id.* at 221.

81. Travis et al., *supra* note 79, at 35–36 (discussing difficulties ex-offenders face finding suitable housing when they are released from prison).

82. *Id.*

83. CENTER FOR HOUSING POLICY, THE HOUSING NEEDS OF EX-PRISONERS (1996), *available at* http://www.jrf.org.uk.

84. *Id.*

85. *Id.*

86. Travis et al., *supra* note 79, at 35 (discussing exceptions housing authorities may make to the ban on public housing for tenants who can prove that they are receiving rehabilitation treatment); *see also* 42 U.S.C. § 13662(b)(2) (2002) (providing that public housing agency or owner may consider whether applicant is rehabilitated).

87. Steven R. Paisner, *Compassion, Politics, and the Problems Lying on Our Sidewalks: A Legislative Approach for Cities to Address Homelessness,* 67 TEMP. L. REV. 1259, 1271–73 (1994) (summarizing interests and concerns of city and its inhabitants in the context of homelessness).

88. Evelyn Nieves, *In Famously Tolerant City, Impatience with Homeless,* N.Y. TIMES, Jan. 18, 2002, at A14 (describing hard-line approaches of New York, San Francisco, and other cities).

89. NATIONAL COALITION FOR THE HOMELESS, ILLEGAL TO BE HOMELESS: THE CRIMINALIZATION OF HOMELESSNESS IN THE UNITED STATES (2002), *available at* http://www.nationalhomeless.org.

90. Lorne Sossin, *The Criminalization and Administration of the Homeless: Notes on the Possibilities and Limits of Bureaucratic Engagement,* 22 N.Y.U. REV. L. & SOC. CHANGE 623, 638–39, 647 (1996).

91. Fair Housing Act, Pub. L. No. 90 284, 82 Stat. 81 (1968) (codified as amended at 42 U.S.C. §§ 3601–3631 (1994)).

92. Prior to the 1988 amendments, the act lacked the necessary enforcement provisions to effect real change in the behavior of those responsible for housing discrimination. *See* James Kushner, *The Fair Housing Amendments Act of 1988: The Second Generation of Fair Housing,* 42 VAND. L. REV. 1049, 1050 (1989).

93. 392 U.S. 409 (1968).

94. Civil Rights Act, 14 Stat. 27 (1866) (codified at 42 U.S.C. § 1982 [1994]) (providing that all citizens have same right enjoyed by Whites to inherit, purchase, lease, sell, hold, and convey real and personal property). As a result of the decision in *Jones,* this provision does not require state action.

95. Margery Austin Turner & Ron Wienk, *The Persistence of Segregation in Urban Areas: Contributing Causes, in* HOUSING MARKETS AND RESIDENTIAL MOBILITY 193, 199 (G. Thomas Kingsley & Margery Austin Turner eds., Urban Inst. Press 1993).

96. LEGAL ACTION CTR., HOUSING LAWS, *supra* note 74.

97. Jody David Armour, *Affirmative Action: Diversity of Opinions: Hype and Reality in Affirmative Action,* 68 U. COLO. L. REV. 1173, 1177–78 (1997).

98. Gary Orfield, *Housing and the Justification of School Segregation,* 143 U. PA. L. REV. 1397, 1401 (1995); Robert D. Bullard, *Environmental Racism and "Invisible" Communities,* 96 W. VA. L. REV. 1037, 1042 (1994) (discusses housing and environmental hazards); WILLIAM JULIUS WILSON, THE TRULY DISADVANTAGED: THE INNER CITY, THE UNDERCLASS, AND PUBLIC POLICY 42 (Univ. of Chicago Press 1987).

99. RONALD E. WIENK, MEASURING RACIAL DISCRIMINATION IN AMERICAN HOUSING MARKETS: THE HOUSING MARKET PRACTICES SURVEY (U.S. Dep't of Housing and Urban Dev., Office of Pol'y Dev. and Research 1979) (offering extensive investigation of forty major urban areas documenting racial discrimination in housing patterns).

100. MARGERY AUSTIN TURNER ET AL., HUD HOUSING DISCRIMINATION STUDY: SYNTHESIS 11, 28 (U.S. Dep't of Housing and Urban Dev., Office of Pol'y Dev. and Research 1991).

101. Joe R. Feagin, *Excluding Blacks and Others from Housing: The Foun-*

dation of White Racism, 82 CITYSCAPE: J. POL'Y DEV. 79 (1999) (discussing sociological effects of segregation during the demographic shifts).

102. *Id.*

103. Michael H. Schill, *Local Enforcement of Laws Prohibiting Discrimination in Housing: The New York City Human Rights Commission,* 23 FORDHAM URB. L.J. 991 (1996) (discussing other aspects of housing discrimination, such as discrimination on the basis of sexual orientation, familial status, and physical capabilities).

104. According to 2000 census data, in U.S. metropolitan areas as a whole, 65 percent of Blacks would have to move to attain a uniform racial residential distribution. LEWIS MUMFORD CTR., ETHNIC DIVERSITY GROWS, NEIGHBORHOOD INTEGRATION LAGS BEHIND 1–2, 5 (2001), *available at* http://mumford1 .dyndns.org/cen2000/WholePop/WPreport/MumfordReport.pdf (last visited July 29, 2007).

105. MASSEY & DENTON, *supra* note 18, at 64 tbl.3.1.

106. Jeffrey Rosen, *Bus Stop: The Lost Promise of School Integration,* N.Y. TIMES, Apr. 2, 2000, § 4, at 1.

107. *Id.*

108. Brown v. Bd. of Educ., 347 U.S. 483 (1954).

109. *Id.* (listing only three exceptions: New Jersey, North Dakota, and Tennessee).

110. Harry J. Holzer & Keith R. Ihlanfeldt, *Spatial Factors and the Employment of Blacks at the Firm Level,* NEW ENG. ECON. REV., May–June 1996, at 65.

111. TIMOTHY BATES, BANKING ON BLACK ENTERPRISE: THE POTENTIAL OF EMERGING FIRMS FOR REVITALIZING URBAN ECONOMIES 140 (Joint Ctr. for Political and Economic Studies 1993).

112. DONALD TOMAKOVIC DEVEY, GENDER AND RACIAL INEQUALITY AT WORK: THE SOURCES AND CONSEQUENCES OF JOB SEGREGATION 24 (ILR Press 1993).

113. John Kain, *The Spatial Mismatch Hypothesis: Three Decades Later,* 3 HOUSING POL'Y DEBATE 371 (1992); Michael Fix et al., *An Overview of Auditing for Discrimination, in* CLEAR AND CONVINCING EVIDENCE: MEASUREMENT OF DISCRIMINATION IN AMERICA 1, 18–25 (Michael Fix & Raymond J. Struyk eds., Urban Inst. Press 1994); *The Meaning of Race for Employers, in* THE URBAN UNDERCLASS 203, 209–13 (Christopher Jencks & Paul Peterson eds., Brookings Inst. 1991).

114. 42 U.S.C. §§ 3601–3619, 3631 (1988 & Supp. V 1993) (prohibiting discrimination in the sale or rental of housing). Additional laws prohibiting discrimination are § 1982 of the Civil Rights Act of 1866, 42 U.S.C. § 1982 (1988), and the Equal Credit Opportunity Act, 15 U.S.C. § 1691 (1988 & Supp. V 1993) (prohibiting discrimination in credit transactions).

115. 42 U.S.C. § 3604(a) (making it illegal to refuse to sell or rent "to any person because of race, color, religion, sex, familial status, or national origin"). Sales of single-family homes by persons who own three or fewer houses are exempt from the Fair Housing Act if the seller does not use the services of a real estate broker and does not advertise. *See* § 3603(b)(1). Similarly, landlords who live in and own buildings occupied by no more than four families are also exempt from the prohibitions of the Fair Housing Act. *See* § 3603(b)(2).

116. H.R. Rep. No. 100 711, at 15 (1988), *as reprinted in* 1988 U.S.C. C.A.N. 2173, 2176 ("Twenty years after the passage of the Fair Housing Act, discrimination . . . in housing continue[s] to be pervasive."). In 1999, HUD secretary Andrew Cuomo stated that "[f]or more than 30 years, discrimination in housing has been prohibited under law. Yet audits of the rental and sales market show that an estimated 2.5 million instances of discrimination still occur annually nationwide." FY 2000 VA HUD Appropriations: Hearing before the Sen. Appropriations Subcomm. on VA, HUD and Indep. Agencies of the Senate Comm. on Appropriations, 106th Cong. (1999) (statement of Andrew Cuomo, Secretary, Dep't of Housing and Urban Development).

117. Fair Housing Act, Pub. L. No. 90 284, § 813, 82 Stat. 81, 88 (1968) (current version at 42 U.S.C. §§ 3601–3619 (1988 & Supp. V 1993)). The attorney general was authorized to file civil actions in cases of pattern or practice discrimination and in cases where issues of general public importance were raised. *See id.* "Pattern and practice" is defined as a discriminatory practice that affects groups of people rather than just one individual. F. Willis Caruso & William H. Jones, *Fair Housing in the 1990s: An Overview of Recent Developments and Prognosis of Their Impact,* 22 J. Marshall L. Rev. 421, 524–25 (1989).

118. Immediately after the enactment of the 1968 legislation, the Department of Justice established a section within the Civil Rights Division that was in charge of enforcing the act.

119. Massey & Denton, *supra* note 18, at 195–200.

120. *See* Gary Orfield, *Housing and the Justification of School Segregation,* 143 U. Pa. L. Rev. 1397, 1404 (1995).

121. Julian Bond, *Historical Perspectives on Fair Housing,* 29 J. Marshall L. Rev. 315, 327 (1996). As Bond explains,

Between 1968 and 1978, the Justice Department prosecuted an average of thirty-two fair housing cases a year. This number is huge when compared to the Reagan Presidency caseload. During Reagan's first year as President, not one fair housing case was filed. In 1982 only two were filed. At the same time, the number of fair housing complaints had escalated sharply. Between 1979 and 1982, the number of complaints filed with HUD nearly doubled, from 2800 in 1979 to 5100 in 1982. The number of cases filed by the Reagan Justice Department tripled from two to six in

1983. At the end of Reagan's eight years in office, the total number of housing cases filed equaled the annual average during each of Carter's four years in office.

It took twenty years, but Congress amended the Fair Housing Act in 1988. These 1988 Amendments gave the nation and the victims of housing discrimination a fair housing law whose promise was capable of being fulfilled. . . .

Finally, that battle, stretching over decades, had been won. But, there are still more battles to be fought and won. Data from the 1990 Census show that America remains an overwhelmingly segregated society. Northern cities on average are severely segregated. At the average rate of change across all northern areas, it will take seventy-seven years just to achieve a moderate level of segregation. Although southern metropolitan areas are less segregated than the Northern areas, it will take thirty-six years for them to reduce their segregation to the moderate range. *Id.*

122. President George W. Bush, State of the Union Address (Jan. 20, 2004), *available at* http://www. whitehouse.gov. This initiative proposes that agencies, including the Department of Labor, the Department of Housing and Urban Development, and the Department of Justice, coordinate programs and services aimed to "help ex-offenders find and keep employment, obtain transitional housing and receive mentoring." U.S. DEP'T OF LABOR, PRESIDENT BUSH'S PRISONER RE-ENTRY INITIATIVE: PROTECTING COMMUNITIES BY HELPING RETURNING INMATES FIND WORK, *available at* http://www.dol.gov/cfbci/reenryfactsheet .htm; Lila T. Mills, *Ashcroft Touts Efforts to Help Ex-Prisoners Re-Enter Society,* CLEV. PLAIN DEALER, Sept. 21, 2004, at B2.

123. Herman Joseph & John Langrod, *The Homeless, in* SUBSTANCE ABUSE: A COMPREHENSIVE TEXTBOOK 1141 (Joyce H. Lowinson et al. eds., Lippincott Williams & Wilkins 2005).

124. *Id.*

125. 24 C.F.R. Section 966.4(1)(5)(vii).

NOTES TO CHAPTER 5

1. Olinda Moyd, *Mental Health and Incarceration: What a Bad Combination,* 7 U.D.C. L. REV. 201, 210–11 (2003).

2. 429 U.S. 97 (1976).

3. *Id.* at 98.

4. *Id.*

5. *Id.*

6. *Id.* at 101.

7. *Id.*

8. *Id.* at 104.

9. *Id.*

10. *Id.*

11. *Id.*

12. *Id.*

13. *Id.*

14. 501 U.S. 294 (1991).

15. *Id.* at 302–3.

16. *Id.*

17. *Id.*

18. 511 U.S. 825 (1994).

19. *Id.* at 838–39.

20. *Id.* at 837.

21. Inmates of Allegheny County Jail, 612 F.2d 754, 763 (3d Cir. 1979); Bowring v. Godwin, 551 F.2d 44, 47 (1977); *see also* Newman v. Alabama, 503 F.2d 1120 (5th Cir. 1974), *cert. denied,* 421 U.S. 948 (1975) (criticizing the Alabama penal system for failing to employ mental health professionals to provide treatment to inmates).

22. Fred Cohen, *Captives' Legal Right to Mental Health Care,* 17 L. & Psy-chol. Rev. 1, 39 (1993).

23. E. F. Torrey, *Jails and Prisons: America's New Mental Hospitals,* 85 Am. J. Pub. Health 1611, 1611–13 (1995).

24. Paula M. Ditton, U.S. Dep't of Just., Mental Health and Treat-ment of Inmates and Probationers (1999); Richard L. Elliot, *Evaluating the Quality of Correctional Mental Health Services: An Approach to Surveying a Correctional Mental Health System,* 15 Behavioral Sci. L. 427, 427–39 (1997).

25. Arrestee Drug Abuse Monitoring Program, U.S. Dept of Just., 1999 Annual Report on Drug Use among Adult and Juvenile Arrestees 9 (2000), *available at* http://www.ncjrs.org.

26. Christopher J. Mumola, *Incarcerated Parents and Their Children,* August 2000, NCJ 182335, *available at* www.ojp.usdoj.gov/bjs/abstract/iptc.htm.

27. Harry K. Wexler et al., *Outcome Evaluation of a Prison Therapeutic Community for Substance Abuse Treatment,* 17 Crim. Just. & Behav. 71, 72 (1990).

28. Paul Gendreau & Robert R. Ross, *Revivification of Rehabilitation: Evidence from the 1980s,* 4 Just. Q. 349, 349–407 (1987).

29. Steven Belenko, *The Challenges of Integrating Drug Treatment into the Criminal Justice Process,* 63 Alb. L. Rev. 833, 834–38 (2000).

30. Steven Belenko et al., *Criminal Justice Responses to Crack,* 28 J. Res. Crime & Delinq. 55, 70–72 (1991).

31. Steven Belenko, *supra* note 29, at 855-56.

32. D. A. Andrews et al., *Does Correctional Treatment Work? A Clinically*

Relevant and Psychologically Informed Meta-Analysis, 28 CRIMINOLOGY 369, 369, 384–85 (1990); Gendreau & Ross, *supra* note 28, at 350–51.

33. *Id.* at 861.

34. *Id.*

35. *Id.*

36. Steven Belenko, *supra* note 29, at 858 (citing Bureau of Just. Stat., U.S. Dep't of Just., *Nation's Probation and Parole Population Reached New High Last Year* 2 (1997) (highlighting number of parolees and probationers reincarcerated for violations). D. A. Andrews et al., *supra* note 32, at 369 (explaining that imprisonment without rehabilitation will have no effect on recidivism).

37. THEODORE M. HAMMETT ET AL., U.S. DEP'T OF JUST., 1996, 1997 UPDATE: HIV/AIDS, STD'S, AND TB IN CORRECTIONAL FACILITIES 85–86 (1999) [hereinafter HAMMETT ET AL., 1996, 1997 UPDATE].

38. DIV. OF TUBERCULOSIS ELIMINATION, U.S. DEP'T OF HEALTH AND HUMAN SERVS., QUESTIONS AND ANSWERS ABOUT TB (1999), *available at* http://www.cdc.gov/nchstp/tb/faqs/qa.htm (last visited July 29, 2007).

39. *Id.*

40. Joan Petersilia, *When Prisoners Return to Communities: Political, Economic, and Social Consequences,* FED. PROBATION, June 2001, at 3.

41. *Id.*

42. Scott A. Allen et al., *Hepatitis C among Offenders: Correctional Challenge and Public Health Opportunity,* FED. PROBATION, Sept. 2003, at 22.

43. NAT'L INSTS. OF HEALTH, CONSENSUS DEVELOPMENT CONFERENCE STATEMENT: MANAGEMENT OF HEPATITIS C, 2002 (2002), *available at* http://consensus.nih.gov.

44. ASS'N OF STATE AND TERRITORIAL HEALTH OFFICIALS, HEPATITIS C AND INCARCERATED POPULATIONS: THE NEXT WAVE FOR CORRECTIONAL HEALTH INITIATIVES (2002), *available at* http://www.astho.org.

45. Theodore M. Hammett et al., *The Burden of Infectious Disease among Inmates of and Releasees from U.S. Correctional Facilities, 1997,* 92 AM. J. PUB. HEALTH, 1789–94 (2002).

46. *Id.*

47. *Id.*

48. At the end of 1995, there were 24,226 HIV-positive inmates in state and federal prisons. The HIV prevalence rate was 2.4 percent in state prisons and 0.9 percent in federal prisons. *See* LAURA MARUSHCAK, U.S. DEP'T OF JUST., HIV IN PRISONS AND JAILS, 1995, 1 (1997).

49. Theodore M. Hammett et. al., *supra* note 45, at 5.

50. MARUSCHAK, *supra* note 48, at 4 (stating that in 1995 .51 percent of all prisoners had AIDS, compared to .08 percent of the U.S. population).

51. THEODORE M. HAMMETT ET AL., U.S. DEP'T. OF JUST., 1994 UPDATE: HIV/AIDS AND STD'S IN CORRECTIONAL FACILITIES 14 (1995).

52. D. Stuart Sowder, Note: *AIDS in Prison: Judicial Indifference to the AIDS Epidemic in Correctional Facilities Threatens the Constitutionality of Incarceration*, 37 N.Y.L. SCH. L. REV. 663, 666–67 (1992); Art Golab, *State Lacks AIDS Policy for Prisons, Lawmaker Says*, CHI. SUN-TIMES, Dec. 24, 1995, at 9.

53. Joanne Mariner, *Body and Soul: The Trauma of Prison Rape*, in BUILD-ING VIOLENCE 125, 126 (John P. May ed., Sage Publications 2000).

54. ROBERT DUMOND, THE IMPACT AND RECOVERY OF PRISON RAPE, *available at* http://www.spr.org.

55. HUMAN RIGHTS WATCH, NO ESCAPE: MALE RAPE IN U.S. PRISONS, DE-LIBERATE INDIFFERENCE VIII (2001), *available at* http://www.hrw.org (reporting that nearly half of the fifty states fail to collect data on rapes occurring in their jails and prisons).

56. Cindy Struckman-Johnson & David Struckman-Johnson, *Sexual Coercion Rates in Seven Midwestern Prison Facilities for Men*, 80 PRISON J. 379, 381 (2000).

57. James Robertson, *Prison Rape Elimination Act of 2003: A Primer*, 40 No. 3 CRIM. LAW BULLETIN 5 (May 2004).

58. PETER M. BRIEN & ALLEN J. BECK, U.S. DEP'T OF JUST., HIV IN PRISONS, 1994 (1996). Data on HIV/AIDS were provided by the departments of corrections in fifty states and the District of Columbia and by the Federal Bureau of Prisons. Since 1991 respondents have reported their HIV testing policies and the number of HIV infected inmates in their custody at year end. *Id.*

59. *Id.* There were 1,953 female state inmates infected with HIV, compared to 19,762 male inmates.

60. *Id.* "In three States more than 10% of female inmates were known to be HIV positive—New York (20%), Connecticut (15%), and Massachusetts (12%)." *Id.*

61. Brenda V. Smith & Cynthia Dailard, *Female Prisoners and AIDS: On the Margins of Public Health and Social Justice*, 9 AIDS & PUB POL'Y J. 78, 80 (1994); Crystal Mason, *Comments by Crystal Mason: HIV-Positive Women in Prison*, 9 BERKELEY WOMEN'S L.J. 149, 150 (1994).

62. HAMMETT ET AL., 1996–1997 UPDATE, *supra* note 37, at 10 (reporting that the rate of HIV infection is higher among women in almost all correctional systems surveyed).

63. Anne S. De Groot et al., *Setting the Standard for Care: HIV Risk Exposures and Clinical Manifestations of HIV in Incarcerated Massachusetts Women*, 24 NEW ENG. J. ON CRIM. & CIV. CONFINEMENT 353, 360 (1998).

64. *Id.* at 358–59.

65. Susan Y. Chu et al., *Impact of the Human Immunodeficiency Virus Epidemic on Mortality in Women of Reproductive Age, United States*, 264 JAMA 225, 227 (1990).

66. *See generally* HENRY J. STEADMAN & JOSEPH J. COCOZZA, MENTAL ILL-

NESS IN AMERICA'S PRISONS (Nat'l Coalition for the Mentally Ill in the Criminal Justice System 1993).

67. Paul F. Stavis, *Why Prisons are Brim-Full of the Mentally Ill: Is Their Incarceration a Solution or a Sign of Failure?*, 11 GEO. MASON U. CIV. RTS. L.J. 157, 159 (2000).

68. Linda A. Teplin, *Psychiatric and Substance Abuse Disorders among Male Urban Jail Detainees*, 84 AM. J. PUB. HEALTH 292, 292–93 (1994).

69. Richard L. Elliott, *Evaluating the Quality of Correctional Mental Health Services: An Approach to Surveying a Correctional Mental Health System*, 15 BEHAV. SCI. & L. 427–39 (1997).

70. Unfortunately, the standard of care the Court set forth in *Estelle* is ambiguous because the Court did not provide, and has not provided, a substantive definition of such terms as "deliberate indifference." Other courts have grappled with these terms: Newman v. Alabama, 503 F.2d 1120 (5th Cir. 1974), *cert. denied*, 421 U.S. 948 (1975).

71. 974 F.2d 1050 (9th Cir. 1992).

72. *Id.* at 1059–60.

73. 551 F.2d 44, 48 (4th Cir. 1977).

74. *Id.* at 47–48.

75. Henry J. Steadman et al., *A SAMHSA Research Initiative Assessing the Effectiveness of Jail Diversion Programs for Mentally Ill Persons*, 50 PSYCHIATRIC SERV. 1620, 1620 (1999).

76. Stacy S. Lamon et al., *New York City's System of Criminal Justice Mental Health Services*, in SERVING MENTALLY ILL OFFENDERS 144, 145 (Gerald Landsberg et al. eds., Springer 2002).

77. George L. Kelling & James Q. Wilson, *Fixing Broken Windows*, ATLANTIC MONTHLY, Mar. 1982, at 29. The broken windows theory maintains that low-level disorder—such as loitering, public intoxication, and littering—contributes to more serious crime if left uncorrected. *Id.*

78. Terence P. Thornberry & Jack E. Call, *Constitutional Challenges to Prison Overcrowding: The Scientific Evidence of Harmful Effects*, 35 HASTINGS L.J. 313, 343 (1983) (citing Garvin McCain, Verne C. Cox, & Paul B. Paulus, *The Effect of Prison Overcrowding on Inmate Behavior* (U.S. Dep't. of Justice, Nat'l Inst. of Justice 1980) (finding that "prisons with large populations and those that experience sharp increases in inmate population experience an increase in . . . psychiatric commitments").

79. Research increasingly shows how even less serious mental disorders (e.g., depression and attentional disorders) can be risk factors for violence and criminality. AMERICAN PSYCHIATRIC ASS'N, DIAGNOSTIC AND STATISTICAL MANUAL OF MENTAL DISORDERS: DSM-IV-TR (4th ed. 2000), the standard diagnostic reference for mental health professionals.

80. E. Fuller Torrey, Editorial: *Jails and Prisons: America's New Mental*

Hospitals, 85 Am. J. Pub. Health 1611, 1611–12 (1995) (quoting M. J. Grinfeld, *Report Focuses on Jailed Mentally Ill*, Psychiatric Times, July 1993, at 1); H. Richard Lamb & Linda E. Weinberger, *Persons with Severe Mental Illness in Jails and Prisons: A Review*, 49 Psychiatric Serv. 483, 486 (1998).

81. Estelle v. Gamble, 429 U.S. 97 (1976).

82. Pugh v. Locke, 406 F. Supp. 318, 325 (M.D. Ala. 1976) (describing sexual exploitation of mentally ill inmate), *aff'd as modified sub nom.* Newman v. Alabama, 559 F.2d 283 (5th Cir. 1977), *rev'd in part and remanded sub nom.* Alabama v. Pugh, 483 U.S. 781 (1978).

83. Robert E. Drake et al., *Review of Integrated Mental Health and Substance Abuse Treatment for Patients with Dual Disorders*, 24 Schizophrenia Bull. 589, 601–3 (1998); John F. Edens et al., *Treating Prison Inmates with Co-Occurring Disorders: An Integrative Review of Existing Programs*, 15 Behav. Sci. & L. 439, 440 (1997).

84. Mark J. Heyrman, *Mental Illness in Prisons and Jails*, 7 U. Chi. L. Sch. Roundtable 113, 118 (2000).

85. Karen M. Abram & Linda A. Teplin, *Co-Occurring Disorders among Mentally Ill Jail Detainees: Implications for Public Policy*, 46 Am. Psychologist 1036, 1039, 1044 (1991).

86. Mark R. Munetz et al., *The Incarceration of Individuals with Severe Mental Disorders*, 34 Community Mental Health J. 361, 369 (2001).

87. Fox Butterfield, *Prisons Brim with Mentally Ill, Study Finds*, N.Y. Times, July 12, 1999, at A10 (citing Ditton, *supra* note 24, at 1.).

88. Bureau of Just. Stat., U.S. Dept of Just., Sourcebook of Criminal Justice Statistics, 1996 (1996).

89. H. Richard Lamb, *Involuntary Treatment for the Homeless Mentally Ill*, Notre Dame J.L. Ethics & Pub. Pol'y 269, 277 (1989) (observing that "the estimates of the seriously mentally ill in the urban homeless population range from 25 to 50 percent . . . and that the true percentage is most likely in the upper end of that range"); H. Richard Lamb et al., Treating the Homeless Mentally Ill: A Report of the Task Force on the Homeless Mentally Ill (Am. Psychiatric Ass'n 1992); Bruce G. Link et al., *Lifetime and Five-Year Prevalence of Homelessness in the United States*, 84 Am. J. Pub. Health 1907 (1994); Felicity Barringer, *U.S. Homeless Count Is Far Below Estimates*, N.Y. Times, Apr. 12, 1991, at A11 (noting underestimates of homelessness because of difficulties in enumerating homeless populations).

90. Kim Barker, *New Court Tries Prevention*, Seattle Times, Feb. 21, 1999, at B1.

91. Lee Rood, *Iowa Imprisons More Mentally Ill*, Des Moines Reg., Oct. 17, 1999, at 1A.

92. *Id.* at 6A.

93. Phyllis L. Solomon et al., *Homelessness in a Mentally Ill Urban Jail Population*, 43 HOSP. & COMMUNITY PSYCHIATRY 169, 170 (1992).

94. Jeffrey L. Metzner, *Guidelines for Psychiatric Services in Prison*, 3 CRIM. BEHAV. & MENTAL HEALTH 252–67 (1993).

95. Joseph J. Cocozza & Kathleen Skowyra, *Youth with Mental Health Disorders: Issues and Emerging Responses*, JUV. JUST., Apr. 2000, at 3.

96. Shaun Parsons et al., *Prevalence of Mental Disorder in Female Remand Prisons*, 12 J. FORENSIC PSYCHIATRY 194, 196 (2001); Mark I. Singer et al., *The Psychosocial Issues of Women Serving Time in Jail*, 40 SOC. WORK 103, 107 (1995).

97. Henry J. Steadman, *Estimating Mental Health Needs and Service Utilization among Prison Inmates*, 19 BULL. AM. ACAD. PSYCHIATRY & L. 297–307 (1991).

98. Kathleen Jordan et al., *Prevalence of Psychiatric Disorders among Incarcerated Women*, 53 ARCH. GEN. PSYCHIATRY 513, 514 (1996).

99. ARRESTEE DRUG ABUSE MONITORING PROGRAM, U.S. DEP'T OF JUST., 1998 ANNUAL REPORT ON DRUG USE AMONG ADULT AND JUVENILE ARRESTEES 1 (1998), *available at* http://www.ncjrs.org.

100. Thomas W. Haywood et al., *Characteristics of Women in Jail and Treatment Orientations: A Review*, 24 BEHAV. MODIFICATION 307, 310 (2000).

101. Emil R. Pinta, *The Prevalence of Serious Mental Disorders among U.S. Prisoners, in* FORENSIC MENTAL HEALTH: WORKING WITH OFFENDERS WITH MENTAL ILLNESS 12 (Gerald Landsberg & Amy Smiley eds., Civic Research Inst. 2001).

102. Devon R. Charles et al., *Suicidal Ideation and Behavior among Women in Jail*, 19 J. CONTEMP. CRIM. JUST. 65, 75 (2003).

103. LAWRENCE A. GREENFIELD & TRACY L. SNELL, U.S. DEP'T OF JUST., SPECIAL REPORT: WOMEN OFFENDERS 8 (1999), *available at* http://www.ojp.usdoj .gov/bjs/pub/pdf/wo.pdf (last visited July 29, 2007).

104. Sandra E. Taylor, *The Health Status of Black Women, in* HEALTH ISSUES IN THE BLACK COMMUNITY 44, 56 (Ronald L. Braithwaite & Sandra E. Taylor eds., 2d ed. 2001).

105. CRIM. JUST. INST., INC., THE CORRECTIONS YEARBOOK 2001: STATISTICS ON PRISON POPULATIONS, *available at* http://www.cji-inc.com.

106. OFFICE OF THE SURGEON GEN., U.S. DEP'T OF HEALTH AND HUMAN SERVS., MENTAL HEALTH: CULTURE, RACE, AND ETHNICITY (2001) [hereinafter MENTAL HEALTH: CULTURE, RACE, AND ETHNICITY], *available at* http://www .surgeongeneral.gov.

107. Marc A. Zimmerman et al., *Resilience among Urban African American Male Adolescents: A Study of the Protective Effects of Sociopolitical Control on Their Mental Health*, 27 AM. J. PSYCHOL. 733 (1999).

108. John C. Boger, *Race and the American City: The Kerner Commission in Retrospect: An Introduction*, 71 N.C. L. Rev. 1289, 1329 (1993).

109. U.S. Dep't of Health and Human Servs., Mental Health: A Report of the Surgeon Gen. 82, 84, 406–8 (2000) [hereinafter Mental Health Report 2000].

110. Alvin F. Pouissaint & Amy Alexander, Lay My Burden Down: Suicide and the Mental Health Crisis among African Americans 95–96 (2000) (reviewing historical and current unequal health and mental health care given to African Americans).

111. Arthur L. Whaley, *Racism in the Provision of Mental Health Services: A Social-Cognitive Analysis*, 68 Am. J. Orthopsychiatry 47, 52 (1998).

112. "Bias in clinician judgment is thought to be reflected in over diagnosis or misdiagnosis of mental disorders." Mental Health Report 2000, *supra* note 109, at 88. "African-Americans have fewer mood/anxiety and substance abuse diagnoses but significantly more organic/psychotic diagnoses. These differences probably reflect ethnocentric clinician bias in the diagnostic assessment of youth from cultural/racial backgrounds." Carl C. Bell & Harshad Mehta, *The Misdiagnosis of Black Patients with Manic Depressive Illness*, 72 Nat'l. Med. Assoc. 141 (1980).

113. Jewelle Taylor Gibbs & Diana Fuery, *Mental Health and Well-Being of Black Women: Toward Strategies of Empowerment*, 22 Am. J. Community Psychol. 559 (1994).

114. Elaine J. Copeland, *Oppressed Conditions and the Mental Health Needs of Low-Income Black Women: Barriers to Services, Strategies for Change*, 1 Women & Therapy 13, 26 (1982).

115. Robert Whitaker, Mad in America: Bad Science, Bad Medicine, and the Enduring Mistreatment of the Mentally Ill 171–72 (2002).

116. Kenneth P. Lindsey & Gordon L. Paul, *Involuntary Commitments to Public Mental Institutions: Issues Involving the Overrepresentation of Blacks and Assessment of Relative Functioning*, 106 Psychol. Bull. 171, 172 (1989); *see also* the numerous studies cited in Susan Stefan, *Issues Relating to Women and Ethnic Minorities in Mental Health Treatment and Law*, in Law, Mental Health, and Mental Disorder 255 (Bruce D. Sales & Dan W. Shuman eds., 1996).

117. Sue E. Estroff et al., *Everybody's Got a Little Mental Illness: Accounts of Illness and Self among People with Severe Persistent Mental Illness*, 5 Med. Anthropology Q. 331, 362 (1991).

118. DSM III R specifically cautions clinicians concerning this problem. American Psychiatric Association, Diagnostic and Statistical Manual of Mental Disorders, 3d rev. (2000).

119. V. R. Adebimpe, *Overview: White Norms and Psychiatric Diagnosis of Black Psychiatric Patients*, 138 Am. J. Psychiatry 279, 279, 281–83 (1981); B.

Jones & B. Gray, *Problems of Diagnosing Schizophrenia and Affective Disorders among Blacks*, 37 HOSP. & COMMUNITY PSYCHIATRY 61, 61–65 (1986).

120. P. Solomon, *Racial Factors in Mental Health Service Utilization*, PSYCHOSOCIAL REHABILITATION J., Mar. 1988, at 10.

121. Ruth L. Greene et al., *Mental Health and Help-Seeking Behavior, in* AGING IN BLACK AMERICA 185 (James S. Jackson et al. eds., 1993); Vickie M. Mays et al., *Mental Health Symptoms and Service Utilization Patterns of Help-Seeking among African American Women, in* MENTAL HEALTH IN BLACK AMERICA 161 (Harold W. Neighbors & James S. Jackson eds., 1996).

122. Erica Goode, *Disparities Seen in Mental Care for Minorities*, N.Y. TIMES, Aug. 27, 2001, at A1.

123. Stephanie Hartwell, *An Examination of Racial Differences among Mentally Ill Offenders in Massachusetts*, 52 PSYCHIATRIC SERVS. 234, 236 (2001).

124. MENTAL HEALTH: CULTURE, RACE, AND ETHNICITY, *supra* note 106, at 32.

125. *Id.* at 32.

126. Evalina W. Bestman, *Intervention Techniques in the Black Community, in* CROSS-CULTURAL TRAINING FOR MENTAL HEALTH PROFESSIONALS 213 (Harriet P. Lefley & Paul B. Pedersen eds., 1986); Robert L. Bragg, *Discussion: Cultural Aspects of Mental Health Care for Black Americans, in* CROSS-CULTURAL PSYCHOLOGY 179 (Albert Gaw ed., 1982); Lawrence E. Gary, *Attitudes of Black Adults toward Community Mental Health Centers*, 38 HOSP. & COMMUNITY PSYCHIATRY 1100, 1105 (1987); Gerald G. Jackson, *Cross-Cultural Counseling with Afro Americans, in* HANDBOOK OF CROSS-CULTURAL COUNSELING AND THERAPY 231 (Paul Pedersen ed., 1985).

127. *Frontline:* "A Crime of Insanity" (PBS television broadcast, Oct. 17, 2002).

128. JAMES J. STEPHAN, U.S. DEP'T OF JUST., STATE PRISON EXPENDITURES, 1996, 1, 3 (1996).

129. *Therapy instead of Jail*, PALM BEACH POST, Apr. 19, 1999, at 18A.

130. *Frontline:* "A Crime of Insanity," *supra* note 127.

131. *Id.*

132. M. DeAnna Doherty, *Mentally Ill Inmates, in* INTERNATIONAL ENCYCLOPEDIA OF JUSTICE STUDIES (2002), *available at* http://www.iejs.com/Corrections/Mentally_Ill_Inmates.htm (last visited July 29, 2007).

133. *Id.*

134. DITTON, *supra* note 24, at 9.

135. Mentally Ill Offender Treatment and Crime Reduction Act: Hearing on S. 1194 before the Sen. Comm. on the Judiciary, 108th Cong. (2003) (statement of Reginald A. Wilkinson, Director, Ohio Dep't of Rehabilitation and Correction), *available at* http://www.drc.state.oh.us/WEB/Articles/article77.htm.

136. *Id.*

137. MENTAL HEALTH: CULTURE, RACE, AND ETHNICITY, *supra* note 106.

138. *Id.*

139. *Id.*

140. *Id.*

141. Erica Goode, *Disparities Seen in Mental Care for Minorities,* N.Y. TIMES, Aug. 27, 2001, at A1.

142. Race Matters.Org, Minorities' Care for Mental Illness Is Called Inferior, *available at* http://www.racematters.org.

143. *Id.*

144. MENTAL HEALTH: CULTURE, RACE, AND ETHNICITY, supra note 106. The Surgeon General's Report concludes that disparities in access to mental health services are partly attributable to financial barriers.

145. Fred Osher et al., *A Best Practice Approach to Community Reentry from Jails for Inmates with Co-Occurring Disorders: The APIC Model,* 49 CRIME & DELINQ. 79 (2003).

146. Patricia Griffin, *The Back Door of the Jail, in* EFFECTIVELY ADDRESSING THE MENTAL HEALTH NEEDS OF JAIL DETAINEES 91, 94–99 (Henry J. Steadman ed., 1990); Fred Osher et al., *A Best Practice Approach to Community Reentry from Jails for Inmates with Co-Occurring Disorders: The APIC Model,* 49 CRIME & DELINQ. 79 (2003); AM. ASS'N OF CMTY. PSYCHIATRISTS, POSITION STATEMENT ON POST RELEASE PLANNING (2001), *available at* http://www.wpic.pitt.edu.

147. Arthur J. Lurigio & John A. Swartz, *Changing the Contours of the Criminal Justice System to Meet the Needs of Persons with Serious Mental Illness, in* CRIMINAL JUSTICE 2000: POLICIES, PROCESSES, AND DECISIONS OF THE CRIMINAL JUSTICE SYSTEM 45, 88–93 (U.S. Dep't of Just. ed., 2000); Roger H. Peters & Holly A. Hills, *Community Treatment and Supervision Strategies for Offenders with Co-Occurring Disorders: What Works?, in* STRATEGIC SOLUTIONS: THE INTERNATIONAL COMMUNITY CORRECTIONS ASSOCIATION EXAMINES SUBSTANCE ABUSE 81, 116–19 (Edward J. Latessa ed., 1999).

NOTES TO CHAPTER 6

1. Dareh Gregorian & Pia Akerman, *Ex-Con Barber in Hair Tangle,* N.Y. POST, Feb. 21, 2003, at 3; *see also* Clyde Haberman, *Ex-Inmate Denied Chair (and Clippers),* N.Y. TIMES, Feb. 25, 2003, at B1.

2. Gregorian & Akerman, *supra* note 1.

3. HARRY J. HOLZER ET AL., THE URBAN INST., CAN EMPLOYERS PLAY A MORE POSITIVE ROLE IN PRISONER REENTRY? 14 (2002), *available at* http://www.urban.org/UploadedPDF/410803_PositiveRole.pdf (last visited July 29, 2007).

4. *A Stigma That Never Fades*, ECONOMIST, Aug. 10, 2002, at 25, 26.

5. Sharon Dietrich, Maurice Emsellem, & Catherine Ruckelshaus, *Work Reform: The Other Side of Welfare Reform*, 9 STAN. L. & POL'Y REV. 53, 56 (1998). Title VII applies to state and municipal, as well as private, employers.

6. Michael Meltsner et al., *An Act to Promote the Rehabilitation of Criminal Offenders in the State of New York*, 24 SYRACUSE L. REV. 885, 904–5 (1973).

7. Note that the decision in Green v. Mo. Pac. R.R. Co., 523 F.2d 1290 (8th Cir. 1975) is not binding on the Arizona courts or the Ninth Circuit. Therefore, companies in Arizona may maintain policies eliminating all applicants from employment who have been convicted of a criminal offense, absent some legislative action prohibiting such practices. Furthermore, the United States Supreme Court has not addressed this issue.

8. Philip Harvey, *Combating Joblessness: An Analysis of the Principal Strategies That Have Influenced the Development of American Employment and Social Welfare Law during the 20th Century*, 21 BERKELEY J. EMP. & LAB. L. 677, 724–27, 741 fig.7 (2000).

9. CTR. ON BUDGET & POL'Y PRIORITIES, STILL FAR FROM THE DREAM: RECENT DEVELOPMENTS IN BLACK INCOME, EMPLOYMENT, AND POVERTY 28 (1988).

10. Many residents in East Palo were employed in low-wage jobs with little job security. *See* Dan Walters, *A New Chance for Change*, SACRAMENTO BEE, Nov. 28, 1988, at A3; Ramon G. McLeod, *Good Jobs Keep Receding beyond Black Workers' Grasp*, S.F. CHRON., Mar. 29, 1988, at A1.

11. ANDREW HACKER, TWO NATIONS: BLACK AND WHITE, SEPARATE, HOSTILE, AND UNEQUAL 103 (1992) (noting that in 1990, average Black unemployment was 2.76 times greater than White, which was highest differential since 1960).

12. Andrew Hacker reports that the other 998 companies are not preparing any top African American executives for a future chief executive officer position.

[I]n 1997, only 16 percent of employed African Americans held professional or managerial jobs, compared to 31 percent of employed Whites. By contrast, Black workers were overrepresented in the service sector, with its lower wages: 26 percent of employed African Americans worked in service industries in 1997, while only 15 percent of their White counterparts held jobs in this sector.

13. Phillip Harvey, *Human Rights and Economic Policy Discourse: Taking Economic and Social Rights Seriously* 33 COLUMBIA HUM. RTS. L. REV. 363, 433 (Spring 2002).

14. Joleen Kirschenman & Kathryn Neckerman, *"We'd Love to Hire Them,*

But . . . ," *in* THE URBAN UNDERCLASS 203, 203–4 (Christopher Jencks & Paul E. Peterson eds., 1991).

15. WILLIAM JULIUS WILSON, THE TRULY DISADVANTAGED 1–5 (1987) (blaming the rise of the underclass on the disappearance of unskilled jobs from urban areas).

16. WILLIAM JULIUS WILSON, WHEN WORK DISAPPEARS: THE WORLD OF THE NEW URBAN POOR 3–86, 25–50 (1996).

17. *Id.*

18. JOAN PETERSILIA, WHEN PRISONERS COME HOME: PAROLE AND PRISONER REENTRY 4–5 (2003) [hereinafter WHEN PRISONERS COME HOME].

19. *Id.*

20. Fox Butterfield, *Freed from Prison, but Still Paying a Penalty,* N.Y. TIMES, Dec. 29, 2002, at 18; Avi Brisman, *Double Whammy: Collateral Consequences of Conviction and Imprisonment for Sustainable Communities and the Environment,* 28 WM. & MARY ENVTL. L. & POL'Y REV. 423, 433 (2004).

21. *Id.* at 435.

22. Bruce E. May, *The Character Component of Occupational Licensing Laws: A Continuing Barrier to the Ex-Felon's Employment Opportunities,* 71 N.D. L. REV. 187, 193 (1995).

23. *Id.*

24. *Id.* at 194.

25. *Id.* at 196.

26. *Id.* at 197.

27. *Id.*

28. *Id*

29. *Id.*

30. *Id.*

31. *Id.*

32. BILL HEBENTON & TERRY THOMAS, CRIMINAL RECORDS: STATE, CITIZEN, AND THE POLITICS OF PROTECTION 111 (1993).

33. JEREMY TRAVIS ET AL., FROM PRISON TO HOME: THE DIMENSIONS AND CONSEQUENCES OF PRISONER REENTRY 13 (2001) (reporting number of incarcerated women who have children), 31 (listing Alabama, Delaware, Iowa, Mississippi, Rhode Island, and South Carolina as states that impose permanent bars for public employment on ex-offenders).

34. Garcia v. Duffy, 492 So. 2d 435, 438 (Fla. 2d DCA 1986.

35. *Id.* at 992.

36. Babi-Ali v. City of New York, 979 F. Supp. 268, 277 (S.D.N.Y. 1997); Haddock v. City of New York, 553 N.E.2d 987, 992 (N.Y. 1990).

37. Any dollar amount on the liability limit would be arbitrary. However, the limit should be high enough so that plaintiffs will receive a meaningful recovery, but not so high as to strip employers of the benefit of their compliance.

38. Fla. Laws ch. 99 225, 1400, 1412–13 (1999) (to be codified at Fla. Stat. § 768.096).

39. *Id.*

40. Eric Rasmussen, *Stigma and Self-Fulfilling Expectations of Criminality,* 39 J.L. & ECON. 519, 540 (1996) (noting that "[t]he private sector . . . unofficially punishes known criminals by stigmatizing them").

41. Civil Rights Act of 1964, 42 U.S.C. § 2000e-2(a)(1) (1991).

42. 42 U.S.C. § 2000e-2(k)(1)(A)(i).

43. Debbie A. Mukamal & Paul N. Samuels, *Statutory Limitations on Civil Rights of People with Criminal Records,* 30 FORDHAM URB. L.J. 1501, 1503 (2003).

44. Equal Employment Opportunity Comm'n, Policy Guidance on the Consideration of Arrest Records in Employment Decisions under Title VII of the Civil Rights Act of 1964, as amended, 42 U.S.C. §§ 2000e to 2000e-17 (1990).

45. Green v. Missouri Pac. R.R., 523 F.2d 1290 (8th Cir. 1975) is the leading case on an employer's use of a criminal conviction in the application process. *Green* involves an employer's absolute policy of refusing consideration for employment to any person convicted of a crime other than a minor traffic offense. *Id.* at 1292. The plaintiff, an African American who had a prior conviction for refusing military induction, applied and was rejected for a clerk's position solely on the basis of that conviction. *Id.* The court held, first, that the plaintiff's statistics (5.3 percent of African American applicants, compared to 2.2 percent of White applicants, were rejected under the policy) sufficed to make out a prima facie case of adverse impact. *Id.* at 1300. The court then held that, although criminal convictions lawfully may be considered, "[w]e cannot conceive of any business necessity that would automatically place every individual convicted of any offense, except a minor traffic offense, in the permanent ranks of the unemployed." *Id.* at 1298. The court in *Green* struck down the policy. Although blanket rejection rules like the one in *Green* have been found unlawful, more narrowly tailored selection criteria relating to convictions have been upheld. E.E.O.C. v. Carolina Freight Carriers Corp., 723 F. Supp. 734, 752 (S.D. Fla. 1989) (holding that employer's policy of not hiring employees with theft convictions justified as legitimate means to reduce risk of employee theft).

46. N.Y. Correct. Law § 752 (McKinney 2001) ("Unfair discrimination against persons previously convicted of one or more criminal offenses prohibited."); Conn. Gen. Stat. Ann. § 46a 80 (West 2001) ("Denial of employment based on prior conviction of crime. Dissemination of arrest record prohibited."); Wis. Stat. Ann. § 111.335 (West 2001) ("Arrest or conviction record; exceptions and special cases.").

47. Wis. Stat. Ann. § 111.31 (West 2003).

48. § 111.31(2)–(3).

49. The Wisconsin legislature codified its rationale for enacting WFEA. In pertinent part, the Wisconsin legislature declared its policy as follows:
The legislature finds that the practice of unfair discrimination in employment against properly qualified individuals by reason of . . . arrest record [and] conviction record . . . substantially and adversely affects the general welfare of the state. Employers . . . that deny employment opportunities and discriminate in employment against properly qualified individuals solely because of . . . arrest record [and] conviction record . . . deprive those individuals of the earnings that are necessary to maintain a just and decent standard of living. § 111.31(1).

50. Haw. Rev. Stat. Ann. § 378 2 (Michie 1999).

51. § 378 2.5.

52. N.Y. Correct. Law § 752 (Mckinney 1998); N.Y. Exec. Law § 296 (Mckinney 1998). These statutes have only been held applicable to those seeking employment and not current employees. *See* Green v. Wells Fargo Alarm Serv., 192 A.D.2d 463, 464 (N.Y. App. Div. 1993).

53. N.Y. Correct. Law § 752.

54. § 752.

55. § 752.

56. § 752.

57. 200 A.D.2d 224 (N.Y. App. Div. 1994).

58. *Id.* at 225.

59. *Id.* at 227.

60. "Direct relationship" is defined in N.Y. Corr. Law § 750(3) (McKinney 2003) as one in which the "nature of criminal conduct for which the person was convicted has a direct bearing on his fitness or ability to perform one or more of the duties or responsibilities necessarily related to the license or employment sought." Since the housing caretaker position, unlike a correction officer position, for example, would not as such involve plaintiff in violent confrontations and obviously does not require plaintiff to carry arms, his fitness to perform these duties is not implicated.

61. *Id.*

62. Ford, 200 A.D.2d at 229–30.

63. *Id.* at 229.

64. 713 F. Supp. 677 (S.D.N.Y. 1989).

65. While this action was brought in federal court, the case has since been favorably cited by New York state courts. *See* Ford, 200 A.D.2d at 228.

66. Soto-Lopez, 713 F. Supp. at 678.

67. *Id.*

68. *Id.*

69. 712 N.E.2d 669, 670 (N.Y. 1999).

70. 181 A.D.2d 614 (N.Y. App. Div. 1992).

71. In re City of New York v. City Civil Serv. Comm'n, 532 N.Y.S.2d 626 (N.Y. Sup. Ct. 1988).

72. Joan Petersilia, *Parole and Prisoner Reentry in the United States, in* PRISONS 479, 519 (Michael Tonry & Joan Petersilia eds., 1999) [hereinafter *Parole and Prisoner Reentry*].

73. Ted Palmer, *Aspects of Successful Integration, in* CHOOSING CORRECTIONAL OPTIONS THAT WORK 139–40 (Alan Harland ed., 1996).

74. PETERSILIA, WHEN PRISONERS COME HOME, *supra* note 18, at 4–5.

75. Leroy D. Clark, *A Civil Rights Task: Removing Barriers to Employment of Ex-Convicts*, 38 U.S.F. L. REV. 193 (2004); Monica Scales, *Employer Catch-22: The Paradox between Employer Liability for Employee Criminal Acts and the Prohibition against Ex-Convict Discrimination*, 11 GEO. MASON L. REV. 419 (2002); Sheri-Ann S. L. Lau, *Employment Discrimination Because of One's Arrest and Court Record in Hawaii*, 22 U. HAW. L. REV. 709 (2000); James R. Todd, *It's Not My Problem: How Workplace Violence and Potential Employer Liability Lead to Employment Discrimination of Ex-Convicts*, 36 ARIZ. ST. L.J. 725 (2004).

76. N.Y. Correct. Law § 753(1) (McKinney 2003).

77. An employer cannot discriminate against an applicant on the basis of a criminal conviction record, unless (1) there is a direct relationship between one or more of the previous criminal offenses and the specific license or employment sought; or (2) the issuance of the license or the granting of the employment would involve an unreasonable risk to property or to the safety or welfare of specific individuals or the general public. N.Y. Correct. Law § 752 (Mckinney 1987).

78. N.Y. Correct. Law § 753(1).

79. Bonacorsa v. Van Lindt, 523 N.E.2d 806 (N.Y. 1988).

80. N.Y. Correct. Law § 701 (McKinney 2003). As both appellate levels of the New York courts pointed out in Morrisette v. Dilworth, 89 A.D.2d 99 (N.Y. App. Div. 1982), the granting of such a certificate is "not a pardon," *id.* at 101, and "does not eradicate or expunge the underlying conviction." 452 N.E.2d 1222, 1223 n.2 (N.Y. 1983).

81. Ford v. Gildin, 200 A.D.2d 224, 229 (N.Y. App. Div. 1994).

82. For example, the jury in Haddock v. New York awarded $3.5 million to the plaintiff. This was later reduced to $2.5 million by the Appellate Division. 553 N.E.2d 987, 990 (N.Y. 1990).

83. 42 U.S.C. § 1981a(b) (1994).

84. 42 U.S.C. § 2000e(b) (1994).

85. Employers with more than fourteen employees but fewer than 101 have their liability capped at $50,000. Large employers, those with more than five hundred employees, have a $300,000 damages cap. *See* 42 U.S.C. § 1981a(b) (1994).

86. Sarvis v. Vt. State Colls., 772 A.2d 494, 500 (Vt. 2001).

87. RE-ENTRY POLICY COUNCIL, REPORT OF THE RE-ENTRY POLICY COUN-CIL: CHARTING THE SAFE AND SUCCESSFUL RETURN OF PRISONERS TO THE COM-MUNITY 294–95 (2005) (The Re-Entry Council was formed by the Council of State Governments and was funded by the United States Departments of Justice, Labor, and Health and Human Services.).

88. Nora V. Demleitner, *Preventing Internal Exile: The Need for Restrictions on Collateral Sentencing Consequences*, 11 STAN. L. & POL'Y REV. 153, 156 (1999).

89. John Hagan & Ronit Dinovitzer, *Collateral Consequences of Conviction for Children, Communities, and Prisoners*, 26 CRIME & JUST. 121, 134 (1999).

90. TRAVIS ET AL., *supra* note 33, at 32.

91. 26 U.S.C.A. § 51(d)(4) (West supp. 2004) (offering tax credits to employers hiring certain categories of workers, including certain felons from low-income families).

92. The Federal Bonding Program was created in 1966 by the U.S. Department of Labor to alleviate employers' concerns that job applicants with criminal records would be untrustworthy workers, by allowing employers to purchase fidelity bonds to indemnify them for loss of money or property sustained through the dishonest acts of their employees. *Available at* U.S. Dep't of Labor, http://www.doleta.gov.

93. Petersilia, *Parole and Prisoner Reentry, supra* note 72, at 519.

NOTES TO CHAPTER 7

1. AScribe Newswire, "Voting Rights Groups Praise Iowa Governor for Restoring Eligibility to Thousands," Ascribe Inc., June 17, 2005

2. *Rachel La Corte, Ex-Felons Face Roadblocks in Regaining Voting Rights, available at* http://seattlepi.nwsource.com/local/231136_gfelono4.html (July 4, 2005.

3. *Id.*

4. *Id.* at 793 tbl. 4a.

5. Kathleen M. Olivares et al., *The Collateral Consequences of a Felony Conviction: A National Study of State Legal Codes Ten Years Later,* FED. PRO-BATION, Sept. 1996, at 10, 13, 16 n.1 (1996).

6. JON SHURE AND RASHIDA MACMURRAY, N.J. POLICY PERSPECTIVE, RE-STORING THE RIGHT TO VOTE: ISN'T IT TIME? (2000), *available at* http://www.njpp.org.

7. THOMAS HOBBES, LEVIATHAN 141–86 (J. Plamenatz ed., 1963); JOHN LOCKE, THE SECOND TREATISE OF GOVERNMENT 366 (rev. ed., J.W. Gough 1976); JOHN RAWLS, A THEORY OF JUSTICE 11–12, 118–92 (Belknap Press of Harvard Univ. Press 1971). These philosophers suggest that the individual en-

gages in a form of "social contract" to form a particular system of government and that this contract must be adhered to for order to be maintained; JAY A. SIGLER, CIVIL RIGHTS IN AMERICA: 1500 TO THE PRESENT 383–84 (1998).

8. Note: *The Disenfranchisement of Ex-Felons: Citizenship, Criminality, and "The Purity of the Ballot Box,"* 102 HARV. L. REV. 1300 (1989).

9. 380 F.2d 445 (2d Cir. 1967).

10. *Id.* at 451.

11. Anthony C. Thompson, *Navigating the Hidden Obstacles to Ex-Offender Reentry,* 45 B.C. L. REV. 255, 282 (2004).

12. JAMES Q. WILSON, THINKING ABOUT CRIME 118 (rev. ed. 1983).

13. RONALD DWORKIN, TAKING RIGHTS SERIOUSLY 190–91 (1977).

14. JOHN BRAITHWAITE & PHILIP PETTIT, NOT JUST DESSERTS: A REPUBLICAN THEORY OF CRIMINAL JUSTICE 46 (1990).

15. Marc Mauer, *Felon Disenfranchisement: A Policy Whose Time Has Passed,* 31 A.B.A. HUMAN RIGHTS 1 (Winter 2004).

16. Nora V. Demleitner, *Continuing Payment on One's Debt to Society: The German Model of Felon Disenfranchisement as an Alternative,* 84 MINN. L. REV. 753, 770–71 (2000).

17. Alec C. Ewald, *Civil Death: The Ideological Paradox of Criminal Disenfranchisement Law in the United States,* 2002 WIS. L. REV. 1045 (2002).

18. For a brief history of the southern constitutional conventions, see chapters 6 and 7 of J. MORGAN KOUSSER, THE SHAPING OF SOUTHERN POLITICS: SUFFRAGE RESTRICTION AND THE ESTABLISHMENT OF THE ONE-PARTY SOUTH (1974) and chapter 12 of C. VANN WOODWARD, ORIGINS OF THE NEW SOUTH, 1877–1913 (1951).

19. WOODWARD, *supra* note 18, at 331–32.

20. By 1908, all eleven ex-Confederate states had adopted the poll tax, "and the Afro-American was always its chief intended victim." J. Morgan Kousser, *The Undermining of the First Reconstruction: Lessons for the Second, in* MINORITY VOTE DILUTION 27, 34 (Chandler Davidson ed., 1984).

21. Grandfather clauses guaranteed the franchise to men who had voted—or whose fathers or grandfathers had voted—before the Civil War. This was an attempt at a race-neutral provision that effectively disenfranchised Blacks while attempting to garner the votes of poor or uneducated Whites. WOODWARD, *supra* note 18, at 332–35.

22. Karen M. Arrington, *The Struggle to Gain the Right to Vote: 1787–1965, in* VOTING RIGHTS IN AMERICA 25, 30 (Karen M. Arrington & William L. Taylor eds., 1992).

23. *Id.*

24. Andrew L. Shapiro, Note: *Challenging Criminal Disenfranchisement under the Voting Rights Act: A New Strategy,* 103 YALE L.J. 537, 542 (1993) (referencing Hunter v. Underwood, 471 U.S. 222 [1985]) (citations omitted).

25. Hunter v. Underwood, 471 U.S. 222 (1985),

26. Shapiro, *supra* note 24.

27. Eric Lichtblau, *Confusing Rules Deny Vote to Ex-felons, Study Says*, N.Y. TIMES, Feb. 20, 2005, § 1, at 24.

28. *Letting Ex-Cons Vote "the Right Thing to Do,"* SOUTH FLORIDA SUN-SENTINEL, April 8, 2007, Local Section.

29. JAMIE FELLNER & MARC MAUER, HUMAN RIGHTS WATCH AND THE SEN-TENCING PROJECT, LOSING THE VOTE: THE IMPACT OF FELON DISENFRANCHISE-MENT LAWS 8 (1998), *available at* http://www.hrw.org/reports98/vote.

30. Alec C. Ewald, *supra* note 17, at 1054.

31. Kate Zernike, *Iowa Governor Will Give Felons the Right to Vote*, N.Y. TIMES, June 18, 2005, at A8.

32. John Hopkins, *An Appeal for Blanket Voting Rights to Freed Cons*, VIR-GINIAN-PILOT, Jan. 11, 2006, *available at* http://home.hamptonroads.com/stories/story.cfm?story=97951&ran=243974 (last visited July 29, 2007).

33. N.M. Stat. § 31-13-1 (2006).

34. PATRICIA ALLARD & MARC MAUER, THE SENTENCING PROJECT, REGAIN-ING THE VOTE: AN ASSESSMENT OF ACTIVITY RELATING TO FELON DISENFRAN-CHISEMTN LAWS 1 (1999).

35. *Id.*

36. *Id.* at 7–8. Other states disenfranchising more than one hundred thousand ex-offenders as of 1998 were Alabama, Mississippi, Texas, and Virginia. *Id.* at 8. Florida governor Jeb Bush has questioned the results of the Fellner & Mauer study. *See* Jeb Bush, *In Florida, Ex-Felons Can Regain the Right to Vote*, SARASOTA HERALD TRIB., Jan. 12, 2001, at A14.

37. In Alabama, convicts must submit blood or saliva containing DNA to obtain the restoration of voting rights. Jesse Katz, *For Many Ex-cons, Voting Ban Can Be for Life*, L.A. TIMES, Apr. 2, 2000, at A1. Felons who move to Virginia from one of the two states where felons retain the right to vote must wait five or seven years to vote, while those barred from voting while incarcerated may register immediately. Restoration of Rights, *available at* http://www.soc.state.va.us. (explaining the Virginia governor's clemency policy and noting that prior to restoration of civil rights "an applicant must be free from any supervised probation and not have any convictions or charges pending for a period of five years immediately preceding the application"). For a comprehensive summary of state restoration procedures, see Restoring Your Right to Vote, *available at* http://www.usdoj.gov (listing restoration procedures in each state). Nevada and Kentucky—both of which indefinitely disenfranchise felons—have recently made it easier for ex-offenders to restore their voting rights. Nevada law does not automatically restore voting rights to convicts, but requires that any former felon who applies for such restoration will receive it. NEV. REV. STAT. ANN. 213.157 (Michie Supp. 2001). Kentucky retains gubernatorial discretion

in the restoration process, but has simplified its standards. Ky. Rev. Stat. Ann. § 196.045 (Michie Supp. 2001).

38. 75 Ala. 583 (1884).

39. *Id.*

40. Trop v. Dulles, 356 U.S. 86, 96–97 (1958).

41. 605 F. Supp. 802 (M.D. Tenn. 1985).

42. *Id.* at 813.

43. *Id.* at 804–14 (referring to Voting Rights Act as amended in 1982).

44. *Id.* at 814.

45. Wesley v. Collins, 791 F.2d 1255, 1260–61 (6th Cir. 1986).

46. Richardson v. Ramirez, 418 U.S. 24 (1974).

47. *Id.* at 41–56.

48. *Id. Richardson* was decided on the basis of language in section 2 of the Fourteenth Amendment that explicitly mentions the disenfranchisement of convicted criminals. Section 2 of the Fourteenth Amendment provides, in part,

[W]hen the right to vote at any election . . . is denied to any of the male inhabitants of [a] State, being twenty one years of age, and citizens of the United States, or in any way abridged, except for participation in rebellion, or other crime, the basis of representation therein shall be reduced in the proportion which the number of such male citizens shall bear to the whole number of male citizens twenty one years of age in such State. U.S. Const. amend. XIV, § 2 (emphasis added).

Strong arguments have been made that the Court incorrectly applied this section in *Richardson.*

49. Alice E. Harvey, *Ex-Felon Disenfranchisement and Its Influence on the Black Vote: The Need for a Second Look,* 142 U. Pa. L. Rev. 1145, 1149–59 (1994).

50. Fellner & Mauer, *supra* note 29, at 1.

51. Allard & Mauer, *supra* note 34, at 1.

52. *Id.*

53. *Id.*

54. 947 F. Supp. 954 (S.D. Miss. 1995).

55. *Id.* at 973–76.

56. *Id.*

57. 42 U.S.C. § 1973 (2000); Fellner & Mauer, *supra* note 29, at 19.

58. City of Mobile v. Bolden, 446 U.S. 55 (1980).

59. Voting Rights Act Amendments, Pub. L. No. 97 205, § 3 (1982); United States Department of Justice, Civil Rights Division, Voting Section, Congress, amended section 2 of the act to allow a constitutional claim of minority vote dilution without proof of a racially discriminatory purpose.

60. Fellner & Mauer, *supra* note 29, at 19–20.

61. Va. Const. art. II, § 1.

62. 85 F.3d 919 (2d Cir. Cir. 1996) (*per curiam*).

63. *Id.* at 920.

64. *Id.*

65. *Id.* at 921–22.

66. *Id.* at 937 (Feinberg, J., dissenting).

67. Rogers v. Lodge, 458 U.S. 623, 624 (1982).

68. Farrakhan v. Locke, 987 F. Supp. 1304, 1313 (E.D. Wa. 1997).

69. Adam H. Kurland, *Partisan Rhetoric, Constitutional Reality, and Political Responsibility: The Troubling Constitutional Consequences of Achieving D.C. Statehood by Simple Legislation,* 60 Geo. Wash. L. Rev. 475, 499 (1992).

70. *Former Felons Have a Right to Vote,* N.Y. Times, Oct. 17, 2002, at A32.

71. Pamela Karlan, *Convictions and Doubts: Retribution, Representation, and the Debate over Felon Disenfranchisement,* 56 Stan. L. Rev. 1147, 1157 (2004).

72. *Id.*

73. *Id.*

74. In New York State, seven conservative upstate Republicans represent state senatorial districts that comply with "one person, one vote" only because incarcerated prisoners are included within the population base. For example, one of the upstate districts is represented by Dale Volker. As a reporter explained, Volker "says it's a good thing his captive constituents can't vote, because if they could, '[t]hey would never vote for me.'" Jonathan Tilove, *Minority Prison Inmates Skew Local Populations As States Redistrict,* Newhouse News Serv., Mar. 12, 2002, *available at* http://prisonpolicy.org/news/newhouse news031202.html.

75. Jeff Manza et al., The Truly Disenfranchised: Felon Voting Rights and American Politics 1, 18–19 (2001) (unpublished paper), *available at* http://www .northwestern.edu; Sasha Abramsky, *A Growing Gap in American Democracy,* N.Y. Times, July 27, 2002, at A23.

76. Manza et al., *supra* note 75, at 18–19.

77. Tenn. Code Ann. § 40-29-105 (1996). In Tennessee, the individual must obtain a judgment from a local trial court in order to restore his or her voting rights. Individuals convicted of murder, rape, treason, or voter fraud are ineligible to have voting rights restored. *Id.* § 40-29-105(c)(2)(B).

78. Tex. Elec. Code Ann. § 11.002.

79. Del. Const. art. V, § 2. An amendment to the Delaware Constitution in 2000 provides for automatic restoration of felon voting rights after five years have elapsed. Convictions for murder, sexual crimes, and "crimes against the public" are not eligible for automatic restoration. *Id.*

80. Neb. Rev. Stat. § 29-112 (2006). The Nebraska legislature initially passed Legislative Bill 53 on March 3, 2005; however, Governor Dave Heine-

mann vetoed it. The legislature responded by overriding the veto by a vote of thirty-six to eleven. *See* Nate Jenkins, *Lawmakers Override Felon Voting Veto,* LINCOLN (NEBRASKA) J. STAR, Mar. 11, 2005, at B1.

81. Md. Code Ann., Elec. Law § 3-102 (West 2006).

82. Nev. Rev. Stat. § 213.157 (2006) (automatically restoring voting rights upon completion of the sentence for felons convicted of a first-time nonviolent felony).

83. *See* Conn. Gen. Stat. § 9-46a (2006).

NOTES TO CHAPTER 8

1. Editorial: *Probation Violators Should Be Jailed,* LEDGER (Lakeland, FL), Aug. 14, 2004, at A18.

2. Luisa Yanez, *Ex Probation Supervisor: "Why Fire Me over Killings?"* MIAMI HERALD, Aug. 12, 2004, at 1B. WLNR 194611929.

3. Andrew Lyons, *Officials Pointing Fingers over Paperwork Mixup,* DAYTONA NEWS-JOURNAL, August 11, 2004, section A.

4. Loren A. N. Buddress, *Federal Probation and Pretrial Services: A Cost-Effective and Successful Community Corrections System,* FED. PROBATION, Mar. 1997, at 6.

5. Sunny A. M. Koshy, *The Right of [All] the People to Be Secure: Extending Fundamental Fourth Amendment Rights to Probationers and Parolees,* 39 HASTINGS L.J. 449, 466 (1988).

6. N.Y. Exec. Law § 259 i[2](c) (McKinney 1998) (necessitating calculation of potential recidivism); *see also* Morrissey v. Brewer, 408 U.S. 471, 482 [1972]).

7. Melinda K. Blatt, *State Liability for Injuries Inflicted by Parolees,* 56 U. CINN. L. REV. 615, 615 (1987); TRAVIS O'LEARY, *A History of Parole, in* PROBATION, PAROLE, AND COMMUNITY CORRECTIONS 109 (Robert M. Carter ed., 1984).

8. N.Y. Exec. Law § 259 I[2][c] (McKinney 1978).

9. Joan Petersilia, *Parole and Prisoner Reentry in the United States, in* PRISONS 479, 506–7 (Michael Tonry & Joan Petersilia eds., 1999).

10. 730 Ill. Comp. Stat. 5/3 14 2(d) (1993).

11. Thomas Peters & David Norris, *Reconsidering Parole Release Decisions in Illinois: Facts, Myths, and the Need for Policy Changes,* 24 J. MARSHALL L. REV. 815, 835–39 (1991); William Recktenwald & Rob Karweth, *Parole System a Bad Joke That May Get Worse,* CHI. TRIB., Apr. 7, 1991, at 1.

12. Thomas J. Bamonte, *The Viability of Morissey v. Brewer and the Due Process Rights of Parolees and Other Conditional Releases,* 18 S. ILL. U. L.J. 121, 134 (1993).

13. *Id.*

14. Jeremy Travis & Kirsten Christiansen, *After Incarceration, Failed Reentry: The Challenges of Back-end Sentencing*, 13 GEO. J. ON POVERTY L. & POL'Y 249, 250–51 (Summer 2006).

15. 408 U.S. 471 (1972).

16. 411 U.S. 778 (1973).

17. 408 U.S. at 482.

18. *Id.*

19. Richard P. Seiter, *Prisoner Reentry and the Role of Parole Officers*, FED. PROBATION, Dec. 2002, at 50–51.

20. David N. Adair, *Revocation of Supervised Release: A Judicial Function*, 6 FED. SENTENCING REP. 190 (1994).

21. When I say "technical violations," what I mean is a violation of a condition of parole (something that is on its face not a criminal act but results in reincarceration).

22. Thomas J. Bamonte & Thomas M. Peters, *The Parole Revocation Process in Illinois*, 24 LOY. U. CHI. L.J. 211, 225–27 (1993).

23. *Id.* at 229–30.

24. *Id.* at 235–36.

25. *Id.* at 242–43.

26. Violent Crime Control and Law Enforcement Act, Pub. L. No. 103 322, 108 Stat. 1796 (1994).

27. Petersilia, *supra* note 9, at 28.

28. ERIC LOTKE, NAT'L CTR. OF INST. & ALTERNATIVES, HOBBLING A GENERATION: YOUNG AFRICAN-AMERICAN MALES IN WASHINGTON, D.C.'S CRIMINAL JUSTICE SYSTEM FIVE YEARS LATER 1 (1997).

29. Christopher Uggen, Jeff Manza, & Melissa Thompson, *Citizenship, Democracy, and the Civic Reintegration of Criminal Offenders*, 605 ANNALS AM. ACAD. POL. & SOC. SCI. 281, 286 tbl.1 (2006) (showing that in 1968, African Americans made up 32 percent of the total adult prison/parole population and that in 1978, African Americans made up 34 percent of the total adult prison/parole population in the United States).

30. In the fall of 1997, 1,532,800 African Americans were enrolled in higher education institutions, compared to 2,149,900 African Americans who were under correctional supervision—i.e., in jails, in prison, or on parole or probation. NAT'L CTR. FOR EDUC. STAT., DIGEST OF EDUCATION STATISTICS 2000, at 236 tbl.207 (2000), *available at* http://nces.ed.gov/programs/digest/doo/ (last visited July 29, 2007); BUREAU OF JUST. STAT., U.S. DEP'T OF JUST., PRISONERS IN 1997, at 2 tbl.1.3 (2000), *available at* http://www.ojp.usdoj.gov/bjs/abstract/p97.htm (last visited July 29, 2007).

31. MARK MAUER, RACE TO INCARCERATE 19 (1999) (documenting dramatic rise in incarceration in United States and critically examining politics of crime control).

32.

[O]f the more than 150,000 drug offenders incarcerated in state prisons in 1991. . . . [a]lmost 127,000 of these offenders, or 84 percent, had no history of a prior incarceration for a violent crime, and one half of the offenders had no prior incarcerations at all. One third of the drug offenders sentenced to state prison had been convicted of the less serious possession offenses.

Id. at 157 (citing JAMES LYNCH & WILLIAM SABOL, URBAN INST., DID GETTING TOUGH ON CRIME PAY? [1997].).

33. MAUER, *supra* note 31, at 124–25.

34. *Id.*

35. *Id.*

36. JONATHAN SIMON, POOR DISCIPLINE: PAROLE AND THE SOCIAL CONTROL OF THE UNDERCLASS, 1890–1990 252, 253 (1993).

37. See Walter Scanlong, *It's Time I Shed My Ex-Convict Status,* NEWSWEEK, Feb. 21, 2000, at 10.

38. Bruce E. May, *Real-World Reflection: The Character Component of Occupational Licensing Laws: A Continuing Barrier to the Ex-Felon's Employment Opportunities,* 71 N.D. L. REV. 187, 187–88 (1995).

39. Kate Munro, *Employers Challenged,* N.H. SUNDAY NEWS, Mar. 8, 1998.

40. Eric Rasmusen, *Stigma and Self-Fulfilling Expectations of Criminality,* 39 J.L. & ECON. 519, 520 (1996).

41. Joan Petersilia, *When Prisoners Return to Communities: Political, Economic, and Social Consequences,* 65 FED. PROBATION 3, 4 (2001).

42. Bruce Morgan, *Jail Time,* TUFTS MED., Winter 2000, at 17.

43. Leena Kurki, *Restorative and Community Justice in the United States,* 27 CRIME & JUST. 235, 237 (2000).

44. *Id.*

45. Anthony C. Thompson, *It Takes a Community to Prosecute,* 77 NOTRE DAME L. REV. 321 (2002).

46. *Id.*

47. Francis T. Cullen et al., *Environmental Corrections: A New Paradigm for Effective Probation and Parole Supervision,* FED. PROBATION, Sept. 2002, at 28.

48. *Id.*

49. *Id.*

50. Edward E. Rhine, *Why "What Works" Matters under the "Broken Windows" Model of Supervision,* FED. PROBATION, Sept. 2002, at 38, 40.

51. Jeremy Travis, Laurie O. Robinson, & Amy L. Solomon, *Prisoner Reentry: Issues for Practice and Policy,* 17 CRIM. JUST. 12, 12–13 (2002).

52. *Id.*

53. *Id.*

54. *Id.*

NOTES TO CHAPTER 9

1. Excerpted from Terry Saunders, *Staying Home,* 41 No. 1 JUDGES J. (Winter 2002).

2. Jeremy Travis, Laurie Robinson, & Amy Solomon, *Prisoner Reentry: Issues for Practice and Policy,* CRIMINAL JUSTICE MAGAZINE, Spring 2002, at 12.

3. *Id.* at 15.

4. *Id.*

5. Franz Maruna & Thomas LeBel, *Welcome Home? Examining the "Reentry Court" Concept from a Strengths-Based Perspective,* 4 W. CRIMINOLOGY REV. 91 (2003).

6. Joan Petersilia & Susan Turner, *Intensive Probation and Parole,* 17 CRIME & JUST. 281, 282 (1993).

7. PETER FINN & ANDREA K. NEWLYN, U.S. DEP'T OF JUSTICE, MIAMI'S "DRUG COURT": A DIFFERENT APPROACH 3 (1993).

8. John S. Goldkamp, *The Drug Court Response: Issues and Implications for Justice Change,* 63 ALB. L. REV. 923, 943 (2000).

9. *Id.* at 927–28.

10. James Q. Wilson and George L. Kelling, *Broken Windows: The Police and Neighborhood Safety,* ATLANTIC MONTHLY, Mar. 1982.

11. Todd R. Clear & David R. Karp, *The Community Justice Movement, in* COMMUNITY JUSTICE: AN EMERGING FIELD 5–7 (David R. Karp ed., 1998).

12. Anthony C. Thompson, *Courting Disorder: Some Thoughts on Community Courts,* 10 WASH. UNIV. J. L. & POL'Y 63, 98 (2002).

13. Morris Hoffman, *Therapeutic Jurisprudence, Neo-Rehabilitation, Judicial Collectivism: The Least Dangerous Branch Becomes Most Dangerous,* 29 FORDHAM URB. L.J. 2,063 (2002).

14. Attorney General Janet Reno, Remarks at John Jay College of Criminal Justice on the Reentry Court Initiative (Feb. 10, 2000), transcript *available at* http://www.usdoj.gov.

15. *Reentry Courts,* 17 CRIM. JUST. 15, 15 (Spring 2002).

16. 287 U.S. 45 (1932).

17. Kim Taylor-Thompson, *Tuning Up Gideon's Trumpet,* 71 FORDHAM L. REV. 1461, 1470 (2003).

18. 304 U.S. 458 (1938).

19. *Id.* at 468.

20. 316 U.S. 455 (1942).

21. *Id.* at 465.

22. 372 U.S. 335 (1963).

23. 407 U.S. 25 (1972).

24. KAREN FREEMAN-WILSON, ROBERT TUTTLE, & SUSAN P. WEINSTEIN, U.S. DEP'T OF JUST., ETHICAL CONSIDERATIONS FOR JUDGES AND ATTORNEYS IN DRUG COURT 24–25 (2001) [hereinafter ETHICAL CONSIDERATIONS].

25. Taylor-Thompson, *supra* note 17, at 1465.

26. Saunders, *supra* note 1, at 36.

27. FREEMAN-WILSON, TUTTLE, & WEINSTEIN, ETHICAL CONSIDERATIONS, *supra* note 24, at 2.

28. FREEMAN-WILSON, TUTTLE, & WEINSTEIN, ETHICAL CONSIDERATIONS, *supra* note 24, at 10.

29. FREEMAN-WILSON, TUTTLE, & WEINSTEIN, ETHICAL CONSIDERATIONS, *supra* note 24, Canon 3 and commentary.

30. Thompson, *supra* note 12, at 85.

31. Greg Berman & John Feinblatt, *Beyond Process and Precedent: The Rise of Problem-Solving Courts*, 41 JUDGES' J. 5, 6 (2002).

32. Greg Berman & John Feinblatt, *Problem-Solving Justice: A Quiet Revolution*, 86 JUDICATURE 182, 213 (2003).

33. Phylis Skoot Bamberger, *Specialized Courts: Not a Cure-All*, 30 FORDHAM URB. L.J. 1091 (2003).

34. Dora L. McNew, *An Introduction to Community Corrections*, 11 HAMLINE J. PUB. L. & POL'Y 31, 32 (1990).

35. McNew, *supra* note 34, at 41–42.

36. Christine Lindquist, Jennifer Hardison, & Pamela K. Latimore, *Reentry Courts Process Evaluation (Phase 1), Final Report* (October 2003), section 4.3.4. at 41-42.

37. *Id.*

38. *Id.*

39. *Id.* at 40.

40. Shadd Maruna & Thomas P. LeBel, *Welcome Home? Examining the Reentry Court Concept from a Strengths-Based Perspective*, 4 No. 2 W. CRIMINOLOGY REV. 91–107, 92 (2003).

41. JEREMY TRAVIS, U.S. DEP'T OF JUST., BUT THEY ALL COME BACK: RETHINKING PRISONER REENTRY RESEARCH IN BRIEF SENTENCING AND CORRECTIONS ISSUES FOR THE 21ST CENTURY (2000).

42. Peggy B. Burke, *Collaboration for Successful Prisoner Reentry: The Role of Parole and the Courts*, 5 CORRECTIONS MGMNT. Q. 16 (2001).

43. James Austin, *Prisoner Reentry: Current Trends, Practices, and Issues*, 47 CRIME AND DELINQ. 314, 329–32 (2001).

44. Maruna & LeBel, *supra* note 40, at 93.

NOTES TO THE CONCLUSION

1. Todd R. Clear et al., *Incarceration and the Community: The Problem of Removing and Returning Offenders*, 47 CRIME & DELINQ. 335 (2001).

2. Bill McCarthy & John Hagan, *Getting into Street Crime: The Structure and Process of Criminal Embeddedness*, 24 SOC. SCI. RES. 63 (1995); Craig

Haney, *Psychology and the Limits of Prison Pain: Confronting the Coming Crisis in Eighth Amendment Law,* 3 PSYCHOL. PUB. POL'Y AND LAW 499 (1997).

3. JEREMY TRAVIS & MICHELLE WAUL, PRISONERS ONCE REMOVED: THE IMPACT OF INCARCERATION AND REENTRY ON CHILDREN, FAMILIES, AND COMMUNITIES (2003).

4. Jeffrey Fagan et al., *Reciprocal Effects of Crime and Incarceration in New York City Neighborhoods,* 30 FORDHAM URB. L.J. 1551 (2003).

5. *Id.* at 1556.

6. *Id.* at 1561.

7. *Id.* at 1556 (citing D. J. Silton, Note: *U.S. Prisons and Racial Profiling: A Covertly Racist Nation Rides a Vicious Cycle,* 20 LAW & INEQ. 53, 65 (2002).

8. Joan Petersilia, *What Works in Prisoner Reentry: Reviewing and Questioning the Evidence,* 68 FED. PROBATION 4 (2004).

9. John Hagan & Ronit Dinovitzer, *Collateral Consequences of Imprisonment for Children, Communities, and Prisoners, in* PRISONS 116, 119–20 (Michael Tonry & Joan Petersilia eds., Univ. of Chicago Press 1999).

10. *Id.*

11. Daniel Brook, When *God Goes to Prison,* LEGAL AFF., June 2003, at 22, 24.

12. *Id.*

13. *Id.*

14. *Id.*

15. *Id.* at 27.

16. *Id.*

17. *Id.*

18. *Id.*

19. *Id.*

20. *Id.*

21. *Id.* at 28.

22. *Id.*

23. *Id.*

24. David Cole, *Faith and Funding: Toward an Expressivist Model of the Establishment Clause,* 75 S. CAL. L. REV. 559, 562–63 (2002).

25. *Id.* at 573.

26. *Id.* at 568.

27. *Id.* at 568 & n.32 (citing then–police commissioner of Boston, William Bratton, attributing much of success in preventive crime fighting to work of ministers).

28. *Id.* at 570–71.

29. *Id.* at 566–78.

30. Chuck Colson & Pat Nolan, *Prescription for Safer Communities,* 18 NOTRE DAME J. L. ETHICS & PUB. POL'Y 387, 393 (2004).

31. *Id.* at 393.

32. *Id.*

33. Byron R. Johnson et al., *Religious Programs, Institutional Adjustment, and Recidivism among Former Inmates in Prison Fellowship Programs*, 14 Just. Q. 145, 154–163 (1997).

34. Byron R. Johnson, Manhattan Inst. for Pol'y Research & Univ. of Penn. Ctr. for Research on Religion and Urban Civil Society, The Role of African-American Churches in Reducing Crime among Black Youths, *available at* http://www.manhattan-institute.org.

35. John J. DiIulio Jr., *Godly People in the Public Square*, Pub. Int., Oct. 1, 2000, at 110.

36. Robert Wuthnow, *How Religious Groups Promote Forgiving: A National Study*, 39 J. for Sci. Study Religion 25, 125 (2000).

37. Robert Wuthnow, Acts of Compassion: Caring for Others and Helping Ourselves (1991).

38. Mark Chaves & Lynn M. Higgins, *Comparing the Community Involvement of Black and White Congregations*, 31 J. for Sci. Study Religion 425, 438–39 (1992).

39. Anthony C. Thompson, *Navigating the Hidden Obstacles of Offender Reentry*, 45 B.C. L. Rev. 255 (2004).

40. *Id.*

41. Brent Staples, *How Denying the Vote to Ex-Offenders Undermines Democracy*, N.Y. Times, Sept. 17, 2004, at A26.

42. *Id.*

43. *Id.*

44. The term "cultural competence" refers to the skill set of a counselor, social worker, or other interventionist and/or the various prevention and intervention strategies that place emphasis on acknowledging and incorporating the "lived experiences" and "social realities" of a distinct subgroup (racial, ethnic, religious, sexual orientation, or age-specific) who are members of a larger treatment population to facilitate personal change and transformation. O. J. Williams, *African American Men Who Batter: Treatment Considerations and Community Response*, *in* The Black family: Essays and Studies 265–79 (R. Staples ed., 5th ed. 1999).

45. O. J. Williams & L. R. Becker, *Domestic Partner Abuse: The Results of a National Survey*, 9 Violence & Victims 287 (1994).

46. Todd R. Clear & George F. Cole, American Corrections (2000).

Index

About the Author

Anthony C. Thompson is Professor of Clinical Law at the New York University School of Law. Prior to his 1995 arrival at NYU, he served for nine years as a public defender in California, where he represented both adults and juveniles in criminal cases. He serves on the board of directors of the National Council for Crime and Delinquency, a national think tank on race and justice based in Oakland, California, and is also cochair of the board of trustees of the Reentry Institute at the John Jay College of Criminal Justice in New York City.